The Essential Guide to
Digital Set-top Boxes and Interactive TV

ISBN 0-13-017360-6

90000

9 780130 173607

Essential Guide Series

THE ESSENTIAL GUIDE TO DATA WAREHOUSING

Lou Agosta

THE ESSENTIAL GUIDE TO TELECOMMUNICATIONS, SECOND EDITION

Annabel Z. Dodd

THE ESSENTIAL GUIDE TO DIGITAL SET-TOP BOXES AND INTERACTIVE TV

Gerard O'Driscoll

The Essential Guide to Digital Set-top Boxes and Interactive TV

GERARD O'DRISCOLL

Prentice Hall PTR
Upper Saddle River, NJ 07458
www.phptr.com

Editorial/Production Supervision: *MetroVoice Publishing Services*
Acquisitions Editor: *Mike Meehan*
Editorial Assistant: *Diane Spina*
Buyer: *Maura Goldstaub*
Art Director: *Gail Cocker-Bogusz*
Interior Series Design: *Meg Van Arsdale*
Cover Design: *Bruce Kenselaar*
Cover Design Direction: *Jayne Conte*
Project Coordinator: *Anne Trowbridge*

© 2000 Prentice Hall PTR
Prentice-Hall, Inc.
Upper Saddle River, NJ 07458

The publisher offers discounts on this book when ordered in bulk quantities.
For more information, contact

Corporate Sales Department,
Prentice Hall PTR
One Lake Street
Upper Saddle River, NJ 07458
Phone: 800-382-3419; FAX: 201-236-7141
E-mail (Internet): corpsales@prenhall.com

Printed in the United States of America

10 9 8 7 6 5 4 3 2 1

ISBN 0-13-017360-6

Prentice-Hall International (UK) Limited, *London*
Prentice-Hall of Australia Pty. Limited, *Sydney*
Prentice-Hall Canada Inc., *Toronto*
Prentice-Hall Hispanoamericana, S.A., *Mexico*
Prentice-Hall of India Private Limited, *New Delhi*
Prentice-Hall of Japan, Inc., *Tokyo*
Pearson Education Asia Pte. Ltd., *Singapore*
Editora Prentice-Hall do Brasil, Ltda., *Rio de Janeiro*

This book is dedicated to my wife, Olive, and our young baby who is due any day. To my loving and caring mother, Mary O' Driscoll. To my father, Liam O' Driscoll, who taught me the meaning of hard work in the days before the arrival of the Celtic tiger to Ireland. To Owen and Brian, who are not only my younger brothers but are also great friends of mine. The final dedication goes to my drinking buddies in the Electronic Production class of 1988.

Contents

Preface

The boundaries between the IT world, Internet systems and broadcast television technologies have blurred. The result of this blurring effect has been the development of a new computing paradigm that is focused on the home entertainment market. The evolution of this new paradigm in tandem with a demand for new interactive TV applications has created the need for a special interface or gateway device that can be used to pass digital content between high-speed broadband networks and millions of homes across the world. A low cost consumer electronics device called a digital set-top box is poised and ready to take center stage in this new digital world we are about to enter.

Most industry analysts agree that in the near future, people will choose a digital set-top box to access myriad new services that are available from this new paradigm. Consumers can use their digital set-top boxes to sit down and enjoy watching cinema style pictures with CD quality sound. Advanced versions of these devices have intuitive and easy to use interfaces that allow people to access instant video on demand, e-commerce services and a range of entertainment services that are being dreamed up by the entrepreneurs of the future.

The first couple of chapters in this book will present you with a description of how the set-top business has evolved over the past couple of years.

Digital set-top boxes nowadays contain a number of components that are very similar to a desktop PC. So in chapter two we guide you through the terms and concepts that relate to each of these components.

The proliferation of digital technologies has sparked off the development of a number of software and hardware technologies. This book explores the various industry initiatives and standard bodies that are working on defining open set-top box technologies around the world.

Many companies, including Microsoft, PowerTV, PlanetWeb, OpenTV, Liberate Technologies, Canal+ and Sun Microsystems are vying to gain an early lead in defining the features of digital set-top boxes, as well as the lucrative interactive TV services that go along with them.

This book presents you with a detailed description of the set-top products that are available from these companies.

Additionally we help you understand the confusing array of computer technologies that has become synonymous with the world of digital set-top boxes—middleware, ECMAScript, JavaTV, HTML, TVPAK, JavaScript, DirectX, Windows 2000, XML and much more.

The proliferation of these new technologies into the homes of the future will serve as a springboard to new and exciting opportunities for software developers who want to move away from the world of PC software development to the lucrative world of developing enhanced TV applications. The middle of this book covers the methodologies used by existing developers and presents a brief overview of the development kits that are available for the various set-top software platforms.

In addition to the software development community, interactive TV is opening up new markets for the enormous pool of talented people involved in creating content. In chapter twelve of this book you will gain an insight into mechanisms that are used to author and deliver content that has been optimized for the TV world.

People often don't realize that behind the simple end user interface they see on their television set, there is a complex network architecture that is required to support the various applications.

This book goes behind the scenes and looks at the servers and technologies that are needed to support a range of broadband Internet, Intranet, and TV-centric applications.

Toward the end of the book we look at the security mechanisms and smart card technologies used by network service providers to control access to digital TV pay services.

Our final chapter looks ahead to the digital set-top box becoming a telecommunications hub for the homes of the future. The book concludes with a snapshot of the types of technologies that are currently under development for the next generation of advanced digital set-top boxes—home networking, advanced 3D, voice activation, and personalization technologies.

What Will I Learn?

After reading this book, you should be able to:

- Understand the architecture of an end to end digital TV system.
- Understand how set-top boxes evolved from simple consumer devices capable of receiving analog television only to becoming a central hub within the house for accessing a range of interactive and Internet services.
- Learn about how a set-top box works.
- Understand the hardware architecture of a digital set-top box and the standard reference platforms being developed in the United States and Europe—OpenCable and DVB.
- Explain real-time operating systems that have been optimized for a TV environment.
- Provide a description of the main responsibilities of middleware and understand the new and existing set-top middleware standards.
- Outline in detail the virtual machines that run on a set-top box (HTML, JavaScript, and Personal Java).
- List and explain the most popular middleware solutions.
- Learn the differences between developing applications for a TV environment versus a PC environment.
- Explain the most popular development environments (OpenTV, PowerTV, TVPAK, Java, PlanetWeb, MediaHighway, MHEG-5, and Liberate technologies).

- Describe the end to end architecture of Internet services that can be accessed by a digital set-top box (browsing, e-mail, chat, and Webcasting).
- Explore the relationship between set-tops and client/server computing.
- Describe the end to end architecture of a range of broadband Intranet applications including: home banking, e-commerce, games, and education.
- Describe the end to end architecture of a range of broadband TV broadcast services including: electronic program guides, pay per view, video on demand, near video on demand, parental control, and teletext.
- List and explain the various types of servers that are required to support these advanced Internet, Intranet, and TV centric services.
- Outline the differences between designing rich multimedia content for a TV environment versus a PC.
- List and explain the most popular authoring tools used to produce enhanced TV content.
- Define the role of smart cards in relation to digital television.
- Discuss the various home networking technologies that allow set-top boxes to network with a range of consumer electronic devices including: PCs, printers, cameras, hi-fi units, etc.
- Understand personalization technologies.

KEEPING UP TO DATE WITH SET-TOP BOX DEVELOPMENTS . . . .

Since the set-tops universe expands at an astonishing rate, this book can only provide a time-dated snapshot of the entire industry. Set-top box manufacturers and software developers are constantly adding new features and components. To stay in tune with the evolution of advanced digital set-top boxes please visit the set-tops family of sites at: www.set-tops.com.

Who Should Read this Book

A wide range of information technology (IT), telecommunications, and interactive digital TV professionals interested in promoting the convergence of the PC, TV, and Internet through advanced digital set-top boxes will find the information in this volume of interest. These include the following:

- Members of the software development community who are imagining and developing enhanced TV applications for the next computing paradigm—10 million Windows programmers and 1 million Java developers.
- Business development executives, system integrators, and technical managers who want to learn about the capabilities of advanced digital set-top boxes.
- Content developers and Web designers who want to learn about the tools and technologies available for developing interactive TV content.
- Executives in cable companies, broadcast providers, and satellite providers who want to grow revenue streams and profits through the deployment of advanced TV and Internet-based applications.

Acknowledgments

I am indebted to the many people for their information, feedback, and assistance during the development of this book. First of all, I would like to thank the staff at Prentice Hall for having the vision to see the need for this book and the professionalism to follow through and publish the world's first book on this new industry.

In particular, I would like to thank my Executive Editor Michael E. Meehan for keeping me focused on the task at hand. A special thanks to Astrid Dobbelaar of Phillips who generously developed a white paper on the future of advanced electronic program guides for this book.

Tina Cuccia and Ken Soohoo provided me with some invaluable technical information on PlanetWeb's software products. Thanks also to David Higham of OpenTV for supplying me with a wide variety of white papers and product details. Mike Cook of the Digital TV Group in the UK supplied me with some detailed diagrams associated with troubleshooting digital set-top boxes in a terrestrial environment. Amanda Ingalls of SpyGlass supplied me some product information.

People from the various international standard bodies have been extremely helpful. In particular, I would like to thank Dr. Dirk Jaeger of EuroCableLabs in Germany and Eric Kirsten and Mike Schwartz of CableLabs in the United States. Moreover, I would like to thank Jean-Pierre Evain for helping me to improve my description and understanding of the new Multimedia Home Platform (MHP) standard. I would also like to acknowledge Thomas Neumayr for sending me some details of products that are being developed by Liberate Technologies. I would also like to thank Charles Dawes of Cable and Wireless in the U.K. for compiling the case study in Chapter 9.

Special gratitude goes to Scott Suckling and the team at MetroVoice Publishing who were responsible for project managing, page composition, and copyediting this volume. Most of all I would like to thank my wife, Olive, for her support in completing this book.

1 Overview of Digital TV

In this chapter...

The tremendous potential of digital television is attracting interest from telecommunications providers, computer manufacturers, network providers, consumer electronic companies, and broadcasters around the world. Pay Per View, high speed Internet access, video on demand, cable telephony, and e-commerce represent a portion of the new money spinning ventures in which industry firms are investing increasing amounts of dollars and resources. This chapter acts as a foundation block for the technology discussions that follow in later chapters. Here, we introduce the basic concepts and benefits of digital television. Then we introduce the various international standard bodies that are involved in establishing sets of technical specifications for implementing digital TV systems throughout the world. Finally, this chapter provides you with some detailed information about how the components of the digital broadcasting environment work together.

TERMINOLOGY . . . .

Before entering a detailed discussion about digital television systems, it is important that you understand a number of industry-specific terms. Here's a short list of the most important ones.

Head-end • An industry term that is used to describe a TV operator's main operations center.

Set-top box • A set-top box may be defined as a consumer electronics device used to decode and tune digital signals and convert them to a format that is understood by your television.

MHz • MHz is an abbreviation for megahertz. One MHz represents a million cycles per second. The speed of a processor in a digital set-top box (defined below) is measured in MHz.

Bandwidth • If you have ever waited for a page to download into your PC on a Saturday evening, then you're already familiar with the concept of bandwidth. Think of bandwidth as a pipe that carries information. The less bandwidth you have, the longer the time it will take to download a Web page onto your PC.

Return path • Many of the digital TV services on offer require some form of interaction between the subscriber and either the program provider or the network operator. This interaction may consist of transmitting a couple of user commands but can be as extensive as the communications required by a telecommunications link to the Internet. The term "return path" is used to describe the physical channel that facilitates this two-way interaction.

Protocol • A protocol is a formal description of the messages that need to be exchanged and the rules that need to be followed for two or more systems to exchange information.

Network service provider • Many of the cable, microwave multipoint distribution services (MMDS), terrestrial, satellite, and broadcasting companies are beginning to move into the telecommunications sector to offer a variety of services that have not been associated with their traditional TV-based offerings. Consequently, in this book we sometimes refer to this group of companies as service providers or network service providers. A network service provider will not only manage the network infrastructure, but will also control the various services that run over its high-speed networks.

WHAT IS DIGITAL TELEVISION? . . . .

Digital television, commonly known as digital TV, is a completely new way of broadcasting and is the future of television. It is a medium that requires new thinking and new revenue-generating business models. Digital TV is the successor to analog TV and eventually all broadcasting will be done in this way.

Around the globe, cable, satellite, and wireless operators are moving to a digital environment. Affiliates of the four major networks in the United States—ABC, NBC, CBS, and Fox were slated to begin digital broadcasts by November 1999. By 2006, the Federal Communications Commission (FCC) in the U.S. has mandated that no more analog television signals be broadcast. In Europe, the digital TV train is also rolling out of the station, with broadcasters in France, Ireland, Spain, Germany, Holland, and the U.K. planned to launch digital technologies in 1999. Most industry analysts are predicting that the transition to digital TV will be an evolution rather than a revolution, changing the way of life for hundreds of millions of families around the world.

Companies are acknowledging that the convergence between personal computers, TV sets, and the Internet has already begun and are positioning themselves to maximize revenue from this new computing paradigm.

For consumers, the digital age will improve their viewing experience through cinema-quality pictures, CD-quality sound, hundreds of new channels, the power to switch camera angles, and improved access to a range of exciting new entertainment services. Digital TV also gives subscribers the opportunity to enjoy more programming through cinema-style wide screen TVs. Gone are the days of choosing between a small range of channels. Television will become more fun and powerful to use, yet at the same time simpler and friendlier.

For the broadcaster, a move to a digital environment decreases the bandwidth utilization per channel, facilitates the offering of Internet applications to their subscribers, and opens a new era of business opportunities.

The new digital technologies will allow cable companies, satellite providers, and wireless broadcasters to offer a variety of powerful revenue-generating services, including:

- Internet access at blazing speeds;
- multi-user network games;
- video on demand;
- streaming video and audio;
- home banking services;
- e-commerce applications;
- PC software upgrades;
- Broadcasting rich multimedia content; and
- electronic newspapers.

Digital television also opens up a new world of opportunities for companies who want to develop content and applications for the new paradigm. This includes the creative communities within the television and film industry, Internet content providers, and software development houses, as well as new companies that will be created around this new industry.

To fully understand digital TV, we need to look at its origin and how various compression and transmission technologies were used to revolutionize the television experience. For the past 50 years, broadcasters have been using analog signals as a means of transmitting TV to the mass market. During this period, we experienced the transition from the black-and-white sets to color TV sets. The migration required viewers to purchase new TV sets and broadcasters had to acquire new transmitters, posts and production equipment.

The switch from black-and-white to color had palpable benefits for everyone. Today, the industry is going through a profound and amazing transition: migrating from conventional TV to a new era of digital technology. Television operators are upgrading their existing networks and deploying advanced digital platforms to open a new world of opportunities for consumers, content providers, and entrepreneurs.

First, digital TV offers high speed data transfer rates, which make the delivery of rich multimedia content a reality. Second, many cable, terrestrial, and satellite companies are establishing themselves as Internet service providers, which will enable TV viewers to browse the Internet on their TV sets.

Finally, the new medium will allow viewers from the comfort of their homes to use a simple remote control to electronically purchase goods and services offered by various content providers. Digital TV uses the same language as computers—a long stream of binary digits, each of which is either 0 or 1. With digital television, the signal is compressed and only the updated data is transmitted. As a result, it is possible to squeeze six or eight channels into a frequency range that was previously occupied by only one analog TV channel.

The digital TV cycle begins by recording a particular event or program with digital equipment and is relayed to a redistribution center. In most cases, the redistribution center will be a cable, satellite, MMDS, or terrestrial operator. From here, the operators use specific transmission techniques to broadcast the new digital signal to subscribers on their network.

INTERNATIONAL STANDARD BODIES AND AGREEMENTS . . . .

Making digital television a reality requires the cooperation of a variety of industries and companies, along with the development of many new standards. A wide variety of international organizations have contributed to the standardization of digital TV over the past couple of years. Most standards organizations create formal standards by using specific processes: organizing ideas, discussing the approach, developing draft standards, voting on all or certain aspects of the standards, and then formally releasing the completed standard to the general public. Some of the best-known international organizations that contribute to standardizing of digital television include:

- the European Telecommunications Standards Institute (ETSI);
- Digital Video Broadcasting (DVB);
- the Advanced Television Systems Committee (ATSC);
- the Digital Audio Visual Council (DAVIC);
- the European Cable Communications Association (ECCA);
- CableLabs;
- the W3 consortium; and
- the Federal Communications Commission (FCC).

Their contribution to the standardization process is explained and detailed in the following sections.

European Telecommunications Standards Institute (ETSI)

ETSI is a nonprofit organization whose mission is to determine and produce a wide range of telecommunication standards. It is an open forum that unites approximately 647 members from countries all over the globe, representing administrations, service providers, manufacturers, and end-users. Any European organization proving an interest in promoting European telecommunications standards has the right to represent that interest in ETSI and thus to directly influence the standards-making process. ETSI consists of a General Assembly, a Board, a Technical Organization, and a Secretariat. The Technical Organization produces and approves technical standards. It encompasses ETSI projects, technical committees, and special committees. More than 3,500 experts are at present working for ETSI in over 200 groups. (Additional information about ETSI is available from their web site at http://www.etsi.org/).

Digital Video Broadcasting (DVB)

The DVB project was conceived in 1991 and was formally inaugurated in 1993 with approximately 80 members. Today, the DVB project has made huge advancements and boasts a membership of over 230 organizations in more than 30 countries worldwide.

Members of the group include electronic manufacturers, network operators, broadcasters, software companies, and various regulatory bodies.

The DVB project has been a big success and has generated various standards for delivering digital TV to people throughout Europe, Asia, Australia, and North America.

The work of the DVB project has resulted in a comprehensive list of technical and nontechnical documents that describe solutions for implementing digital television in a variety of different environments.

The international standards and solutions developed by DVB over the past few years can be classified and summarized as follows:

1. DVB-S—An international standard for transmitting digital television using satellites.
2. DVB-C—An international standard for transmitting digital television using digital cable systems.
3. DVB-T—An international standard for transmitting digital television in a terrestrial environment.
4. DVB-MC/S—An international standard for transmitting digital television using microwave multipoint video distribution systems.
5. DVB-SI—An international standard that defines the data structures that accompany a digital television signal.
6. DVB-CA—An international standard that defines digital television security standards.
7. DVB-CI—An international standard that defines a common interface to the digital TV security system.
8. DVB-I—An international standard for deploying interactive TV.
9. DVB-Data—An international standard designed to allow operators to deliver software downloads and high speed data services to their customers.
10. Interfaces—An international standard that defines digital TV interfaces to high speed backbone networks.

The Standard for the
Digital World

Figure 1.1
DVB Logo

Copies of these standards are available for download on ETSI's web site.

DVB-compliant digital equipment is widely available and is easily identified by the DVB logo illustrated in Figure 1.1. The DVB has had its greatest success in Europe, however the standard has implementations in North and South America, Africa, Asia, and Australia. For additional information about DVB, visit their web site at http://www.dvb.org/.

Advanced Television Systems Committee (ATSC)

The ATSC committee was formed to establish a set of technical standards for broadcasting standard and High Definition Television (HDTV). Pictures based on this standard can have 3 to 5 times the sharpness of today's analog broadcasts.

The committee is composed of 136 member organizations, standard bodies, IT corporations, educational institutions, and electronic manufacturers. It has been formally adopted in the United States, where an aggressive implementation of digital TV has already begun. In addition to the U.S., Canada, South Korea, Taiwan, and Argentina have also adopted the ATSC digital TV standard for terrestrial broadcasts. A sample of the ATSC standards are outlined in Table 1.1.

Table 1.1 *ATSC Standard Documents*

Document Number	Standard Description	Brief Overview	Web Address of Detailed Document
A/52	ATSC Digital Audio Compression	Specifies coded representation of audio information and the decoding process, as well as information on the encoding process	www.atsc.org/Standards/A52/
A/53	ATSC Digital Television Standard	Specifications and characteristics for an advanced TV (ATV) system	www.atsc.org/Standards/A53/
A/54	ATSC Guide	Description of ATV system	www.atsc.org/Standards/A54/
A/64	Transmission measurement and compliance for digital television	Description of measurement and ATSC compliance system	www.atsc.org/Standards/A64/

This table only displays a snapshot of the ATSC standards. To review the complete listings of ATSC standards, we recommend you visit the ATSC Web page at http://www.atsc.org/Standards/stan_rps.html for a more detailed listing.

For the latest information and updates about ATSC, visit their web site at http://www.atsc.org/.

Digital Audio Visual Council (DAVIC)

The organization was formed in 1994 with the aim of defining standards for the end-to-end transfer of digital audio, video, and Internet-based content.

DAVIC is a nonprofit standards organization currently located in Switzerland. The organization currently has a membership of over 180 companies from 25 countries around the globe, representing companies and individuals from all sectors of the audio-visual industry. DAVIC members meet on a regular basis to define specifications and use their web site (www.davic.org) to collaborate and implement various international projects.

European Cable Communications Association (ECCA)

ECCA is the European Association of cable operators. The main goal of the Association is to foster cooperation between operators, and to promote their interests at a European level. ECCA gathers European cable operators, consisting of more than 40 million subscribers. The first informal cooperation between European cable operators started in 1949. As these informal meetings became more frequent, a formal structure for European cooperation was required and on September 2, 1955, the Alliance Internationale de la Distribution par câble (AID) was set up by representatives of Switzerland, Belgium, and The Netherlands. In 1993, AID was renamed the European Cable Communications Association, thus stressing the communication role of its members as well as its European goals.

ECCA now has 29 members in 17 countries. It also has 5 associate members in central and eastern Europe. ECCA has considerably contributed to European policies related to cable on the regulatory as well as on the technical standards field.

On the regulatory, ECCA has done a lot of work on areas such as digital TV, copyright, must-carry, and open-access issues. In addition to these projects, ECCA members have also compiled the following technical specifications.

Eurobox

On initiative of the ECCA organization, a common specification for cable set-top boxes following DVB standards was agreed upon by a large number of cable operators in Europe (the Eurobox platform).

The Eurobox platform was set up in 1997, and has more than 5.5 million subscribers. A more detailed description of the Eurobox is available in Chapter 5 of this book.

Euromodem

A collective resolution to develop a global standard for high speed cable modems was signed at the ECCA Cable Forum in November 1998. The standard fully complies with European standards and with several DVB specifications. The ECCA group has considered two different types of modems: class A and class B. Class A modems are capable of transmitting data at very high speeds in a downstream direction (maximum of 50.8 Mbits/sec) and 3 Mbits/sec in the upstream direction. They are capable of accessing the Internet at high speeds and support a number of security technologies. Class B is the second type of modem considered by the group. It extends the functionality of class A devices through the support of time critical services such as video conferencing and telephony. At the time of going to press, a number of electronic manufacturing companies were invited to submit plans to manufacture modems compliant with the Euromodem standard.

Cable telephony

On the basis of the full liberalization of the telecommunications sector in Europe, cable companies, satellite providers, and terrestrial broadcasters in different countries are planning to become competitors to the local telephony companies. Therefore, their networks are being or have been upgraded to broadband telecommunications networks, which are able to provide all kinds of services from telephony and local Internet access to high speed broadband connections. ECCA is also actively working in this area. For additional information about ECCA, visit their web site at http://www.ecca.be/.

CableLabs

Cable Television Laboratories, Incorporated (CableLabs), was originally established in May 1988 as a research and development consortium of cable television system operators. To qualify as a member of CableLabs, a company needs to be a cable television system operator. CableLabs currently represents more than 85 percent of the cable subscribers in the United States, 70 percent of the subscribers in Canada, and 10 percent of the subscribers in Mexico. CableLabs plans, funds, and implements a number of research and projects that help cable companies take advantage of future opportunities in the areas of digital TV, telephony, and high speed Internet. For additional information about CableLabs, visit their web site at http://www.cablelabs.com/.

W3 Consortium (W3C)

The W3 Consortium (W3C) was originally founded in 1994 to lead the World Wide Web to its full potential by developing common protocols that promote its evolution and ensure its interoperability. The organization is an international consortium, jointly hosted by the Massachusetts Institute of Technology in the U.S; an organization in Europe called the Institut National de Recherche en Informatique et en Automatique, and Keio University in Japan.

The consortium provides a range of services, including: a repository of information about the World Wide Web for developers and users; reference code implementations to embody and promote standards; and various prototype and sample applications to demonstrate use of new technology. For detailed information about the W3C, visit their web site at http://www.w3c.org/.

Federal Communications Commission (FCC)

The Federal Communications Commission (FCC) is an independent United States government agency, directly responsible to Congress. The FCC was established by the

Communications Act of 1934 and is charged with regulating interstate and international communications by radio, television, wire, satellite, and cable. The FCC's jurisdiction covers the 50 states, the District of Columbia, and U.S. possessions. There are six operating bureaus. The bureaus are: Mass Media, Cable Services, Common Carrier, Compliance and Information, Wireless Telecommunications, and International. These bureaus are responsible for developing and implementing regulatory programs, processing applications for licenses or other filings, analyzing complaints, conducting investigations, and taking part in FCC hearings.

The Cable Services Bureau was established in 1993 to administer the cable Television Consumer Protection and Competition Act of 1992. The Bureau enforces regulations designed to ensure that cable rates are reasonable under the law. It is also responsible for regulations concerning "must carry," retransmission consent, customer services, technical standards, home wiring, consumer electronics, equipment compatibility, indecency, leased access, and program access provisions. The Bureau also analyzes trends and developments in the industry to assess the effectiveness of the cable regulations. For additional information about the FCC, visit their web site at http://www.fcc.gov/.

BUILDING BLOCKS OF A DIGITAL TV SYSTEM . . . .

A TV operator normally receives content from a variety of sources, including local video, cable, and satellite channels. The content needs to be prepared for transmission to the customer's home by passing the signal through a digital broadcasting system. The diagram in Figure 1.2 depicts the basic building blocks of a digital broadcasting system.

Note that the components shown in this diagram are logical units and do not necessarily correspond to the number of physical devices that are deployed in a total end-to-end digital solution. The role of each component shown in Figure 1.2 is briefly outlined in the following categories.

Compression and Encoding

Central to a digital video-broadcasting network is the compression system, whose job is to deliver high quality video and audio to consumers using a small amount of network bandwidth. The main goal of any compression system is to minimize the storage capacity of information. This is particularly useful for service providers who want to "squeeze" many digital channels into a digital stream.

A compression system consists of *encoders* and *multiplexers*. Encoders are devices used to digitize, compress, and scramble a range of audio, video, and data channels. Digital encoders allow TV operators to broadcast several high quality video

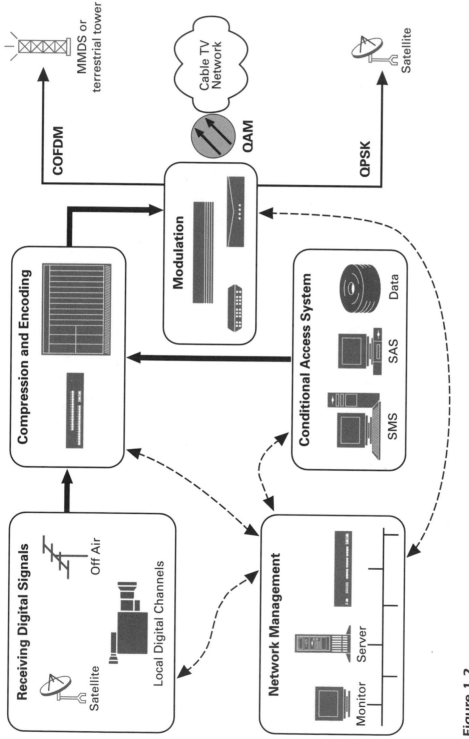

Figure 1.2
Simplified block diagram depicting the basic building blocks of a digital broadcasting system

programs over the same bandwidth that was formerly used to broadcast just one ana-log video program.

Once the signal is encoded and compressed, an MPEG-2 stream is transmitted to the multiplexer (MPEG-2 is an acronym for Moving Pictures Experts Group). This group has defined a range of compression standards and file formats, including the MPEG-2 video animation system. MPEG-2 is generally accepted in 190 countries worldwide as the standard for digital video compression. There are two major MPEG standards available on the market today: MPEG-1 and MPEG-2.

The MPEG-1 file format is normally used by interactive TV developers to cre-ate TV "stills" and has a quality level slightly less than conventional video cassette recorders. The MPEG-2 file format is used in a digital broadcasting environment and features CD-quality audio complemented with a high screen resolution. Once the sig-nal has been compressed into MPEG-2 format, the multiplexer combines the outputs from the various encoders together with the security and program information and data into a single digital stream.

Modulation

Once the digital signal has been processed by the multiplexer, it is now time to amal-gamate the video, audio, and data with the carrier signal in a process called *modula-tion*. The unmodulated digital signal outputted from the multiplexer has only two pos-sible states, either a "zero" or a "one." By passing the signal through a modulation pro-cess, a number of states are added, which increases the data transfer rate. The modu-lation technique used by TV operators will depend on the geography of the franchise area and the overall network architecture.

The three major types of digital modulation are Quadrature Amplitude Modulation, Quadrature Phase Shift Keying, and Coded Orthogonal Frequency Division Multiplexing.

Quadrature Amplitude Modulation (QAM)

QAM is a relatively simple technique for carrying digital information from the TV operator's broadcast center to the customer. This form of modulation modifies the amplitude and phase of a signal to transmit the MPEG-2 transport stream. QAM is the preferred modulation scheme for cable companies because it can achieve transfer rates up to 40 Mbits/sec.

Quadrature Phase Shift Keying (QPSK)

QPSK is more immune then QAM to electromagnetic noise and is normally used in a satellite environment or on the return path for a cable television network. QPSK works on the principle of shifting the digital signal so that it is out of phase with the incoming signal. QPSK will improve the robustness of a network, however, this modulation scheme is only capable of transmitting data at 10 Mbits/sec.

Coded Orthogonal Frequency Division Multiplexing (COFDM)

COFDM operates extremely well in heavily built-up areas where digital transmissions become distorted by obstacles such as buildings, bridges, and hills. COFDM is different to QAM because it uses multiple signal carriers to transfer information from one node on the network to another. At the moment, COFDM may be implemented with either 2,000 (2K) or 8,000 (8K) carrier signals. European terrestrial and MMDS operators mainly use the COFDM modulation scheme. In contrast, COFDM has not been deployed in the United States because the ATSC (Advanced Television Systems Committee) has defined a digital terrestrial system that meets the needs of a less-rugged geographical terrain.

Conditional Access System

Broadcast and TV operators are now interacting with their viewers on many levels, offering them a greater program choice than ever before. Additionally, the deployment of a security system or conditional access (CA), as it is commonly called, provides them with unprecedented control over what they watch and when. A CA system is best described as a virtual gateway that allows viewers to access a new world of digital services.

The main goal of any CA system is to control subscribers' access to digital TV pay services and secure the operators revenue streams. Consequently, only customers that have a valid contract with the network operator can access a particular service. Using today's CA systems, network operators are able to directly target programming, advertisements, and promotions to subscribers by geographical area, market segment, or according to personal preferences. The CA system is therefore a vital aspect of the digital TV business. In technical terms, the key elements of the CA system are illustrated in Figure 1.3.

Restricting access to a particular service is accomplished by using a technique called cryptography. It protects the digital service by transforming the signal into an unreadable format. The transformation process is known as "encryption" in a digital environment and "scrambling" in an analog domain. Once the signal is encrypted, it can only be decrypted by means of a digital set-top box. Decryption is the process

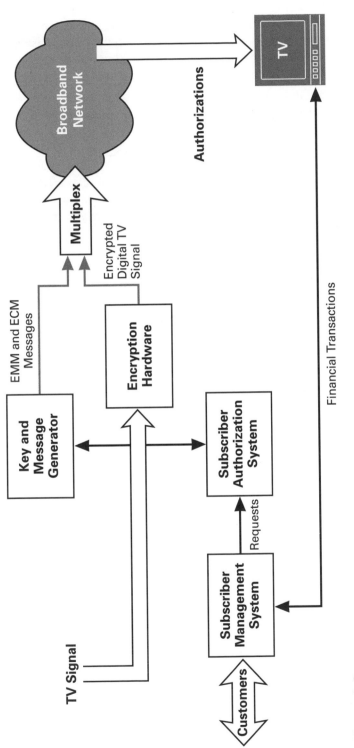

Figure 1.3
Basic principle of an end-to-end conditional access system

used to convert the message back to its original format. This is carried out using a decryption key. A key is best described as a secret value, consisting of a random string of bits, which is used by a computer in conjunction with mathematical formulas called algorithms to encrypt and decrypt information.

The box incorporates the necessary hardware and software subsystems to receive and decrypt the signal. These components are comprised of a de-encryption chip, a secure processor, and some appropriate hardware drivers. The de-encryption chip is responsible for holding the algorithm section of the CA. The secure processor can either be soldered onto the set-top box's printed circuit board or else attached to a smart card. Smart cards are plastic cards that look like credit cards. This processor contains the necessary keys needed to decrypt the various services. Chapter 11 discusses the cryptography aspects of smart card security in more detail.

A given subscriber may decrypt and access the digital signal only if the subscriber has purchased the relevant entitlement. As an example, the entitlement may be provided in the form of an electronic smart card that is plugged into the set-top box. Alternatively, in a pay-per-view scenario, the entitlement may be delivered electronically by entitlement management messages (EMMs) and entitlement control messages (ECMs) within the broadcast stream. An EMM is used to carry authorization details and are subscriber-specific. Consequently, the number of EMMs that need to be sent over the broadband network is proportional to the number of set-tops on the network. In addition to sending EMMs to specific customers, operators can also broadcast EMMs to groups of subscribers in different geographical areas. ECMs, on the other hand, carry program- and service-specific information, including control words that are used by the smart card to decrypt the relevant program. However, if a subscriber is not entitled to watch the program, then a signal is sent to the set-top box to indicate that this program has not been authorized for de-encryption. ECMs and EMMs are generated and broadcasted at the TV operations center using specialized hardware devices. They are then transmitted to the viewer's smart card. The card will check access rights and descramble the requested digital services. It is possible to change the value of an ECM every 10 seconds in order to maximize security on a digital network. A typical smart card is capable of storing up to a hundred entitlement messages, which means that each subscriber on the network is capable of ordering 100 pay-TV events at any one time.

In addition to encrypting digital services, the CA also interfaces with the following subsystems:

Subscriber Management System (SMS)

To exploit the commercial potential of digital broadcasting, TV operators need to interface their technical systems with a subscriber management system (SMS). The SMS provides the support required to accurately manage the digital TV business model. It handles the customer database and sends requests to the subscriber authorization system (SAS)—the technical management part of the CA system. Functions typically provided by an SMS software application system include:

- register, modify, and cancel subscriber records;
- targeted marketing campaigns;
- inventory management of set-tops and smart cards;
- customer experience tracking;
- cross-selling of services;
- interfacing with banks and credit card companies;
- fault management;
- multilingual and multicurrency capability;
- bill preparation and formatting;
- presentation of bills in electronic formats; and
- accounting and auditing facilities.

Many of the software solutions currently available in the marketplace are capable of supporting the increasing variety of interactive services offered to subscribers. The main goal of any SMS system is to ensure that subscribers view exactly what they pay for.

Subscriber Authorization System (SAS)

The main task of the SAS is to translate the requests coming from the SMS into EMMs. These authorization messages are then sent via the digital multiplex to the smart card, which is located in the set-top box. They are sent to customers on a regular interval (for example, every month) to renew subscription rights on the smart card. In the case of Pay Per View (PPV) applications, the SAS sends a certain amount of electronic tokens to the smart card that will allow customers to purchase a variety of PPV events. The SAS contains database(s) that are capable of storing the following items of information:

- pay TV product information,
- data to support the electronic TV guide,
- identification numbers of smart cards,
- customer profiles, and
- scheduling data.

Additionally, SAS security can be enhanced by periodically changing the authorization keys broadcasted to the subscriber base. Some well-known CA systems include:

- CryptoWorks from Philips,
- Viaccess from France Telecom,
- Nagra from NagraVision,
- MediaGuard from Canal+ Technologies,
- VideoGuard from NDS,
- DigiCipher from General Instruments, and
- Iredeto from MindPort.

Network Transmission Technologies

Several different technologies have been deployed to bring broadband entertainment services from a central point to customers on a digital TV network. The different distribution systems (or mix of systems) adopted to broadcast digital TV services in countries around the world has largely been a function of each market's unique characteristics, including elements such as topography, population density, existing broadcast infrastructure, as well as social and cultural factors.

The most popular of these technologies are detailed in the following subsections.

Digital Via Hybrid Fiber-Coax (HFC)

Hybrid fiber-coax (HFC) technology refers to any network configuration of fiber-optic and coaxial cable that may be used to redistribute a variety of broadband entertainment services. These broadband services include telephony, interactive multimedia, high speed Internet access, video-on-demand, and distance learning. The types of services provided to consumers will vary between cable companies.

Many of the major cable television companies in the United States, Europe, Latin America, and Southeast Asia are already using it. Networks built using HFC technology have many characteristics that make it ideal for handling the next generation of communication services. First and foremost, HFC networks can simultaneously transmit broadband analog and digital services. This is extremely important for network operators who are rolling out digital TV to their subscribers on a phased basis. Additionally, HFC meets the expandable capacity and reliability requirements of a new digital TV system. HFC's expandable capacity allows network operators to add services incrementally without major changes to the overall plant infrastructure. HFC is essentially a "pay as you go" architecture that matches infrastructure investment with new revenue streams, operational savings, and reliability enhancements. The HFC network architecture is comprised of fiber transmitters, optical nodes, fiber and coaxial cables, and distribution hubs. An end-to-end HFC network is illustrated in Figure 1.4.

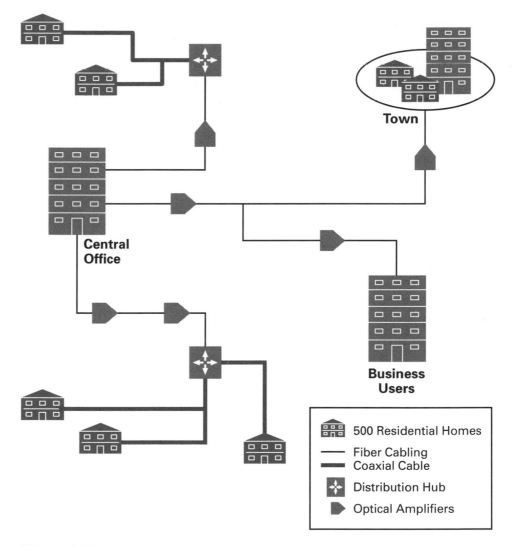

Figure 1.4
End-to-end HFC Network

From the diagram we can see that the signal is transmitted from the central office in a star-like fashion to the fiber nodes using fiber-optic feeders. The fiber node, in turn, distributes the signals over coaxial cable, RF amplifiers, and taps throughout the customer serving area. In conclusion, HFC is the lowest-cost alternative available in terms of cost-per-home-passed. This fact, combined with the other advantages already discussed, ensures that HFC will remain the primary technology for distributing advanced broadband services in a cabled environment.

Digital via Wireless Cable

Wireless cable is a relatively new service used to broadcast TV signals at microwave frequencies from a central point or head-end to small antennas located on the subscriber's roof. It is enabled through the use of two distribution technologies: multichannel multipoint distribution system (MMDS) and local multipoint distribution system (LMDS).

MMDS

Analog-based MMDS began in the mid-1970s with the allocation of two channels for sending business data. The service, however, became very popular for TV subscriber programming and applications were made to allocate part of the ITFS (Instructional Television Fixed Service) band to wireless cable TV. Once the regulations had been amended, it became possible for a wireless cable system to offer up to thirty-one 6 MHz channels in the 2.5 to 2.7 GHz band. During this timeframe, the system was used by nonprofit organizations to broadcast educational and religious programs. In 1983, the FCC allocated frequencies in both of these spectrums, providing 200 MHz bandwidth for licensed network providers. The basic components of an end-to-end digital MMDS system is shown in Figure 1.5.

An MMDS system consists of a head-end that receives signals from satellites, fiber optic cable, off-the-air TV stations, and local programming. At the head-end, the signals are mixed with commercials and other inserts, scrambled, converted to the 2.1 and 2.7 GHz frequency range, and sent to microwave towers. The signals are then rebroadcast from low-powered base stations within a 35-mile diameter of the subscriber's home. Signals are received with home rooftop antennas, which are 18 to 36 inches wide. The receiving antenna should have a clear line of site to the transmitting antenna. A down converter, usually a part of the antenna, converts the microwave signals into standard cable channel frequencies. From the antenna, the signal travels to a set-top box where it is decrypted and from there the signal passes into the television. If the subscriber requires interactivity, then the digital set-top box is also connected to the public telephone network.

Today, there are systems in use all around the U.S. and in many other countries, including Australia, South Africa, South America, Ireland, and Canada. Currently, MMDS is an analog service providing about 20 channels of programming to subscribers. Digital MMDS increases the number of channels to between 130 and 180. Digital MMDS also reduces the line-of-sight restrictions by providing a more efficient signal that will require less signal strength at the set-top box. Digital signals will need about 100 times less signal strength than analog signals, which translates to a substantial increase in the range of service area. Where an analog signal degrades with distance, the digital signal will remain constant and perfect as long as it can be received. In addition to more channels, digital MMDS customers will also be able to receive a variety of Internet, telephony, and interactive TV-based services. MMDS is presently using a standard phone line for the return path, but trials are under way to utilize a portion of the wireless bandwidth for return capabilities.

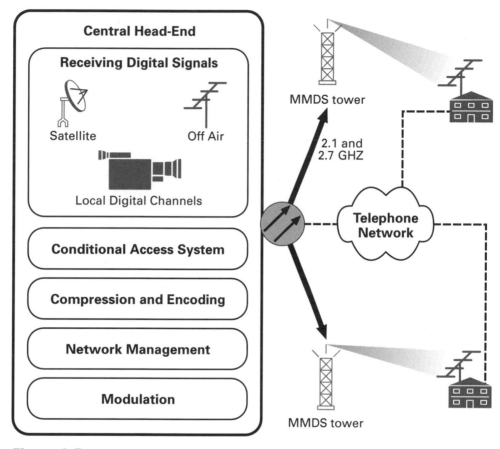

Figure 1.5
End-to-end digital MMDS solution

In Ireland for example, MMDS operators are currently very active in testing and delivering a diversity of advanced digital TV and Internet services using MMDS network transmission techniques to customers across the island. The services on offer to customers include:

- high speed access to the Internet;
- private data networks for companies on the island;
- broadcast video and Pay Per View television;
- Plain Old Telephone Service (POTS); and
- fractional and full leased lines

Future services discussed by Irish operators include video conferencing and delivering multimedia training courses to remote parts of the country using advanced MMDS digital technologies. MMDS operators across the world are adopting similar approaches to their Irish counterparts and are poised to take advantage of the exciting new digital MMDS broadcasting revolution, allowing the delivery of a variety of services to their customer bases.

LMDS

LMDS uses microwave frequencies in the 28 GHz frequency range to send and receive broadband signals, which are suitable for the transmission of video, voice, and multimedia data. Digital LMDS has been commercially deployed and is used to deliver video programming from local and cable channels. Additionally, it is also capable of delivering a plethora of Internet- and telephony-based services to consumers. The system architecture for LMDS is very similar to the MMDS system. The reception and processing of programming and other head-end functions are the same. The signals are then rebroadcasted from low-powered base stations in a 4–6 mile radius of the subscriber's home. Signals are then received using six square-inch antennas, which can be mounted either inside or outside the home. As with the MMDS, the signal travels to the set-top box, decrypted, and formatted for display on the customer's television. In addition to a high video and audio quality, other benefits of LMDS include its bandwidth range of 1 GHz and the availability of a return channel for interactive TV services.

Digital via Terrestrial

Commercially launched in the U.K. in November 1998, terrestrial communications, or DTT as it is commonly called, can also be used to broadcast a range of digital services.

Elements of a terrestrial communications network include:

1. Transmission medium—Services are normally provided via the ultra high frequency band (UHF). The frequencies in this band range from 300 MHz up to 3 GHz. Standard 8 MHz channels are used and shared with analog transmissions.

2. Modulation scheme—DTT uses the COFDM modulation scheme. The main purpose of COFDM is to make the terrestrial signal immune to multipath reflections. In other words, the signal needs to be robust enough to traverse geographical areas that include mountains, trees, and large buildings.

3. Transmission infrastructure—Uses an existing network of broadcast stations and transmitters.

4. Customer's premises equipment—With a modern aerial, there should be no need to replace it to receive the DTT service. If the aerial is a very old one, the viewer would certainly benefit from updating. Additionally, DTT

necessitates the purchase of a new digital set-top box to receive and decode the digital signal.

Digital via Direct Broadcast Satellite (DBS)

Digital television is also available through direct broadcast satellite (DBS), which can provide higher bandwidth than terrestrial, MMDS, or cable transmission.

Direct Broadcast Satellite (DBS) is a service whereby you receive subscription television from a single high-powered satellite. This satellite is typically located about 22,000 miles above the surface of the earth. At the moment, when you subscribe to an analog service you receive a state-of-the art mini-dish that is maintained and owned by the local distributor, along with a decoder for your television set that unscrambles the signals received from the satellite. This year, consumers will be able to receive digital satellite service by installing a new and smaller digital satellite dish and buying a new digital satellite set-top box. Digital via DBS brings consumers more channels to choose from, new features, and new services.

Network Management

As you can see the broadcasting center is made up of many complex components. As these components handle more and more services, network problems must be quickly detected and resolved. To maximize system uptime and monitor the services delivered to customers, a network monitoring and control system is installed at the broadcasting center. The main goal of such a system is to minimize service interruptions to digital TV customers. Features of a typical head-end control system include:

- monitoring the availability of devices,
- gathering statistics,
- reporting alarms and problems to support personnel, and
- remote diagnostics.

The systems available at present are vendor-specific and will run on either Windows NT or UNIX platforms.

SUMMARY . . . .

Digital television brings about many challenges, but with those challenges come a lot of opportunities. Advances in technology over the past few years have meant that the possibility of delivering digital television services to billions of people around the globe has moved from the realms of fantasy into reality.

Digital TV offers a potential mechanism through which every home, school, business, and community center in the world could be included in the information society.

It opens up a new world of opportunity for companies to develop and utilize their existing network infrastructures. This includes broadcasters; cable and satellite companies; the creative community in television and film; Internet content providers; web site producers; and new, innovative companies that will form around the future of digital TV. The broadcast of digital TV and multimedia data works well because of the agreements and partnerships forged by a number of organizations around the world. A complete digital broadcasting system is comprised of a number of building blocks including the compression, encoding, and modulation-system, a CA system for security purposes; network transmission media to deliver the digital services; and, finally, a network management system to detect and resolve problems.

2 Set-top Hardware Architecture

$\mathbf{T}$he television and information technology industries are currently moving to a new consumer-based computing paradigm. A hardware device called a digital set-top box is expected to become a key component in allowing people to access the services on offer from this new paradigm in this new post-PC era. Our intention in this chapter is to present you with a description of how the set-top business has evolved over the past couple of years. When you think of a set-top box, you generally picture a black box that sits on your television set. From a distance, this is a very correct mental image, however, if you look a little closer, you will discover that it consists of a number of components that are very similar to a desktop PC. This chapter will guide you through the terms and concepts that relate to each of these components. Once you are armed with knowledge of the various hardware components, we conclude this chapter with a description of how to install and troubleshoot a terrestrial digital set-top box.

EVOLUTION OF ADVANCED DIGITAL SET-TOPS . . . . . .

The deployment of digital TV and interactive services is already under way in various locations around the globe. During this transition period, which is expected to last about 10 years, TV operators will continue to broadcast analog signals in parallel to the new digital transmissions. Central to this migration from analog to digital broadcasting is a small black device called a set-top box. This small black box that sits on top of a standard television set will enable consumers to use their existing televisions to participate in the digital revolution of the 21st century. These set-top boxes will retail for about $250 and provide consumers with a much better quality picture compared with today's existing analog systems. From their living rooms, consumers will use these devices to watch TV, surf the Internet, e-mail their friends, shop for products, investigate their hobbies, play multimedia games, and more.

Experts are predicting that these low-cost devices will become a gateway to the much-hyped digital information superhighway. The eventual market for set-tops is expected to exceed 4 billion units. According to Dataquest, sales of digital set-top boxes in the year 2000 are expected to reach 25.1 million units, worth an estimated $6.3 billion, and will reach a level of 50 million units annually by the year 2005. The chart in Figure 2.1 illustrates some of the forecasted figures.

Set-top boxes have been with us for many years. The first generation of set-tops were capable of only receiving and unscrambling analog transmissions and displaying the results on your TV set. Modern versions of these devices contain more advanced features and allow TV viewers access to a limited number of interactive services.

The second generation of set-tops is similar to their analog counterparts. However, they empower subscribers to access a range of digital TV services. A typical second generation set-top will perform basic MPEG decoding, have a low-cost CPU, a minimum amount of memory (that is, 1 Mbyte), a low speed return channel

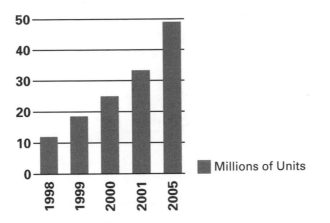

Figure 2.1
Forecasted sales of digital set-top boxes

such as a telephone modem, and limited support for connecting the box to remote devices.

Approximately 8 million of these devices are currently operational in Europe and the United States. In addition to receiving digital TV signals most of these set-tops are also capable of receiving and processing analog signals. Certainly there are a lot of people who are satisfied to sit in front of a television and be passively entertained. But there is, however, another section of the TV community who gets bored quite easily with the old style of watching a TV and are looking to use their television to access a variety of interactive multimedia applications. It is these people that are demanding set-top boxes with advanced computing capabilities.

Toward the end of 1998, a new generation of set-top box began to emerge. This new generation of fully interactive set-tops have adopted a number of PC-like features, including high-speed data interfaces, extra memory, a powerful CPU, high-speed return channel and the ability to process multimedia-based content.

These devices are user friendly and enable TV viewers to access a range of Internet- and TV-centric applications, including: TV mail, video on demand, home shopping, interactive advertising, multi-user games, and electronic program guides.

The practical deployment of these advanced digital set-tops does, however, have some obstacles to overcome before mass-market penetration. For example, up until recently consumers were unwilling to purchase these devices because of the high costs associated with manufacturing a digital set-top box. Consequently, network operators have been increasing the pressure on set-top manufacturers to cut costs. Some operators have even decided to subsidize digital set-tops in order to expand subscriber bases and increase overall market share.

Most vendors and network operators agree that the cost of a set-top box in a retail store should initially cost between $300 and $500. The challenge for manufacturers, therefore, is to design a low-cost set-top box that supports existing applications such as near Pay Per View and basic navigation, but can evolve to support advanced Internet-based applications. In 1999, most analysts are expecting to see an explosion of activity in the set-top industry.

SET-TOP BOX COMPUTING PARADIGM . . . .

The paradigms of computing have been constantly evolving and changing over the past 30 years. It began in the late 1950s with the presence of large, room-size machines known as *mainframes*. They provided users of computers with a centralized location for processing and storing data. Typically, a mainframe consisted of one processor, a small amount of memory, and a limited storage device. Devices called *dumb terminals* were used to input data onto mainframes. They consisted of a keyboard and a screen with no local storage space. The environment of mainframes providing all the data storage and computational activity to a number of dumb terminals became known as the *centralized computing paradigm.* This type of computing is still in limited use today. As the computer industry matured in the 1980s, personal computers (PCs) were created, which allowed individuals to have total control over their own computers. The new power of local processing resulted in a rapid migration away from the mainframe environment to a new PC-based computing model known as *distributed computing.* Instead of centralizing all data processing into a single mainframe machine, distributed computing uses multiple smaller processing computers. While the distributed PC paradigm was growing in its worldwide use, so too was another paradigm—the *network centric computing* paradigm. The concept of the network-centric paradigm is based on a type of computing where the computers on a network have to connect to a server for essential resources.

These three paradigms have been basically restricted to the corporate and business sectors of our community and have resulted in the manufacture and sale of 200 million computers worldwide. As sales of computers continue to skyrocket, a new computing paradigm is beginning to emerge in the mass markets, which is largely based on a set-top box and a standard TV monitor. These set-top boxes will operate on consumer-based networks such as cable TV, and digital TV satellite networks.

These new consumer-based networks of the future will be capable of delivering advanced e-commerce and Internet based services to billions of people around the globe. Before we jump into this new and exciting computing paradigm, it may be useful if we first take a high-level look at the set-top industry. Figure 2.2 presents an illustration of the major participants. The companies shown in the diagram are leaders within their fields. When evaluating various set-top technologies, this figure is an excellent quick reference resource.

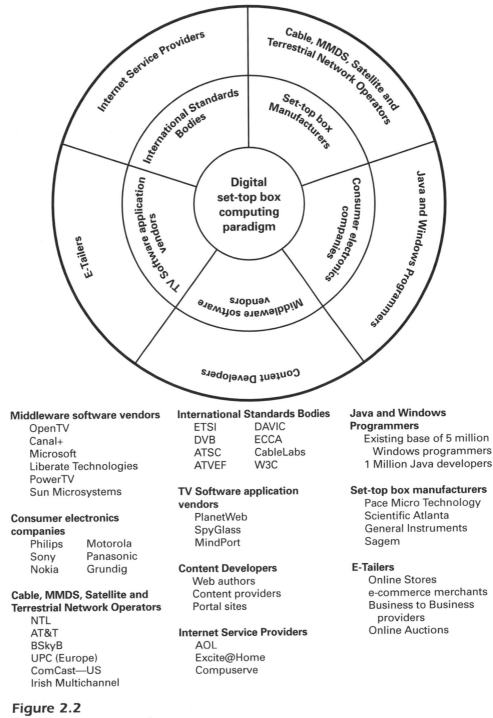

Figure 2.2
Set-top industry overview

Middleware software vendors
OpenTV
Canal+
Microsoft
Liberate Technologies
PowerTV
Sun Microsystems

Consumer electronics companies
Philips   Motorola
Sony   Panasonic
Nokia   Grundig

Cable, MMDS, Satellite and Terrestrial Network Operators
NTL
AT&T
BSkyB
UPC (Europe)
ComCast—US
Irish Multichannel

International Standards Bodies
ETSI   DAVIC
DVB   ECCA
ATSC   CableLabs
ATVEF   W3C

TV Software application vendors
PlanetWeb
SpyGlass
MindPort

Content Developers
Web authors
Content providers
Portal sites

Internet Service Providers
AOL
Excite@Home
Compuserve

Java and Windows Programmers
Existing base of 5 million
    Windows programmers
1 Million Java developers

Set-top box manufacturers
Pace Micro Technology
Scientific Atlanta
General Instruments
Sagem

E-Tailers
Online Stores
e-commerce merchants
Business to Business
    providers
Online Auctions

BASIC CONCEPTS . . . .

When you think of a set-top box, you generally picture a TV set and a black box connected to the set with lots of wires. The true picture of a digital set-top is one of a complex electronics device comprised of many hardware and software components.

It is usually connected to your TV set and the cable connection on the wall. Your local cable, terrestrial, or satellite operator normally installs these devices. This may change soon when set-top boxes enter retail stores across the globe. Set-top boxes can also be described as types of computers that translate digital signals into a format, which can be viewed on a television screen.

The main features of a set-top box may be classified as follows:

- decodes the incoming digital signal;
- verifies access rights and security levels;
- displays cinema-quality pictures on your TV set;
- outputs digital surround sound; and
- processes and renders Internet and interactive TV services.

HOW A SET-TOP WORKS . . . .

Basically, the tuner in the box receives a digital signal from a cable, satellite, or terrestrial network and isolates a particular channel. The signal is then forwarded to a silicon chip called a *demodulator* and converted to binary format. Once in binary format, the demodulator will check for errors and forward the binary signal to another chip called a *demultiplexer*. This chip will then extract the audio, video, and data from the binary stream and send the data to the appropriate decoder chips. This demultiplexer chip may also work with the security subsystem to determine your access rights to various Internet and digital TV services.

Once the demultiplexer has finished with the signal, the three decoders will transform the digital bits into a format suitable for viewing on your television.

UNDER THE HOOD . . . .

At the moment, every network operator has unique set-top box requirements. Therefore, manufacturers are forced to have a distinct design for each operator. Hence, the architecture we describe in this chapter is for a pretty advanced set-top box and is not specific to any network operator or set-top box manufacturer.

The physical components may be roughly divided into the following categories.

- system board,
- tuner(s),
- modulator and demodulator,
- demultiplexer and decryptor,
- decoders,
- graphics processor,
- CPU and memory,
- storage devices,
- physical interfaces, and
- physical characteristics.

If we look more closely at the architecture of a digital set-top in Figure 2.3, you will notice that the hardware architecture is very similar to a standard desktop multimedia computer. This figure shows an expanded and simplified view of a set-top box capable of supporting broadcast analog, broadcast digital, and interactive digital transmission.

System Board

If you were to open up your digital set-top and look inside, you would see a large printed circuit board: the *system board*. All the main hardware components of the set-top are connected to the system board. The digital TV information is carried between set-top hardware components using buses. The system board is made of a fiberglass sheet that has miniature electronic circuitry embedded in it.

This digital information is in the form of bits and bytes. A bit is the smallest unit of information that can be processed by a set-top. A single bit can hold only one of two values: zero or one. A byte contains more meaningful information and is obtained by combining 8 consecutive bits. A byte represents one American Standard Code for Information Interchange (ASCII) character inside the digital set-top. ASCII is a code used to represent English characters as numbers. For example, if a subscriber uses a wireless keyboard to type *A* on the TV screen, this character is processed within the set-top as 01000001. You can think of a bus as a type of highway or pathway in which data travels within a digital set-top box.

The width of this bus determines how much data can be sent between internal set-top box components. For example, an 8-bit bus is capable of transmitting 8 bits of data, whereas a 16-bit bus is capable of transmitting double the amount of information.

In addition to bus width, set-top designers also measure the clock speed of a bus to determine how fast interactive TV applications can run within the box. All buses on the system board consist of two parts: an *address bus* and a *data bus*. As the name sug-

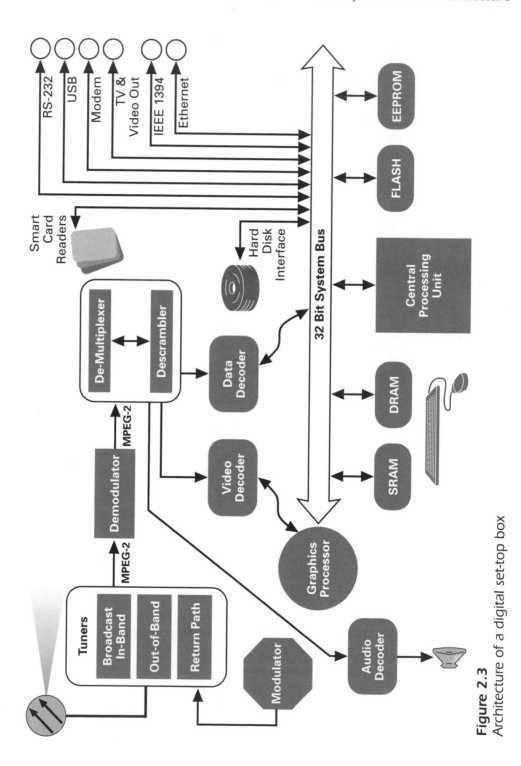

Figure 2.3
Architecture of a digital set-top box

gests, the data bus is used to carry actual digital TV data, whereas the address bus carries information about where the data needs to go.

At present, most set-top boxes are comprised of a mixture of 8- and 16-bit data buses. These bus configurations are suitable for processing video, audio, and limited interactive data services. To meet the growing demands for applications like Internet services, which require high-speed pathways to interconnect set-top components, manufacturers have begun replacing old 8-bit and 16-bit buses with faster 32- and 64-bit buses, such as PCI (Peripheral Component Interconnect). The PCI bus was developed by Intel and is capable of simultaneously transmitting 64 bits of data between hardware components. Most modern PCs include a PCI bus and analysts are predicting that the next generation of digital set-top boxes will also contain PCI bus interfaces.

Tuner(s)

The tuner module is available for accessing QAM-, OFDM-, and QPSK-based networks. In addition to receiving inputs from digital networks, most tuners are also capable of tuning analog broadcasts. Tuners can be divided into three broad categories:

Broadcast In-band (IB) Tuner. Once the signal arrives from the physical transmission media, the IB tuner will isolate a physical channel from a multiplex of channels and convert to baseband. The term *baseband* is used to describe a single channel or digital signal, extracted from a broadband signal which is basically a stream of multiple channels.

Out Of Band (OOB) Tuner. This type of tuner facilitates the transfer of data between the head-end systems and the set-top box. They are widely used in cable set-top boxes for providing subscribers with a medley of interactive services. Implementations of the OOB tuner tend to operate within the 100 to 350 MHz frequency band.

Return Path Tuner. This tuner allows a subscriber to activate the return path and send data back to the interactive services provider. Implementations of this tuner tend to operate within the 5 to 60 MHz frequency band.

Modulator and Demodulator

The baseband output signal from the tuner is forwarded to a demodulator. The function of the demodulator is to sample the analog signal and convert it to a digital bit-stream. The bit-stream contains video, audio, and possibly some data. Once the bit-stream has been recovered, it is checked for errors and forwarded to the demultiplexer. The modulator reverses the actions of a demodulator and is used by the set-top box to deliver a signal to the return path tuner.

Demultiplexer and Decryptor

A standard MPEG-2 data stream will consist of a number of uniquely identified data packets. MPEG-2 uses an identifier called a Packet ID (PID) that identifies a packet as containing a particular format of data: audio, video, or interactive services. European and Japanese TV operators have agreed on 32 unique PIDs for identifying various data formats. The demultiplexer is an application-specific integrated circuit (ASIC) chipset that examines every PID, selects particular packets, decrypts, and forwards to a specific decoder. For example, all packets with the data PID will be forwarded to the data decoder.

The decryption unit is based on a complex algorithm that prevents unauthorized users from viewing programs or accessing Internet-based services. The exact details of the decryption process are operator-specific and thus are shrouded in secrecy.

There is no global decryption standard. However, the Europeans have defined the DVB common scrambling algorithm and Japan has defined their own scrambling scheme. Work is also ongoing in the U.S. to forge a common scrambling algorithm standard.

Decoders

A digital set-top box will normally contain three separate decoders for converting the digital bit-stream back into a format that can be heard and viewed by the subscriber.

A video decoder will transform the video packets into a sequence of pictures, which are displayed on the TV monitor. Video decoder chips are capable of formatting pictures for TV monitors with different screen resolutions and support for *still pictures*. A still picture is defined as a video sequence containing exactly one picture and is normally used for interactive TV advertising.

The compressed audio bit-stream is sent to an audio decoder for decompression. Once the MPEG-2 bit-stream is decompressed, it is presented to a set of speakers. Current digital set-tops are capable of supporting the following audio modes: mono and dual channel, stereo, and joint stereo.

Digital TV customers expect a powerful and convenient system to navigate through the hundreds of channels and interactive services. This detail is also stored within the MPEG-2 stream in table format and is interpreted using a data decoder. Once interpreted, the data is either presented to an external device or sent to the set-top processor.

Graphics Processor

Currently graphic requirements for set-top boxes are pretty low. However, as the demand for Internet browsing and multimedia applications increases by the day, manufacturers are beginning to add graphics processors to their designs.

The main purpose of a graphics processor is to render a range of Internet file formats and proprietary interactive TV file formats. Once rendered by the graphics engine, the graphics file is often used to overlay the standard video display on your TV. The power of these processors will continue to increase as TV providers attempt to differentiate themselves by offering exciting new applications, such as 3D games, to their subscriber base.

Central Processing Unit

The Central Processing Unit (CPU) is the brains of the set-top and is housed in a single chip called a *processor.* In terms of functionality and processing, the CPU is the most important element of a digital set-top box. Functions typically provided by a processor include:

- initializes the various set-top hardware components;
- processes a range of Internet and interactive TV applications;
- monitors and manages hardware interrupts;
- fetches data and instructions from memory; and
- runs various programs.

CPUs are available in different shapes, pin structures, architectures, and speeds. The chip itself contains millions of transistors that are used to manage data transfer within the set-top and perform any necessary computations. The more transistors a CPU has, the faster it can process data.

The architecture of a set-top processor is unique for each manufacturer. However, all processors contain an arithmetic-logic unit, a control unit, and a clock. The arithmetic-logic unit performs all calculations and logical operations on the digital data. The control unit works in close harmony with the arithmetic-logic unit and is responsible for processing input information and executing instructions. It is worth noting that in the world of electronics, all information is broken into data and instructions. When a subscriber, for example, presses a key on their remote control to change the channel, this action is interpreted as an instruction by the processor, which needs to be executed. The clock's main function is to regulate the speed of the processor and synchronize all the parts of the set-top.

The actual speed of a set-top processor is measured in megahertz (MHz), which means million of cycles per second. So a 60-MHz processor has 60 million cycles in one second and in each cycle one or more set-top instructions are executed. The MHz value will give you a rough estimate of how fast a processor in a set-top box can execute instructions. Eighty MHz chips are now becoming standard. However, as demand from service providers increase, some analysts expect to see 150 MHz and 200 MHz chips to be on the market before the end of 1999.

The performance of a processor can also be measured by the width of the data channel. In other words, the more bits a processor handles at a particular moment in time, the more powerful it is. For example, a processor with a 32-bit data channel is twice as fast as a 16-bit processor.

The first generation of digital set-top processors launched in 1995 had a bus capacity of 8 bits. As requirements grew in 1996, manufacturers began to produce set-top boxes with 16-bit CPUs. In 1997, TV service companies recognized the limitations of 16-bit processors and began upgrading their set-top designs to more powerful 32-bit architectures. Predictions for the future include a steady increase in customer expectation for improved set-top box functionality. More and more processor power is required to facilitate Web browsing, video e-mails, and distance learning applications on your TV set. Hence, processors will need to be from a product family that allows set-top box manufacturers to improve performance, while keeping development costs to a minimum.

Many set-top boxes that are currently installed in consumer's homes are based on older and relatively slow CPUs. These boxes have limitations when it comes to handling interactive TV services. In pursuit of solutions for advanced graphics and two-way communication capabilities in set-top boxes, integrated circuit (IC) vendors are unveiling new processors on a regular basis. Some of the most popular families of CPU chips available to set-top box manufacturers are illustrated in Table 2.1.

Table 2.1   A Sample of Processors Used in Digital Set-top Boxes

Processor Family	Vendor(s)	For More Information
ARM	Advanced RISC Machines	http://www.arm.com/
MIPS	Philips and NEC	http://www.philips.com http://www.nec.com/
PowerPC	IBM and Motorola	http://www.ibm.com/ http://www.motorola.com/
Sparc RISC	Sun Microsystems	http://www.sun.com/
STx0	ST Microelectronics	http://eu.st.com/stonline/index.htm
SH-4 Series	Hitachi	http://www.hitachi.com
X86	Intel	http://www.intel.com

Memory Configuration

Just as a computer needs memory to function, a set-top also requires memory to store and manipulate instructions that are issued by the subscriber. Memory comes in chip format and is comprised of millions of integrated circuits. These chips are connected to the system board inside the set-top box. There are two common denotations that are used to represent the size of memory: a kilobyte (KB) is 1,024 bytes and a megabyte (MB) represents 1,048,576 bytes.

The memory modules account for a substantial percentage of the cost of the set-top box. Most elements within the set-top box will require memory to perform various tasks. The graphics engine, video decoder, and the descrambler will all require a certain amount of memory to fulfill their specific functions within the set-top box. Set-top memory can be divided into RAM and ROM, summarized below.

Random Access Memory (RAM)

Most functions performed by the set-top box will require access to RAM. It is used as a temporary storage area for data flowing between the processor and the various hardware components. If you open a set-top box and look inside, you will see that RAM is located on single inline memory modules (SIMMs), which are connected to the system board. SIMMs are best described as small circuit boards that hold a group of memory chips. They are very easy to install and are ideal for digital customers who need to improve the performance of their set-tops.

There are two basic types of RAM in a set-top box: dynamic RAM (DRAM), and Static RAM (SRAM).

Both memory types hold information, but differ in the technologies used to store the data. DRAM will continue to refresh its memory thousands of times a second, whereas SRAM does not refresh its data bits, making it faster but also more expensive. The contents of both types of memory are lost once the consumer powers down the set-top.

In general, set-top box manufacturers will use SRAM to support time-critical tasks such as MPEG processing and DRAM for interactive applications. The size and speed of the RAM has a great influence on the overall performance of a set-top box. A minimum 4 MB of RAM is recommended in most set-top boxes. Applications that involve imaging and graphic manipulations will require more system RAM.

Read Only Memory (ROM)

Once data has been written onto a ROM chip, the network operator or the digital subscriber cannot remove it. ROM is *nonvolatile,* which means it does not lose its contents when the set-top is powered off. Most set-tops contain EEPROMs and Flash ROM, which are variations of the basic ROM technology.

Electrically Erasable Programmable Read Only Memory (EEPROM)

EEPROM is a special type of memory used in set-top boxes to store controls and boot up information. The data is permanently stored on the chip, even when the subscriber powers off the set-top box.

To remove this control information you need to expose the EEPROM chip to ultraviolet light and electrical charges. A set-top box will contain a small amount of EEPROM (usually kilobytes) and has slower access rates than RAM.

FLASH Memory

A Flash memory chip is very similar in functionality to an EEPROM. The only difference between the two is that a Flash memory chip can be erased and reprogrammed in blocks of data bytes instead of one byte at a time. This feature allows operators to update the set-top's operating system and resident software applications over the network without physically visiting the subscriber's home place.

This update can be done in either the foreground or the background. A foreground set-top software update is very intrusive to the viewing experience. A message normally appears on the TV screen notifying the viewer that a code update is available. If the subscriber chooses to proceed with the update, the set-top box is taken off line while the software update occurs.

Foreground updates can take as little as two minutes or as long as a half an hour, depending on the write performance of the Flash memory and the amount of code that needs to be downloaded. Set-tops designed for foreground updates require less Flash memory and often rely on a single flash component. By contrast, a background update does not interrupt the viewing experience. The viewer is not even aware an update is taking place. In this case, the set-top contains two Flash memory devices. The first device stores the existing code while the second is used for updates. The system switches to the flash device with the new code when the power is recycled. An onscreen display will notify the subscriber of the new features that have been installed. While this method of downloading software is more elegant, it is obviously more expensive. Besides using Flash memory to store software code, it can also be used to store subscriber-specific information. Every time a customer makes a purchase or visits a site on the Internet, details of this action are stored in the flash for marketing purposes.

Unlike a hard disk, Flash memory is a solid-state device. It has no mechanical parts and therefore provides subscribers with instant performance without suffering from long seek times.

The recommended minimum memory configuration for a digital set-top box is 8 MB of RAM, 2 KB of EEPROM, and 8 MB of Flash memory.

If you decide to add additional memory, it is important that you purchase memory that matches the speed requirements of your set-top.

Digital set-top boxes were released in 1999 with the following memory configurations.

Memory Type	Quantity
RAM	24 MB
Flash Memory	16 MB
EEPROM	400 KB

Storage Devices

The ability to locally store and retrieve information is expected to become the most important commodity for customers of digital TV services. While the storage space on the first generation of set-tops was limited to Flash memory, today we are beginning to see designers adding interfaces to the motherboard that will allow subscribers to integrate high capacity hard drives into their set-top boxes. The capacity of a hard drive is measured in gigabytes (GB) and may be used by subscribers to store personal documents, favorite Internet sites, and e-mail. The basic architecture is comprised of magnetic-coated circles of material that contain stored information. These circles are called *platters* and are stacked on top of each other to increase the storage capacity of the drive. Information is read from or stored to the hard disk using read and write heads.

Hard disks can be integrated within the set-top or else connected as an external device through high-speed data port interfaces. There are two disk interface technologies that are currently competing for a slice of the set-top market: Small Computer Systems Interface (SCSI; pronounced "scuzzy") and Integrated Drive Electronics (IDE). Drives with an IDE interface are capable of transferring data within a set-top at speeds ranging from 3.3 Mbps to 16.6 Mbps. SCSI hard drives offer subscribers faster access and retrieval times, but they are more expensive than IDE-based drives. Disk drives are capable of retrieving data at high-speeds. In the early days of hard disk manufacturing, drives were only capable of storing around 10 or 20 MB of data. Now, drive capacities have increased dramatically and costs of manufacturing hard disks have plummeted downward. Today, a standard PC will come with a 9-GB drive for storing program and data files. By adding high capacity drives to set-top boxes, digital TV subscribers will be able to download and store digital movies. At the time of this writing, a 17.2-GB drive could be purchased for around $120. This gives customers the ability to store four movies for future viewing.

It is very important for subscribers who decide to connect hard disks to their set-tops to make regular backups. Otherwise, important information could be lost in the event of a fire, a power outage or even a simple user error. High capacity Zip and Jazz disks are very suitable for backing up information because they can be easily connected to the high-speed interface ports at the back of the set-top. At the time of this writing, Seagate Technology, a leading provider of storage products, announced a new home recording technology that allows a hard disk to deliver data to a set-top box at a compatible transfer rate. The new technology, (called SeaStream) could potentially allow TV viewers to use their set-top boxes to simultaneously record multiple programs onto a hard disk.

Physical Interfaces

As set-top hardware designs continue to evolve, the range and choice of physical interfaces available to set-top users is growing by the week. We can classify the physical interfaces of a set-top box into the following categories:

- modems,
- high-speed multimedia interfaces,
- RS232,
- common interface,
- TV and VCR interfaces,
- smart card readers,
- remote controls,
- IR blasters, and
- wireless keyboards.

Modems

Computers use modems to "talk" to each other. In the context of a digital TV environment, modems are added to set-top boxes to facilitate the implementation of two-way interactive services. Many network operators regard interactivity via a modem as the key difference between multichannel broadcasting in the digital domain and multichannel broadcasting in the analog domain. Nowadays, almost all new set-tops come with a built-in modem. However, it is also possible to connect an external modem to the set-top box. From a subscriber's perspective, attaching a lead from the back of the set-top to the telephone or cable socket on the wall activates the modem. Once activated, the modem can utilize the return path for a number of uses, including:

- sending requests to Web servers on the Internet;
- enabling set-top users to upload files and send e-mail; and
- facilitating two-way interactive TV services, such as video on demand.

The modem options available to set-top users are: standard telephone modem for terrestrial, satellite, and MMDS environments; and cable modems for a standard cable network.

Standard Telephone Modems

A telephone modem is a device that translates the digital signals from a computer into analog signals that can be sent down a standard telephone line. At the receiving end, another modem converts the analog signal into a digital one for the receiving computer. This conversion of signals is known as *modulation* and *demodulation*. A telephone modem installed in a set-top box is normally configured to dial out only and will never accept incoming calls. There is a range of modems operating at speeds from 1200 bits per second (or bps) to 56000 bps. Bits per second is a measure of the number of data bits (digital 0s and 1s) transmitted each second in a communications channel. The speed of the modem resident in the set-top box will determine the operator's ability to offer Internet and interactive TV services to their subscribers. Satellite providers, MMDS operators, and terrestrial broadcasters normally deploy telephone modem-enabled set-top boxes to provide interactive services to their subscriber base. The speed of the modem is very important because network operators are able to offer sophisticated interactive services to customers who have set-top boxes with fast telephone modems. There is a direct correlation between the speed of the modem used for the return channel path and the subscriber's overall digital TV experience. Manufacturers have realized this fact and have begun to add faster telephone modems to their set-top designs.

The Comité Consultatif Internationale Téléphonique et Telegraphique (CCITT), (a European committee that develops worldwide data communications standards), has produced a set of recommended standards for modems. Most of the telephone modems currently being installed in set-top boxes will conform to one of the following CCITT standards.

V.22/V.22 bis • Commonly found in set-tops manufactured in 1996, these modems are capable of transmitting and receiving data at speeds of between 1200 bps and 2400 bps.

V.32/V.32 bis • This standard modem is able to send and receive data across a telephone network at 4800 bps or 9600 bps.

V.34/V.34 bis • The V.34 telephone modems are capable of sending and receiving data across phone lines at 28800 bps. The set-tops that have been manufactured in 1998 will more than likely contain this type of modem.

V.42 bis • This is a data compression protocol, which enables a set-top modem to achieve a data transfer rate of 34000 bps. The ability to reach these speeds will very much depend on the quality of the telephone line.

V.90 and K56Flex • It was once believed that the maximum data transfer speed achievable on a telephone line was 34000 bps. This perception has been bypassed and set-tops with modems sending information at 56000 bps were made available in 1999. This measurement is the expected speed, but the actual rate of data transfer depends on line conditions and the speed of the modem at the other end.

All of the modems described above use the standard analog telephone line as an interaction channel. This type of set-top box raises the following deployment issues:

- A subscriber may not have the telephone connection in the same room as the television. In this case, an extension cord needs to run from the set-top box to the nearest telephone line, which leads to additional installation costs for the network operator.

- Unless the subscriber has a second telephone line, it is impossible to make or receive normal telephone calls while the set-top box is communicating with the interactive service provider. To address this issue, some subscribers will either install a second telephone line for interactive services or else replace their existing analog line with an Integrated Systems Digital Network (ISDN) line. An ISDN connection will allow subscribers to make or receive normal telephone calls when the set-top box is communicating.

Cable Modems

Another type of modem widely used in set-top boxes to improve two-way communications is the cable modem. The term *cable modem* refers to a network interface that operates over a standard cable TV system. Cable modems offer service providers the potential of offering high-speed Internet to millions of people around the globe. To achieve mass-market deployment, standards had to be developed.

In the United States, a consortium called Multimedia Cable Network System (MCNS) has developed a standard for bidirectional communications over a cable network called Data Over Cable System Interface Specification (DOCSIS). A number of large networking companies have built products based on the DOCSIS standard and are commercially deployed around the world. The main focus of the DOCSIS standard is offering Internet services to PC users.

In Europe, the DVB consortium has produced a comprehensive set of specifications called DAVIC. The DVB approach is very much focused on transmitting high-speed data in a television environment. At the moment, there are only a handful of vendors who have decided to build products based on the DVB standard. This is expected to change in the near future, with a number of manufacturers committed to building set-tops with DVB-compliant cable modems. Cable modems are primarily used for receiving and transmitting TCP/IP (Transmission Control Protocol/Internet Protocol) traffic, including multimedia content and Web access data. The TCP/IP protocol suite is a widely implemented internetworking standard, described in Chapter 7 in more detail. It sends and receives data in two different fashions. The data that is sent from the head-end to the cable modem (downstream) uses the QAM modulation scheme. The frequency spectrum is between 50 MHz to 750 MHz. When the set-top box needs to send data upstream to the head-end, the cable modem uses the 8 MHz and 40 MHz frequency band. This range of frequencies tends to be quite noisy, with interference coming from CBs and home appliances. Due to this problem, most set-top box manufacturers will use the QPSK modulation scheme in the upstream (return channel) direction.

A standard cable modem will have two connections; one port is connected to the TV outlet on the wall and the other to the subscriber's PC. The cable modem will then communicate over the cable network to a device called a Cable Modem Termination System (CMTS). The speed of the cable modem depends on traffic levels and the overall network architecture. Theoretically speaking, cable modems can achieve downstream speeds in excess of 30 Mbps. However, in reality subscribers can expect to download information between 1 and 1.5 Mbps. Note that when we talk about downstream, we are referring to the signal transfer from the cable head-end to the cable modem. Cable modems are more suitable for applications that require a high-speed return path. For this reason, manufacturers have begun embedding cable modems with digital set-tops. Commercial deployment of cable modem-enabled set-top boxes occurred in the middle of 1999. Cable modem-enabled set-tops are only suitable for a cable TV network and will not function on other networks, such as terrestrial, MMDS, and satellite. To provide interactivity on these networks, subscribers will need to buy or rent a set-top box with a telephone return path.

High-Speed Multimedia Interfaces

As consumer electronic technologies and home PCs continue to converge, consumers and set-top box suppliers are anxious to take advantage of a number of high-speed data transfer technologies. Many of the new set-top box designs are incorporating interfaces that will allow set-tops to communicate in real time with devices such as camcorders, Digital Video Disks (DVDs), CD players, and music keyboards. Manufacturers are capable of adding the following interface options to a digital set-top box.

IEEE 1284 Parallel Port

The IEEE 1284 parallel port provides digital set-top boxes with a high-speed bidirectional connection to a printer. This interface is capable of delivering data to the printer at speeds ranging from 400 Kbps to 1.5 Mbps. This parallel port is quite revolutionary and is nearly 40 times faster than common parallel ports found in desktop and portable notebooks.

Universal Series Bus (USB)

USB is a new external bus standard that was originally specified by Intel to replace older bus standards. USB fully supports plug-and-play technology. With plug-and-play, hardware devices such as mouses, joysticks, and hard disks can be automatically configured as soon as they are physically attached to the set-top box.

Plug-and-play also enables subscribers to add or remove devices while the set-top is up and running.

One USB port can connect up to 127 devices by linking them to the device connected to the port. USB supports two high-speed data transfer protocols: isonchronous and asynchronous. An isonchronous connection from the USB port on the set-top box to a remote device will support data transfers at a guaranteed, fixed rate of delivery. This mode of data transfer allows scanners, video devices and printers to communicate with digital set-top boxes at 12 Mbps. The asynchronous protocol is slower and is used to communicate with keyboards, joysticks, pointing devices, and mouses at 1.5 Mbps.

IEEE 1394 or FireWire Bus Interface Standard

Apple Computers invented FireWire, sometimes referred to as IEEE 1394, a networking standard designed to connect high bandwidth consumer electronic devices such as digital camcorders, videodisc players, and set-top boxes.

Similar to USB, the IEEE 1394 interface also supports plug-and-play technologies. In 1995, the standard was fully ratified by the Institute of Electrical and Electronics Engineers (IEEE). It is possible to connect 53 different devices to a single IEEE 1394 port. The IEEE 1394 specification currently supports the following data transfer rates: S100 (98.3 Mbps), S200 (196.6 Mbps), and S400 (393.2 Mbps). It transfers data at a guaranteed rate, which makes it ideal for devices with a large amount of data movement. To date, relatively few set-top manufacturers have decided to incorporate Firewire into their designs, but the trend is changing.

The set-top box of the future will incorporate FireWire technology and promises to promote the idea of connecting set-tops to various other entertainment devices around the house.

10 Base-T

Some subscribers will want to establish a home network for sharing computer and set-top resources. One way of networking home devices is to purchase a set-top box with a 10 Base-T interface. 10 Base-T, commonly known as Ethernet, is a networking standard that is used by the set-top to communicate with personal computers, scanners, and printers. Connecting a 10 Base-T port to a range of peripheral devices requires the use of specialized cabling and a device called a *hub*. We intend to cover the concept of home networking in more detail in Chapter 13.

RS-232 Serial Interface

The RS-232 port is used for serial communications. *Serial communication* means that a device is transmitting bits of information sequentially over a single physical medium.

Set-top boxes normally come equipped with the RS-232 standard serial interface. The interface uses a D connector with 9 pins and allows connectivity to serial printers, computers, and standard telephone modems.

Common Interface

The common interface (CI) is added to some of the set-top boxes that are manufactured for the European market. CI is a standardized interface that has been defined by the DVB project between the set-top box and a separate hardware module. The most popular type of hardware module is based on the Personal Computer Memory Card International Association (PCMCIA) Type II standard. The PCMCIA card is best described as a credit card-sized peripheral with a thickness of .2 of an inch, a length of 3.4 inches and a width of 2.1 inches. This PCMCIA card has a number of uses, including:

- extending the set-top memory capabilities;
- storing and decrypting CAs for multiple service providers;
- adding hard disk space to the set-top box; and
- adding new tuners to the set-top box.

In the United States CableLabs refer to these cards as point of deployment (POD) modules. They come with an embedded conditional access system and are specific to each network operator. By making the POD module a separable unit from the digital set-top, cable boxes could, in theory, become interchangeable systems that could be sold in the retail channel. SCM Microsystems is a leading developer and supplier of CI modules (for additional information on their products, take a look at their web site at http://www.scmmicro.com).

TV and VCR Interfaces

Set-top boxes communicate with your TV set and video recorder through two output ports called Scart connectors. The interfaces use female-type connectors with 21 pins. The pin assignments are vendor-specific.

Smart Card Readers

A standard set-top box will contain two slots. The first slot is used for a smart card that authorizes subscriber access to various digital television services and the second slot may be used for e-commerce purposes. Electrically, the readers must conform to the ISO/IEC 7816-3 standards. The readers are also capable of supporting a number of data exchange protocols. We will cover smart card technologies in more detail in Chapter 11.

Remote Controls

A remote control is more than a device for changing channels. It is the key that enables subscribers to access a world of digital services and information resources.

The network operator specifies the functions of the remote control. However, a certain amount of control keys will be common across all remote controls. Table 2.2 summarizes some of the most popular remote control buttons and associated actions.

Table 2.2   *Functionality of a Remote Control*

Key description	Set-top action
On/Off	TV is instructed to go into power up or standby mode
Menu	Starts the installation menu for configuring the set-top
Electronic Program Guide (EPG)	Executes navigational system
Volume	Increases and decreases audio
Numeric block of keys	Entering PIN codes and selecting channels
OK	Confirming the selection of a Pay Per View service
Arrows—left, right, up, down	Channel surfing
Home	Navigate back to the start-up screen
Help	Displays help information

The average number of buttons located on a remote control keypad is around 30, but some remote controls are designed with a maximum of 48 different buttons.

The remote control receiver that is embedded in the set-top box supports the reception of the American Standard Code for Information Interchange (ASCII) character set. Once the commands from the remote control are received by the set-top, the receiver delivers the commands to the CPU. The CPU will then execute the particular command and display the results on your TV screen.

The remote control receiver is also capable of receiving information from a keyboard. Subscribers who want to use their set-tops for e-mail, home shopping, and Internet access will need to purchase an alphanumeric keyboard with an InfraRed transmitter. *InfraRed* are light waves used to remotely carry information from keyboards and remote controls to a set-top. This technology forms the basis of a wireless communications protocol developed by Infrared Data Association, or IrDA. The IrDA protocol allows two-way communication between a remote control or a wireless keyboard and a set-top box. It is possible to use the protocol to transmit data at speeds of up to 115200 bits/sec. We can, however, expect to see the data rate transmission speeds increase to 16 Mbits/sec in the near future.

From a physical perspective, the dimensions of a remote control case normally vary from 6.8 inches × 2.2 inches to 8.3 inches × 2.2 inches.

IR Blasters

An IR blaster is a useful device for subscribers who would like to remotely control their television and VCR from a separate location within the home. It is basically a cable that plugs into one of the interfaces at the back of a set-top box that converts the signal transmitted along the wires into IR signals that remote controls can respond to. A high-power IR blaster can be used to blast IR signals up to about 35 feet.

Wireless Keyboards

A wireless keyboard enables cable TV subscribers to access Internet and interactive TV services through their televisions. At the moment, the network operator at an additional cost to the subscriber supplies wireless keyboards. They are ergonomically designed to fit comfortably on a subscriber's lap while sitting on a couch and can operate at a distance of up to 30 feet away from the digital set-top box. Wireless keyboards are plug-and-play, in other words, the digital subscriber can begin using the keyboard without worrying about configuration settings and installing new device drivers. Some of the advanced wireless keyboards also come with an integrated mouse that allows a consumer to move a pointer around the television screen. Power to the keyboard is supplied from local batteries. The life cycle for these batteries is approximately six months, based on a customer using 2,500 keystrokes per day.

Physical Characteristics

The overall physical look and feel of a set-top box is vendor-specific. However, there are some characteristics that are common to most boxes.

The front panel will contain two smart card slots, a front panel display unit, InfraRed sensor, and a Power ON/OFF button. The front panel display consists of a numeric display that displays selected channel or short messages.

The dimensions of a typical set-top box can vary from 12.5 inches × 1.8 inches × 8.6 inches to 1.8 inches × 3.93 inches × 14.5 inches.

The rear panel of a digital set-top box comprises of Scart connectors, input and output ports, high-speed multimedia interfaces (only included with high-end set-tops), stereo connectors, and a modem connection. A graphical view of a typical rear panel is shown in Figure 2.4.

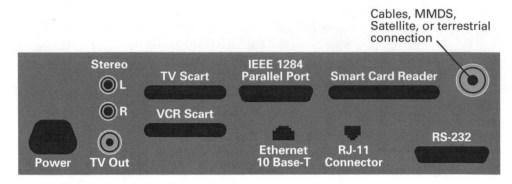

Figure 2.4
Rear panel view of an advanced digital set-top box

Power Supply

As with all electronic devices, set-tops use electrical signals to communicate between various hardware modules. Hence, your set-top box will require a reliable source of power to operate correctly. Electrical power is available in two forms: alternating current (AC) and direct current (DC). Power supplies are used to convert the AC that comes from your wall socket to DC, which is used by your set-top. This conversion process can generate a lot of heat, which could damage the components inside the set-top. As a result, most manufacturers add power supplies with built-in fans that prevent set-tops from overheating. Like many consumer devices, the software that is integrated with the box supports a soft power-down feature using the Power button on the remote control. Soft power-down turns off the television display and frees some hardware resources, but leaves a software program running to respond to a soft power-on request. Soft power-on takes about three seconds—about the same time required for the TV screen to warm up.

INSTALLING A DIGITAL SET-TOP . . . .

The installation cost is a significant issue for TV operators, as this is something that needs to be done in the house of every subscriber. Therefore, we shall take a closer look at the issues and procedures associated with installing a digital set-top box. As described earlier, a set-top box receives the information via satellite, terrestrial, and MMDS transmitters or a cable network, decodes the signal, and displays the picture on your television screen. In most cases, existing reception devices, such as aerials on rooftops, can be used to receive a digital signal. The actual procedures for connecting a set-top box to a digital TV network will depend on the types of equipment that are found in the home. Installers for a cable company could encounter a very simple installation where there is an MMDS aerial feeding one television, up to complicated arrangements of aerials, amplifiers, splitters, VCRs, analog set-top boxes, and a distribution system to multiple television sets throughout the house. It is not possible to cover all the possible combinations, so we will concentrate our energies on a simple installation.

Step 1 • Make sure the set-top box is properly connected to the TV socket on the wall and the viewing smart card is inserted the right way up in the slot on the front of the set-top.

Step 2 • Interconnect the set-top box with other home appliances using the leads that were shipped with the set-top.

Step 3 • Once the set-top has been connected, you can then power the unit up and wait for the box to establish tuning for the various digital services that are available on the network.

Step 4 • A system setup screen should now appear on your television screen, which allows you to:

- see and change picture formats;
- adjust contrast and color levels;
- change the type of sound outputs from your television;
- turn subtitling on or off; and
- test the quality of the incoming digital signal.

Step 5 • Save the new configuration settings to confirm any changes to the default setup.

Step 6 • To activate the return path to access Pay Per View and interactive services, you need to connect a telephone lead to the rear panel of the set-top box.

TROUBLESHOOTING AND INSTALLATION . . . .

Details of how to troubleshoot your set-top box are normally contained within the accompanying instruction manual. Most manuals will list the type of error message that appears on screen, the possible reason for this message, and what to do to correct the problem. Signal-related problems normally require the services of skilled personnel that are employed by your local operator.

The decision tree in Figure 2.5 has been developed by the Digital TV group in the U.K. and enumerates the installation and troubleshooting process for digital terrestrial set-tops.

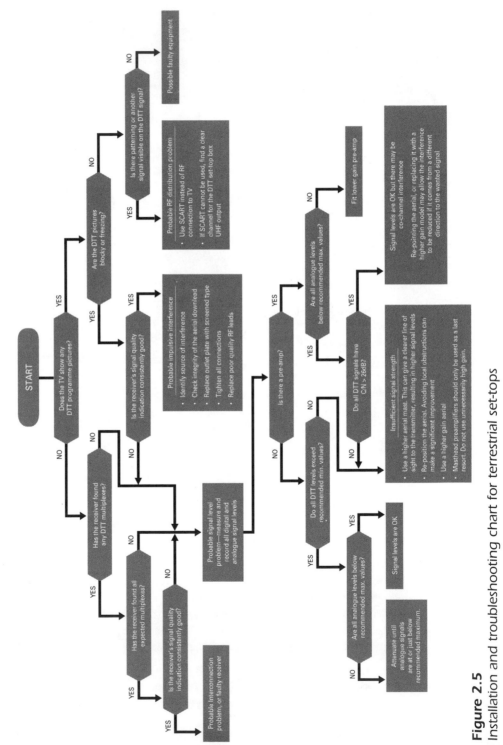

Figure 2.5
Installation and troubleshooting chart for terrestrial set-tops

SUMMARY . . . .

The year 1999 marks the beginning of a new era and paradigm in the TV and computer industry. After 12 years of developing standards and new equipment, both industries are beginning to converge and implementation is finally happening.

The long-heralded convergence of television, computers, communications technologies, and the Internet is happening now. The pace of change within the television and cable business is enormous, with more and more countries around the world committing themselves to the digital revolution. At the center of this new convergence paradigm, is a little black box called a *set-top*. There is a phenomenal wave of activity right now based on building these set-top boxes. They will sit between the digital information superhighway and your television set.

Set-tops have been with us for many years. Today, we are seeing the emergence of set-tops that utilize digital technologies and are capable of processing vast amounts of data. The anatomy of a typical set-top box is built around traditional PC hardware technologies. They contain various flavors of silicon chipsets that are used to handle and process digital video and audio services. To complement the digital services, manufacturers have begun to add a range of PC-like features to their set-top designs, including hard disks, fast processors, and high-speed data ports. As more features become available to subscribers, set-top boxes will require higher performance processors and decoders to keep pace with increased data throughput.

Also of significance to network providers and consumers are the issues that surround the installation and troubleshooting of these complex devices.

3 Set-top Real-time Operating Systems

In this chapter…

So far our discussions about set-top boxes have concentrated on the hardware side of the equation. In this chapter, we commence our examination of the software programs that are required to operate these complex devices. We begin by outlining some of the architectural features of a set-top box real-time operating system—a program that supervises the entire operation of the set-top box. Unlike operating systems for PCs, operating systems for TV-centric devices such as digital set-top boxes do not have a very high profile. Yet every set-top box must have one. This chapter presents seven of the most popular operating systems currently being used by millions of digital set-top boxes.

ARCHITECTURE OF A SET-TOP OS . . . .

Operating systems are one of the most important pieces of software in a set-top box. In fact, every set-top needs an operating system (OS) to function. An OS is a suite of programs used to manage the resources of a particular device. Familiar to most readers is the desktop OS, such as Windows 98, NT workstation, different flavors of UNIX, and the MacOS. The main responsibilities of a desktop OS are:

- allocating and controling the use of the CPU;
- Controling data transfers to hard disks, printers, floppy disks, and other devices;
- ensuring programs run smoothly through the management of computer memory;
- controling communication between computers; and
- managing file systems and data storage.

There are a number of different types of desktop OSs currently on the market and can either be classified as single-tasking or multi-tasking. A single-tasking OS, such as DOS, can only run one program at a time, whereas a multi-tasking OS, like Windows NT, is capable of running multiple programs on a PC at the same time. Computers by their very nature are inherently difficult for humans to work with, since they only understand ones and zeros.

For this reason, all desktop OSs come with an interface that allows end-users and programmers to issue powerful commands to the OS. With the older operating systems like UNIX and DOS, end-users control the PC using a text interface. Over the past 10 years, the use of desktop OSs has simplified because of companies like Microsoft and Apple Computers introducing a graphical user interface. This type of interface enables computer users to execute commands using a mouse to choose from various menus or click on a menu. In regards to storage space, a typical desktop OS will take up between 10 and 200 megabytes of hard disk space.

A set-top box does not have the processing power of a $1,500 multimedia computer and requires an operating system that can handle sophisticated tasks in a small hardware footprint. Similar to a desktop, a set-top needs an operating system to talk to the hardware and manage set-top functions, such as scheduling real-time tasks, managing limited memory resources, and delivering Internet services to subscribers.

The operating system chosen by set-top box manufacturers must be fast and capable of functioning in a real-time environment. In addition to being able to run in a small memory space, a typical set-top OS needs to be extremely reliable because direct user interaction with the OS is very limited.

From a developer's perspective the set-top OS needs to shield the upper application layers from the physical hardware devices. Most of the set-top OSs are typically built in layers, with each layer adding new capabilities.

At the heart of any set-top OS is the *kernel* layer, which is stored in ROM and occupies space ranging from tens of kilobytes to one megabyte of memory. Once the set-top is powered up, the kernel will be loaded first and remains in memory until the set-top is powered down again. The process of booting up a set-top normally takes between 5 and 10 seconds.

It is important that the kernel occupies a small amount of memory. Typically, the kernel is responsible for managing memory resources, real-time applications, and highspeed data transmission. The set-top OS kernel supports multithreading and multitasking. These features allow a set-top box to execute different sections of a program and different programs simultaneously.

In addition to the kernel, a set-top OS needs a *loader* to enable the TV operator to upgrade resident applications or download OS patches to the set-top box. A *resident application* is a program or a number of programs that are built into the memory of the set-top box. For normal updates, the subscriber is given the option to perform the download at a later date, because the process can take several minutes.

A set-top OS requires drivers to control the various hardware devices. Every hardware component in the set-top box—whether it be a smart card reader, a Scart connection, or a modem—must have a device driver. A driver is a program that translates commands from the TV viewer to a format that is recognizable by the hardware component.

Every device contained within the set-top has its own specialized set of commands, which are incorporated into the driver's program. If a manufacturer needs to add extra components to a particular design, then a new driver is written to allow the set-top OS to control the new hardware.

Finally, a set-top OS needs to incorporate a set of Advanced Program Interfaces (APIs) that are required by the development community to write high-level applications for a specific OS. An API is basically a set of building blocks used by software developers to write programs that are specific to a set-top OS environment. For example, in the desktop PC world, Microsoft defined a common API that allowed programmers to build applications for the Windows environment with a standard look and feel. This approach ultimately benefited end-users because it was easier for computer users to learn new Windows applications. The same philosophy has been adopted in the set-top world. The OS for a set-top box is often invisible to the end-user and as a result customers are unable to interface directly with the set-top OS. Similar to the PC market before Windows and DOS became the dominant operating system, the set-top market is comprised of an array of different real-time OSs. A number of real-time systems have emerged to drive the next generation of advanced set-top boxes. We explore the most popular set-top OSs in the following subsections.

CHOICE OF SET-TOP OSs . . . .

There is no standard set-top real-time OS. Instead, many broadcasters and consumer electronic companies are continuing to promote their own in-house solutions. Therefore, it is beyond the scope of this book to review and compare all of the available set-top real-time systems. We will, however, take a closer look at some of the more popular real-time operating systems that are being deployed on digital networks around the globe.

PowerTV OS

Since its inception in 1994, PowerTV has developed an advanced Internet-based software platform for digital set-tops, became leaders in the design and sale of graphic chipsets, and developed a compact set-top OS.

In 1998, nine cable operators in the U.S. and Canada selected the PowerTV set-top OS. These include Time Warner, MediaOne, ComCast, Cox Communications, Adelphia Communications, Marcus Communications, Cogeco, Rogers Cablesystems, and VideoTron.

To meet market demand, PowerTV has partnered with a number of manufacturers, such as Scientific Atlanta, Pioneer, Toshiba and Pace Micro Technologies, to incorporate their technology into their digital set-top boxes.

This particular real-time OS has been specifically developed for the set-top environment. It is designed to exist in low-cost ROM or in Flash memory that can be upgraded easily through network downloads. It interfaces very well with a range of conditional access systems to offer the end-user an integrated, secure platform for the delivery of video and Internet content.

The OS architecture itself is comprised of a number of layers of modules. Figure 3.1 shows the basic layers of the architecture.

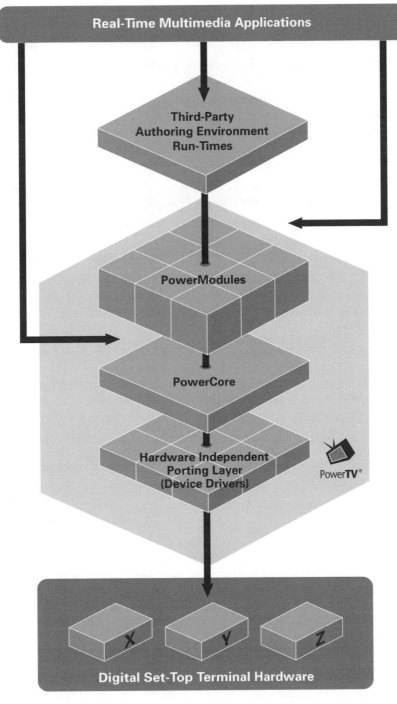

Figure 3.1
A high level view of the PowerTV Real-time OS Architecture

The advantages of adopting a modular approach include minimizing redundancy and optimizing the processing of multimedia- and Internet-based content. As with most real-time OSs the system has a small footprint and normally resides in ROM.

Let's look more closely at the various layers that make up the PowerTV OS. The lowest layer of the OS consists of a number of drivers and software abstractions that interface directly with the physical components of the device. This approach, adopted by PowerTV, allows developers to port the OS to multiple hardware platforms. In the next layer of the OS, we encounter a number of components that make up the heart of the OS: PowerCore. This layer is comprised of a kernel, C utility library, events subsystem, memory manager, and a loader for upgrading system software. The kernel has been optimized to improve processing speed through the use of multithreading and multitasking techniques.

The subsystem, responsible for events, is used to support time-critical applications such as multiuser-networked games. To optimize performance in a set-top with limited memory resources, PowerTV have incorporated a memory manager to allocate resources to specific processes.

Finally, the core PowerTV OS also incorporates a built-in loader that facilitates OS upgrades via network downloads, dynamically linked applications, and add-on modules.

Nearly every network operator will have a set of unique requirements, therefore, PowerTV extends the core OS with a number of plug-in software modules. The PowerTV 2D imaging model provides developers with a set of powerful graphic routines and primitives to create visually compelling set-top applications. The font engine is another add-on module that complements the core OS by supporting a range of font types.

In order to optimize the performance of the OS, PowerTV have incorporated the following OS managers:

TV Manager

The main function of the TV manager is to provide software developers with a standard interface for calling functions associated with channel tuning. The manager speeds up the software development process because programmers do not need to understand the underlying physical mechanisms for delivering the digital signal.

Session Manager

As the name indicates, the session manager is used to establish, maintain, monitor, and close an interactive session between the set-top and the head-end server.

Storage Manager

The management of data storage in a set-top environment is extremely important. The PowerTV OS incorporates a storage manager to compress and decompress data. In addition to optimizing storage on a set-top, the storage manager also facilitates digital signatures and purging of obsolete data items.

Database Manager

Database management in a set-top environment allows developers to use consistent queries and manipulation mechanisms to interrogate local or remote databases.

In addition to the management modules described above, the following extensions can also be dynamically downloaded to your PowerTV set-top.

Media Players

This add-on module allows set-top application developers to associate a particular multimedia data format with a particular media player. For example, the TV operator may decide to broadcast animated content on the network. To display this content on the TV monitor, the PowerTV OS would call the playback mechanism and process the content. This add-on module may also be used to extract data from external devices, including DVD players and VCRs.

Visual Effects

This module is capable of modifying multimedia data to a TV-centric look. This is extremely important for content providers who are developing content for a TV environment.

I/O Streams and Clocking

The I/O module defines a number of standard object-orientated mechanisms for inputting and outputting set-top data. To synchronize facilities within the kernel, PowerTV incorporates a clocking module.

User Interaction

This module enhances the TV viewer's experience by allowing content developers to add new and exciting visual components to existing applications.

In addition to a set-top OS, PowerTV also provides network operators with a software platform that is based on Internet protocols. Chapters 4 and 6 deal with developing applications and content for a PowerTV platform in more detail.

VxWorks

VxWorks is a real-time operating system that was developed by a company called Wind River System. At the time of this writing, Version 5.4 was the latest release of the OS to be integrated with a large range of network-centric devices, including advanced digital set-top boxes, smart phones, car navigation systems, and handheld devices.

VxWorks adheres to a wide range of industry standards. At the heart of the VxWorks OS is a kernel that supports multitasking, priority scheduling, and interrupt handling. To complement the support for open standards, Wind River also ensures that the VxWorks OS is fully scalable. This scalability feature allows software developers to optimize configuration for a wide range of embedded applications.

For developers who want to compile real-time applications for the VxWorks operating system, Wind River supplies the programming community with a range of development and debugging tools.

A unique feature of VxWorks, which is not applicable to the majority of set-top users, but is a very useful tool for software developers, is the presence of a shell. The *shell* allows users to interact with all the facilities of the set-top OS.

VxWorks has extensive networking capabilities, including support for TCP/IP, Telnet, and File Transport Protocol (FTP) across a variety of media. The types of media include Ethernet and Asynchronous Transfer Mode (ATM).

The VxWorks OS has been ported to a broad range of hardware platforms. Although the list of processors supported by VxWorks is growing by the month, the following list presents a sample of platforms currently supported:

- PowerPC and 6800 product family,
- Intel x86 family,
- Sun's Sparc processor family, and
- MIPS and I960.

Another critical component of migrating a real-time OS to a set-top hardware platform is the availability of appropriate drivers. Wind River supplies hundreds of drivers in source and binary format to set-top box manufacturers. The ready availability of a library of drivers speeds up the integration of VxWorks on a particular set-top hardware platform.

To extend the capabilities of the core VxWorks OS, Wind River offers developers a range of accessory products that help to extend the functionality of a set-top box. The VxWorks OS is fully integrated with a number of set-top browsers including: eNavigator from Liberate Technologies, Device Mosaic from Spyglass, and HotJava from Sun Microsystems.

pSOSystem

Another popular real-time OS used to drive advanced set-tops is Integrated Systems Incorporated's (ISI) pSOSystem embedded technologies.

At the core of the pSOSystem system is the multitasking kernel, which is complemented by a rich palette of kernel extensions and specialized applications. The kernel only occupies 15 KB of system memory and delivers a range of real-time operations to the set-top box. As with previous set-top OSs, pSOSystem is highly scalable and is optimized for a variety of processors, including: Motorola 68k, ColdFire and PowerPC families, Intel i960 and x86 families, ARM, MIPS, and Hitachi SH. Networking of a pSOSystem set-top box is facilitated through the addition of the pNA+ product. This is a modular TCP/IP stack that has been designed to support a variety of embedded Internet applications and systems. In addition to basic TCP/IP functionalities, the pSOSystem kernel may be extended to support remote management of set-top boxes.

From a developer's perspective, ISI provides debugger tools and a software development environment that are available to customize implementations. As with other set-top OSs, the pSOSystem system comes with a range of device drivers that are specific to the set-top hardware design.

As digital set-tops begin to evolve into a network computer for the consumer mass market, extensions can be added to the pSOSystem kernel to enable the creation of distributed applications on a TV operator's network.

The pSOSystem is suitable for a single processor, but if in the future manufacturers need to incorporate a second processor in their set-tops, a new multiprocessor OS needs to be implemented. ISI allows this capability with a product called pSOS+m. This multiprocessor implementation allows a set-top application to be spread over a number of processors.

Microware's DAVID OS-9

Microware Corporation was established approximately 20 years ago and concentrates on the development of real-time OSs for the embedded market. The company's flagship product is the multifeatured and multitasking OS-9. OS-9 is a real-time OS that has been adapted to a wide range of applications, including medical instrumentation, robotics, and industrial process control. The OS-9 software solution has a small

ROM/RAM footprint and has been used by Microware in developing a product specific to the digital set-top box called DAVID 0S-9. DAVID is an acronym for Digital Audio/Video Interactive Decoder.

The DAVID 0S-9 software solution can also be incorporated with digital TV sets. Recently, the DAVID software solution has been adopted by airlines to allow passengers to access video on demand and other entertainment services, including interactive shopping, while flying from one location of the globe to the other. As you can see, DAVID technology has a wide range of applications in the TV world.

The DAVID architecture itself is modular-based, which means that set-top designers can add and subtract various subsystems depending on user requirements. The DAVID 2.0 software solutions consist of a Kernel, File Managers and drivers, and APIs. Let's take a closer look at the heart of the DAVID system, which is the kernel. It can fit into a very small footprint of approximately 27 KB and has been ported to a range of hardware platforms, including Motorola 68xxx, Intel 80x86, and IBM/Motorola PowerPC processors. To complement the core OS, MicroWare has added a range of file managers and appropriate drivers. The DAVID system has a file manager dedicated to handling real-time data streams from a wide variety of broadband networks. It also incorporates a file manager dedicated to managing the MPEG video and audio decoders. Other file managers include a multimedia manager for managing interactive content, a sequential character manager for monitoring the user's input, and a file management system for controlling the non-volatile RAM system.

These are the basic core blocks of the DAVID system. Because many network operators have specific requirements, MicroWare is constantly expanding its choice of optional extensions. Examples of these extensions include support for Personal Computer Memory Card International Association (PCMCIA) and data encryption technologies. These extensions are fully modular and can be added or extracted as required by the set-top designer and network operator.

For people who would like to create applications for DAVID enabled devices, MicroWare provides customers with an application developer's package. The tools are available on UNIX and Windows platforms. The software kit is comprised of a library of C functions, sample graphics, application code, and reference material. In addition to MicroWare's software development kit, DAVID also supports the following third-party authoring tools:

- AIMTech Icon Author,
- Apple Media Tool,
- Macromedia Director,
- OptImage Media Mogul,
- Oracle Media Objects,
- Scala Backbone,

- Sybase/Gain Momentum, and
- Wink Communications.

DAVID has already been licensed by more than 20 leading manufacturers for implementation in their digital set-top boxes and TV sets. For example, toward the end of 1998, IBM Japan Ltd. selected Microware's flagship OS-9 real-time system to run on its motherboards. IBM introduced two boards for set-top development: one for digital broadcast satellite (DBS) and the other for digital cable systems. Both models use DAVID technology. In September 1999, Motorola selected DAVID to be the operating system for their new set-top box open architecture, streamaster.

Microsoft's Windows CE

Microsoft has proven in 1998 that they are very anxious to enter the set-top market by investing in a number of cable companies in Europe and the U.S. The software giant already has struck a deal with Tele-Communications Incorporated (TCI) to supply the U.S.-based cable company with 5 million digital set-top boxes running Windows CE. In addition to winning orders, Microsoft has also completed a number of strategic investments and technological advancements including:

- 1997—Microsoft made an announcement to invest over $1 billion in ComCast, a U.S.-based telecommunications and cable company.
- June 1998—Microsoft and Compaq invested $425 million in Road Runner, highspeed Internet access via cable service.
- January 1999—Microsoft partnered with United Pan-Europe Communications (UPC), Europe's largest privately held cable television and telecommunications company, to develop video and Internet-based services. Also in January Microsoft purchased a 5 percent stake in Nortel Inversora SA (NTL). As part of the deal, both companies are jointly developing the British cable operators network in the U.K. and Ireland.
- May 1999—AT&T and Microsoft announced a series of agreements in which the companies will work together to accelerate the deployment of next-generation broadband and Internet services to millions of American homes.
- May 1999—Microsoft purchased a 29.9 percent stake in Britain's second largest cable group—TeleWest Communications.
- June 1999—Microsoft announced the product details of its client and server software systems for the TV industry.
- July 1999—Microsoft said it would buy a $407 million stake in Rogers Communications, the number one cable TV operator in Canada.

Even though Microsoft has made a number of strategic partnerships and investments, the company still faces significant hurdles if it wants to become a dominant player in the set-top OS business. Since the company's inception, Microsoft has developed a family of operating systems. The current members of this family are:

- Windows 95 and 98—Designed as a desktop operating system;
- Windows NT Workstation 4.0—Designed for workstations;
- Windows NT Server—Designed for networks;
- Windows 2000—The latest Windows technology; and
- Windows CE—Designed for Internet-centric devices such as handheld PCs and digital set-tops.

Our energies in this section of the book will focus on examining the features and architecture of the Windows CE operating system. The Windows CE OS is designed to run a variety of devices, and each device runs a specific version of the OS. For example, in the handheld market alone, Microsoft is offering three different versions. Windows CE runs on HP and Sharp handheld computers, version 2.01 is used to run palm-sized devices, and Windows CE 2.11 runs handheld devices with large displays. Windows CE 2.12 is the real-time OS portion of Microsoft's Microsoft TV Platform Adaptation Kit (TVPAK), a client-server software solution specifically designed for the world of digital television. Microsoft TVPAK is comprised of a client-called Microsoft TV and a back-end or head-end system called Microsoft server (see Figure 3.2).

Each of the elements shown in the diagram above are discussed in greater detail in Chapters 4, 6, and 10.

Let's first take a closer look at Windows CE. Microsoft Windows CE is a real-time operating system, designed from the ground up for advanced 32-bit embedded devices such as advanced digital set-top boxes.

Windows CE is modular, which essentially means that real-time system developers can custom design the Windows CE system for specific hardware platforms. To port and customize Windows CE for a digital set-top, developers will need to use the Windows CE platform builder suite of development tools. In addition to porting a customized version of the Windows CE operating system to the set-top box, the builder platform can also be used to develop additional device drivers and real-time applications for a particular set-top hardware platform.

Windows CE has been ported to a number of processor architectures, including ARM, MIPS, PowerPC, and the x86 Intel family. Similar to other set-top operating systems, Windows CE is comprised of a number of layers. The bottom layer is known as the hardware or abstraction layer. It is basically a layer of code that isolates set-top hardware devices from the kernel and is normally specific to a particular hardware platform. The technical functions of this abstraction layer are to manage timers, control power management, and handle interrupt requests from the set-top's processor. In

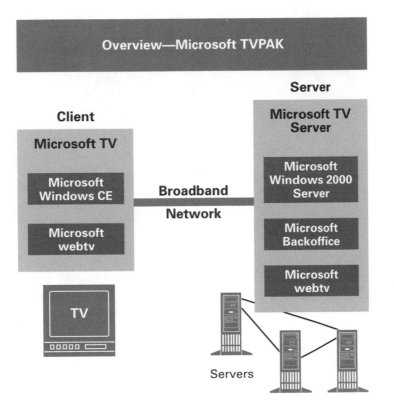

Figure 3.2
Graphical overview of Microsoft TVPAK

addition to the abstraction layer, Windows CE provides device drivers for a variety of set-top hardware components, including:

- keyboards and infrared remote controls;
- Ethernet connectivity;
- serial and parallel data ports;
- PCMCIA slots and cards; and
- USB.

As part of their digital TV strategy, Microsoft has also added a number of drivers to version 2.12 of Windows CE to support the following hardware devices:

- cable modems;
- Smart card readers (CA and e-commerce);
- IP telephony;

- IEEE 1394;
- hard disks;
- tuner(s); and
- Common interface.

The number of set-top drivers is constantly evolving as demands increase for more sophisticated and powerful set-top boxes. At the core of the Windows CE operating system is a multithreaded, preemptive, multitasking kernel. The kernel itself assigns priority to various set-top requests and supports the paging of data between set-top memory modules. The Windows CE kernel borrows much of what is best from other Microsoft 32-bit operating systems, while eliminating features that are not needed for embedded applications. To complement the kernel, Microsoft has also developed a file system that is stored in ROM and used to manage local set-top data.

Similar to Windows 95, 98, and NT, Microsoft has added a registry with a small footprint to the core OS. A *registry* is a database used by the Windows CE operating system to store set-top configuration information. Windows CE has a module that supports the rendering of various fonts and graphic formats.

The ability of a digital set-top box to communicate over the network to servers at the service provider's head-end is extremely important. In addition to supporting built-in modems, Windows CE 2.12 also provides full support for a variety of communication and security protocols.

The implementation of digital TV is a global phenomenon, hence it is critical that the set-top OS is capable of supporting a variety of international languages. Windows CE provides set-top designers with this capability, if required by the network operator.

Additional features available to set-top designers include:

- the ability to create distributed broadband network applications through a technology called Distributed Component Object Model (DCOM). DCOM is a protocol that supports software components communicating directly over a TV network in a reliable, secure, and efficient manner;
- execute Java applications or applets using the Microsoft Virtual Machine for Java for Windows CE; and
- support for DirectX technologies. Microsoft DirectX is a set of interfaces that allow set-top applications to gain access directly to a system's multimedia hardware.

Finally, Microsoft uses Dynamic Link Libraries (DLLs) to connect the various Windows CE modules together. A DLL is best described as a library of executable functions that is accessed on a regular basis by a variety of programs.

The hardware requirements of a Windows CE set-top box is totally dependent on the features and services required by the TV operator. The basic operating system, which is comprised of a kernel, a communications stack, and a graphical module, would require less than 600 KB of ROM and 400 KB of RAM. Once the set-top designer begins to add extensions for cable system integration, the memory and processing requirements begin to increase.

JavaOS for Consumers

The JavaOS for consumers operating system is a small and efficient embedded operating system that executes the Java environment directly on a wide variety of information appliances. JavaOS for Consumers software is specifically targeted at the following types of devices: Internet screen phones, TV set-top boxes, handheld devices, automotive, and Industrial appliances.

It's important for you to have a sense of the "anatomy" of this product. We'll briefly consider the various technologies that make JavaOS what it is. Figure 3.3 shows the basic layers of the architecture.

The foundation block for the JavaOS for Consumers software system is the real-time kernel system that leverages the technologies of the ChorusOS system. The ChorusOS system is a highly scalable and reliable embedded operating system that has established itself among the world's top suppliers of telecommunications equipment. The ChorusOS operating system is used in public switches and PBXs, as well

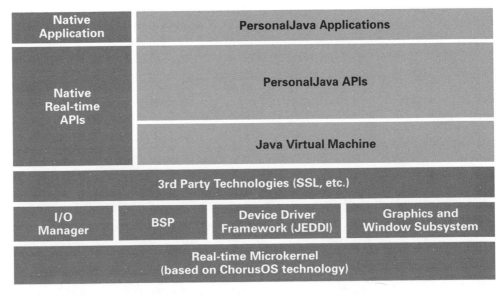

Figure 3.3
JavaOS for Consumers software architecture

as within access networks, cross-connect switches, voice-mail systems, cellular base stations, webphones, and cellular telephones.

The layer just above the kernel layer includes the drivers that are used to operate the various hardware components within the set-top box. The layer above the driver layer is called the third-party layer. Its primary objective is to facilitate the inclusion of third party technologies to the operating system. For instance, some network providers may want to provide e-commerce services to their subscriber base. Consequently the JavaOS for Consumers software includes support for a security protocol called Secure Sockets Layer (SSL). SSL is a security scheme used to combat snooping of confidential information. Our chapter on set-top Internet applications investigates the SSL protocol in more detail. The top layers of the JavaOS for Consumers (PersonalJava, Java Virtual Machine, and applications) have been designed specifically for network-connectable devices such as set-top boxes and will be discussed in greater detail in the next chapter.

Linux

Linux is a freely available variant of the UNIX computer operating system. It was originally developed in the early 1990s by Linus Torvalds and was designed to run on a number of hardware platforms, including Intel and Motorola processors.

There are no license fees associated with Linux, subsequently many set-top box manufacturers are seriously considering the integration of this operating system into their product families. At the time of this writing, America OnLine (AOL) announced the development of a Linux-based TV set-top box with Compaq computers. Linux is a powerful system, and a complete architectural description of the operating system is beyond the scope of this particular publication. Linux is, however, very well documented with several online books devoted to the subject of this emerging system. It may one day become a formidable challenger to Microsoft's vision of Windows on every television set in the world.

SUMMARY . . . .

Similar to a desktop, a set-top box also needs an operating system to operate. Unlike desktop PCs, set-tops are constrained devices with limited hardware resources at their disposal. Consequently, the architecture of a set-top OS is different to an OS that has been designed for the world of computers. It needs to be robust and reliable because television viewers are not overly familiar with "rebooting" their sets. Another requirement of a set-top OS is its capability to concurrently process a number of tasks ranging from processing incoming MPEG digital streams to validating security messages.

Finally, the architecture of a set-top OS needs to embrace open computer and Internet standards wherever possible.

The set-top field OS already includes some formidable foes angling to get into next-generation of digital set-top boxes, including Sun's JavaOS for Consumers and a host of embedded operating systems from companies such as PowerTV, Wind River, ISI, and Microware. Microsoft is also a big player in the space of Internet-enabled devices with its Windows CE operating system. In recent months, Linux, a UNIX variant, has made several steps toward becoming a mainstream set-top OS.

4 Set-top Middleware and APIs

In this chapter…

Television viewers experienced the launch of video on demand, TV mail, and a plethora of killer applications in 1999. Meanwhile, network operators across the globe were busy putting their software platforms in place to run these advanced services. Central to the new software architecture is a connection layer that acts as a communications bridge between the set-top OS and the subscriber application, called *middleware*. Middleware is a relatively new term in the set-top business. It represents the logical abstraction of the middle and upper layers of the communications software stack used in set-top software and communication systems. This chapter will provide an introduction to the basics of set-top middleware systems, discussing the various industry initiatives and standard bodies that are working on defining an open set-top middleware standard. We conclude the chapter with a description of the most popular middleware products that are currently available on the market.

MIDDLEWARE CONCEPTS . . . .

Middleware equates to the application, presentation, and session layers of the Open Systems Interconnect (OSI) seven-layer model. OSI is a networking framework that defines a set of protocols for implementing communications between two devices.

Middleware is used to isolate set-top application programs from the details of the underlying hardware and network components. Thus, set-top applications can operate transparently across a network without having to be concerned about the underlying network protocols. This considerably reduces the complexity of development because applications can be written to take advantage of a common API.

Suppose that a set-top software developer decides to write an application that uses computer resources at the network operator's headquarters. To effectively deploy this distributed application, the programmer will need to ensure that the resident application interacts with a communication stack, such as TCP/IP. Under the middleware approach, the developer is able to avail of TCP/IP features without requiring a significant amount of knowledge on the architecture of the underlying protocols. Recent reductions in memory and processor costs are enabling manufacturers to design set-tops that are capable of running a range of sophisticated middleware software products.

VIRTUAL MACHINES . . . .

To avoid the recreation of content specifically for proprietary platforms, many of the middleware software vendors have begun extending their functionality through the addition of presentation and application virtual machines. A *virtual machine,* also called an engine, can be defined as a self-contained environment that behaves as if it is a separate set-top box. The virtual machine layer acts as the run-time environment for the interactive set-top applications. Therefore, programmers can develop set-top applications and author content without worrying about the underlying hardware architecture.

Network operators can easily download new virtual machines to a customer's set-top box. For example, a network operator can download the OpenTV virtual machine to provide interactive TV programming. When the customers want the ability to browse the Internet, an HTML virtual machine can subsequently be downloaded to their set-top boxes. This capability is crucial for supporting new set-top software standards. The most popular virtual machines are explained in the following subsections.

HTML Virtual Machine

The HTML virtual machine is the most popular presentation engine currently available and allows set-top boxes to process and display a wide range of content that has been developed for the World Wide Web. The main function of the set-top HTML virtual machine is to process and organize Web content for easy viewing on a standard television screen. To understand how this virtual machine works, it is first necessary that we take a closer look at the HTML language. HyperText Markup Language, or HTML, as it is commonly known, is a platform-independent language used to format pages for the World Wide Web. HTML is derived from the Standard Generalized Markup Language (SGML). SGML is the international standard designed to facilitate the flow of information across a variety of hardware and software platforms. An HTML document is stored as plain ASCII text and can be created with any text editor. Special HTML editors are available, which operate on a WYSIWYG basis, such as Microsoft Frontpage 98. HTML is a language of commands. By embedding certain commands within a standard text document, it is possible to create a Web page.

The browser that is used on the set-top will then format the document for display on the TV screen according to the commands it has been given. These commands are not visible when a subscriber views a Web page on their TV screen. In addition to using HTML as a formatting language, it can also be used by content providers to:

- add live audio and video multimedia components to a set-top page;
- integrate links to other set-top pages and sites on the World Wide Web;
- create interactive forms that allow digital TV customers to provide TV network operators with feedback; and
- add rich graphical images.

The commands that are used in the HTML language are known as elements or tags. All elements appear between angle brackets (<>). For example, the element <em> is a command that is understood by a set-top browser. The command instructs the browser to display a particular piece of text in italics on the TV screen. Other HTML tags used by designers include titles, Java applets, forms, tables, and image maps.

HTML uses two different types of tags: StartTag and EndTag. They appear in the form of `<StartTag> Text </EndTag>`. If a content provider wanted, for example, to underline the sentence "Visit set-tops.com new portal site," the developer would type `<U>Visit set-tops.com new portal site</U>`. There are a number of other basic elements that are used for formatting an HTML document.

`<P>`	Used to start new paragraphs.
` `	Functions as a carriage return, moving text to the next line.
`<B>`	Displays a block of text in bold format on a TV screen.
`<Body>`	Indicates to the browser where the actual text is to begin.
`<H2>` and `<H3>`	Indicate text size.
`<HR>`	Creates a horizontal line break.
`<A>`	Used to insert links to other pages on the Internet.

HTML continues to evolve as a standard for publishing sophisticated documents on the Web. The original 1990 specification, called HTML 1.0, is now obsolete. Most Web documents in existence conform to the HTML 2.0 specification, which was drafted in 1994. In May 1996, the W3 Consortium announced the release of the HTML 3.2 standard. And 1997 saw the emergence of HTML 4.0.

Current implementations of the HTML virtual machine on a set-top platform support version 3.2 of the standard, but most middleware software suppliers are planning to offer HTML 4.0 virtual machines toward the end of 1999. Once a Web page is received from the broadband network, the virtual machine will parse the HTML code and produce a vendor-specific data representation. Note that the parsing of HTML can be both processor- and memory-intensive for the set-top. Another component within the machine will then lay out the various HTML components (images, tables, text, etc.) and optimize the page for viewing on a standard television set. The HTML engine integrates with a number of set-top software components, including the real-time OS, the CA module, and the browser.

JavaScript Virtual Machine

The set-top box uses this engine to run applications written in the JavaScript programming language. JavaScript is an open, cross-platform, object-based scripting language created by Sun Microsystems and Netscape Communications Corporation in order to extend the power of HTML documents. A scripting language is a simple programming language that is used to create scripts. A *script* is a series of instructions and rules that tells a program, such as a set-top browser, how to perform a particular action, and is similar to a macro. JavaScript is a scripting language rather than a programming language. Scripting languages use less complex rules than programming languages. This means that they are easier to learn and use. Nevertheless, it can perform many of the functions of a full-fledged programming language.

JavaScript, being in an object-based language, uses predefined objects that you can control and alter in limited ways. This allows JavaScript instructions to be short and compact, which is one reason JavaScript has become popular for use in Internet applications for controlling elements within a Web page. With JavaScript, an HTML page may contain animated graphics. For instance, the "rollover" effect occurs when a set-top user moves his/her remote control over an image on the TV screen and the image changes. JavaScript has many other uses:

- Authors can create animated advertising banners.
- Authors can create forms to validate data that users input on the TV screen (incorrectly written e-mail addresses or improperly selected menu items).
- Useful for providing subscribers with feedback statements.
- When a customer switches on their TV sets, it is possible to use JavaScript to greet them by name.
- Make calculations based on a customer's order and proceed to compile an onscreen invoice.

JavaScript code is embedded within an HTML document and is interpreted along with the HTML code on the page. You usually incorporate JavaScript scripts in the body of an HTML document between the <BODY> and </BODY> tags. The actual script is enclosed within <SCRIPT> and </SCRIPT> tags in the body of the document. Because JavaScript is a scripting language rather than just a formatting language, it can perform more complex tasks than HTML alone.

Current implementations of the JavaScript virtual machine support version 1.2 of the language. However, some of the middleware vendors have added new extensions to enhance the overall TV viewing experience. The JavaScript language is similar to Java, a powerful, high-level language developed specifically for the Web. JavaScript has inherited many features belonging to the Java programming language. For instance, JavaScript and Java have a similar basic structure and syntax. Although Java and JavaScript are related, they serve fundamentally different purposes. For example, Java uses a compiler to read a program and convert into binary code. You must use a compiler every time you alter the program, which is a time-consuming process. In contrast, JavaScript is a purely interpreted language, meaning source code files are executed directly in the virtual machine that's stored within the set-top box.

Personal Java Virtual Machine

Personal Java, or P-Java, is an application development and middleware environment that has been developed by Sun Microsystems. It was designed specifically for a myriad of consumer devices such as network computers, smart telephones, game consoles, and TV set-top boxes. It executes software written in the Java programming language. Personal Java is comprised of a lightweight version of the Java Virtual Machine (JVM), a set of core libraries, and optional libraries that may be used as needed. Toward the end of 1998, Tele-Communications Incorporated, the largest cable operator in the United States, signed an agreement with Sun Microsystems to standardize Personal Java as the application development environment for all its future advanced digital set-top boxes. Millions of TCI set-top boxes powered by Personal Java will offer software developers an exciting new platform to create a range of compelling applications for the interactive TV market.

Over 25 vendors, including the major real-time operating system manufacturers and companies developing applications for advanced consumer devices, have licensed P-Java technology.

At the time of this writing, current resellers of the Personal Java application environment included: Acorn, Aplix, Chorus (Sun), Geoworks, Lucent Technologies, Microtec, Microware, U.S. Software, and Wind River Systems.

Figure 4.1 illustrates the primary system components of version 3.0 of the Personal Java middleware environment.

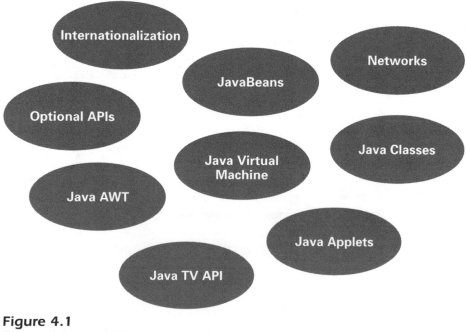

Figure 4.1
Personal Java middleware components

The role of each one of these components is briefly outlined in the following paragraphs.

Java Virtual Machine (JVM)

The Java virtual machine (JVM) is a program that interprets Java bytecodes into machine code. The JVM is what makes Java portable—a vendor such as Microsoft or Sun writes a JVM for their operating system, and any Java program can run on that virtual machine. It is a self-contained operating environment that behaves as if it is a separate computer within the digital set-top box. In other words the JVM has no access to the set-top's real-time OS. This type of virtual system has two benefits for set-top users and manufacturers:

A set-top Java application will run in any JVM, regardless of the underlying hardware platform and real-time OS.

Because the JVM has limited contacts with the set-top real time OS, there is little possibility of a Java program damaging other files or applications on the box.

In addition to interpreting interactive TV Java applications, the JVM is also used by the set-top box to verify the integrity of code. The JVM is currently being incorporated into the next generation of advanced digital set-top boxes.

JavaBeans

The JavaBean API is a specification developed by Sun Microsystems that defines how Java components interact across a distributed network. JavaBeans are reusable software components that are designed to be very easy to use, are compact, and are portable across multiple hardware platforms. The main strength of the JavaBeans components comes from the fact that they are written in the Java language.

It enables developers to write reusable components once and run them anywhere, therefore benefiting from the platform-independent power of Java technology. JavaBeans components are sometimes simply called "Beans." The software you'll need to understand and explore Beans is available free on the Web. The Beans Development Kit (BDK) contains the software and tools that developers need to compile, debug, and run JavaBeans. The BDK also contains various tutorials and demonstration source code. It is available for download at http://splash.javasoft.com/beans/software/bdk_download.html

Java Classes

Classes are the fundamental units in Java. A class is a collection of data and related methods that operate on that data. In fact, all data and functionality in a Java program are organized into classes. The Personal Java VM interfaces with a wide variety of input/output, networking, security, and utility classes.

Java AWT

Short for Abstract Windows Toolkit, this Personal Java API enables programmers to develop applications with a TV-centric look and feel. The AWT contains a number of features such as windows, buttons, pop-up menus, and scroll bars. Low-resolution displays, such as TV sets, are fully supported by the Java AWT feature set.

The Java AWT also includes interfaces that help Java applications to adapt to mouseless environments, such as TV systems operated by remote control.

Java Applets

Applets are small programs that are downloaded from the TV operator's head-end servers and executed on the digital set-top box.

Internationalization Support

When developing applications for a Personal Java environment, it is important that programs can be developed independently of the location, time zone, or language of the digital TV subscriber. The Personal Java VM supports a rich set of APIs for developing global-based, interactive set-top applications. These internationalization APIs are based on the Unicode 2.0 character encoding standard and include the ability to adapt text, numbers, dates, currency, and user-defined objects to any country's or region's conventions.

Optional APIs

These include Remote Method Invocation (RMI), which is used by programmers to create distributed Java-to-Java applications. A standard database access interface is also provided through Java Database Connectivity (JDBC). This provides set-top personal Java developers with a uniform access interface to a wide range of relational databases.

Java TV API

The Java TV API is an extension to the Personal Java development environment, which allows programmers to create TV-centric programs and services.

It also provides control over a number of features that are unique to digital set-top boxes, such as accessing various digital channels, retrieving data from the service information database, and loading an Electronic Programming Guide (EPG).

The Java TV API and its underlying Personal Java platform provide the ideal development and deployment platform for digital interactive television services such as, video-on-demand (VOD), enhanced broadcasting, electronic commerce, network games, and online education. The Java TV API, along with the Personal Java platform, will be the standard application programming environment for TCI's digital set-top boxes, regardless of real-time OS. The diagram in Figure 4.2 describes a typical Java TV and Personal Java environment when implemented on a digital set-top box.

Details of Java TV were announced at the JavaOne conference in 1999 and were recently posted to Sun's web site at: http://java.sun.com/products/javatv/javatvspec 0_9_0.html.

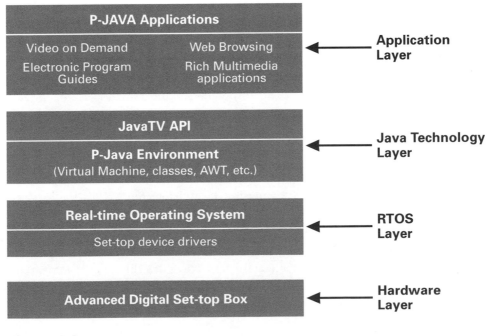

Figure 4.2
Java TV API running on a digital set-top box

MHEG-5

MHEG (pronounced M-heg) is an acronym for Multimedia and Hypermedia information coding Experts Group. This group is developing, within the International Organization of Standardization, several standards which deal with the coded representation of multimedia/hypermedia information. MHEG defines the term *multimedia* as a representation of several media types, such as audio, video, text, and graphics. In the context of our discussions about MHEG, hypermedia is best described as an enhancement that allows digital TV subscribers to navigate through a screen of objects using specialized links. Besides defining hypermedia and multimedia objects, the MHEG standard is also concerned with the interchange of these objects from storage devices to telecommunication and broadcast TV networks. Typical applications of MHEG include:

- digital multimedia teletext;
- electronic program guides;
- video-on-demand;
- e-commerce applications; and
- online games.

Chapter 6 takes a closer look at the tools and skills that are required to develop MHEG-based set-top applications.

MHEG is designed to be supported by systems with minimal resources, which makes it a very suitable middleware product for digital set-top boxes. MHEG is composed of a total of seven parts. Our attention will concentrate on part 5 (MHEG-5) of the standard. An MHEG-5 application, which is basically a set of multimedia and hypermedia objects that reside on a computer at the TV operator's head-end, is converted into bit-stream format and broadcasted over a broadband network. On the receiving end, a digital set-top box with a software component called an MHEG-5 engine, or virtual machine, extracts the multimedia/hypermedia from the incoming digital stream, interprets the data, and displays on the subscriber's television screen. In addition to handling incoming data, the MHEG-5 engine is also responsible for synchronisation and supporting local interactivity with the subscriber. The memory requirement (footprint) of the MHEG-5 engine is only about 300 KB. Thus, a set-top box with a processor running at a speed of 40 Million Instructions per second (MIPS) combined with 2 MB of RAM can easily support this software module.

From a commercial perspective, the U.K. digital terrestrial broadcasters have adopted MHEG-5. Subsequently, people in the U.K. who want to receive digital terrestrial channels combined with multimedia content will need to purchase or lease a set-top box running an MHEG-5 engine.

Promotion of the MHEG-5 middleware standard has been the responsibilities of two organizations based in Europe.

Digital TV Group (DTG) • The DTG was set up in the spring of 1995 to take the DVB framework and turn it into a working system within the ambitious timetable for digital terrestrial broadcasting set by the U.K. government. Membership of the DTG is open to all companies with a genuine commitment to digital terrestrial broadcasting in the U.K. and there are now over 80 member companies. The group manages a range of technical and regulatory issues that surround the broadcast and reception of digital terrestrial TV.

Digital Terrestrial Television Action Group (DigiTag) • DigiTAG was launched formally in September 1996. The aim of the group is to encourage and facilitate the implementation and introduction of digital terrestrial television services using the Digital Video Broadcasting Project's standards (DVB-T). It has over 60 members from broadcasting, network operations, regulatory, and manufacturing organizations throughout Europe, as well as other parts of the world.

What is the future of MHEG-5? A new part to the standard (MHEG-6) has been created to extend its core functionality. The creation of this extension allows MHEG-5-based applications to perform complex data processing tasks and to access services on remote devices such as servers, located in an operator's head-end. The additional functionality is based on Java technologies.

Further enhancements to the standard have come about through the development of an MHEG-5 European specification called EuroMHEG. This specification has been created to extend the current MHEG-5 U.K. profile (version 1.04) to meet the requirements of the European community by providing consumers with the following features:

- return channel functionality;
- fonts downloaded directly to the set-top;
- improved methods of inputting text (i.e., support for wireless keyboards);
- generic access to CA and SI subsystems to support advanced EPGs; and
- a framework for processing online e-commerce transactions.

As well as the technical advancements to the MHEG-5 standard, organizations like DigiTag, Philips, and DTG are working very closely with DVB to promote the interests of MHEG-5.

For a more detailed description of the MHEG-5 open standard, see "Information Technology—Coding of Multimedia and Hypermedia Information—Part 5: Support for Base-level Interactive Applications," available from your national standardization body.

MIDDLEWARE STANDARDS . . . .

As you can see from our previous chapter, a set-top can be equipped with an array of real-time operating systems. Therefore the emergence of an open middleware standard that enables set-top developers to port applications to all of the different operating systems currently available for the digital set-top is extremely important. Adopting industry standards leads to competitive pricing from multiple software suppliers and helps to reduce overall set-top deployment costs.

Standard bodies have realized this fact and are working towards an open middleware standard. The debate for a common middleware platform has however split the digital TV industry into three specific groups. Two of these groups are pursuing the Java Virtual Machine-based interoperability strategy for such devices as advanced digital set-tops and integrated digital TVs. The other group hopes to achieve interoperability through the use of Internet based technologies such as the JavaScript and HTML virtual machines. The DVB organization in Europe and a subgroup of ATSC in the United States called DASE (DTV Application Software Environment) is proposing a middleware standard based on the Java Virtual Machine. Both groups are currently hammering out key elements now for common Java and JavaTV API environments. Final specifications for the new standards are expected from these groups towards the middle of 2000. The competing group is led by proponents of Advanced Television Enhancement Forum (ATVEF)—a US based alliance comprising of companies from the IT industry, cable and satellite operators, and consumer electronic companies. The ATSC organization is proposing a middleware standard based on a derivative of HyperText Markup Language (HTML) virtual machine and the JavaScript virtual machine. Let's examine in more detail, these platforms that are expected to become the building blocks of the new digital world.

Multimedia Home Platform

At the beginning of 1996, the Multimedia Home Platform (MHP) launching group was born from a European project called UNITEL, chaired by the European Broadcasting Union, with the collaboration of key representatives of the High Level Strategy Group (HLSG). The group is comprised of manufacturers, broadcasters, and television operators. The main aim of this group was to raise awareness of the benefits associated with developing a common platform for accessing a wide range of digital multimedia services. Considering the growing interest for these activities, it was proposed to transfer these activities into the DVB project. Subsequently in 1997, two working groups were set up by DVB:

1. A commercially orientated group called DVB-MHP. The main responsibility of this group is to define user and market requirements for enhanced TV, interactive TV, and Internet access in a dual broadcasting/Internet environment. Enhanced Broadcasting combines digital broadcast of audio/video services with downloaded applications that can enable local interactivity. It does not need an interaction channel. The application area, Interactive Broadcasting, enables a range of interactive services associat-

ed or independent from broadcast services. This application area requires an interaction channel. The application area of Internet access is intended for the provisioning of Internet services. It also includes links between those Internet services and broadcast services.

2. A technical group called DVB-TAM (Technical Aspects associated with MHP). This group has primarily been concentrating on the definition of a common API specification.

Multimedia Home Platform (MHP) set-top boxes enable the reception and presentation of applications in a vendor, author, and broadcaster neutral framework. Applications from various service providers will be interoperable with different MHP implementations in a horizontal market.

The DVB MHP solution is intended to cover the whole range of implementations including Integrated Receiver Decoders (IRDs), integrated TV sets, multimedia computers, and local clusters of such devices connected via in-home digital networks (IHDN).

The MHP consists of a user terminal (PC, integrated TV, digital set-top box, associated peripherals, and a range of digital appliances that connect to your in-house network), a standard middleware, and a suite of APIs that are capable of supporting a range of services.

Let's take a closer look at the architecture of the MHP platform. The MHP model consists of 3 layers (Figure 4.3).

Resources

A software or hardware (and associated software like the boot, operating system, memory manager, drivers) resource is a well-defined capability or asset of a system

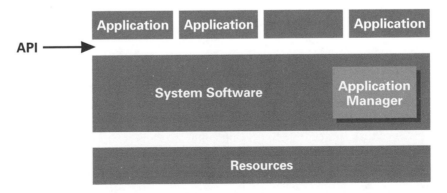

Figure 4.3
The MHP layer model

entity, which can be used to contribute to the realization of functions assembled into a service such as an MPEG decoder, a graphics system, or a modem.

From an abstract point of view it makes no difference if the logical resources are mapped into one or several hardware entities. Resources are provided to the MHP transparently. An application should be able to access all locally connected resources as if they are elements of a single entity unless specifically specified restrictions apply (as in the case of an unidentified application).

System Software and API

The system software, also called platform software or middleware, isolates the application through an abstract view of the software and hardware resources. This ensures the integrity (the look and feel) and interoperability of an application across various MHP implementations.

The system software includes the interactive engine, the run-time engine or virtual machine, an application manager, the libraries, and the databases. The system software, or firmware, is by definition platform-dependent and entirely under the control of each respective manufacturer.

It is the application manager's responsibility to manage the lifecycle of all applications:

- check the code and data integrity;
- synchronize the commands and information;
- adapt the presentation graphic format to suit the platform display;
- obtain and dispose of the system resources;
- manage the error signaling and exceptions;
- initiate and terminate any new sessions;
- allow the sharing of variables and contents; and
- conclude in an orderly and clean fashion.

The API can be described as a set of high-level functions, data structures, and protocols that represent a standard interface for platform-independent application software. It uses object-oriented languages and it enhances the flexibility and reusability of the platform functionalities. The Application Programming Interface is the reference that will be used to develop applications that will be interpreted to activate hardware and/or software functions (see Figure 4.4).

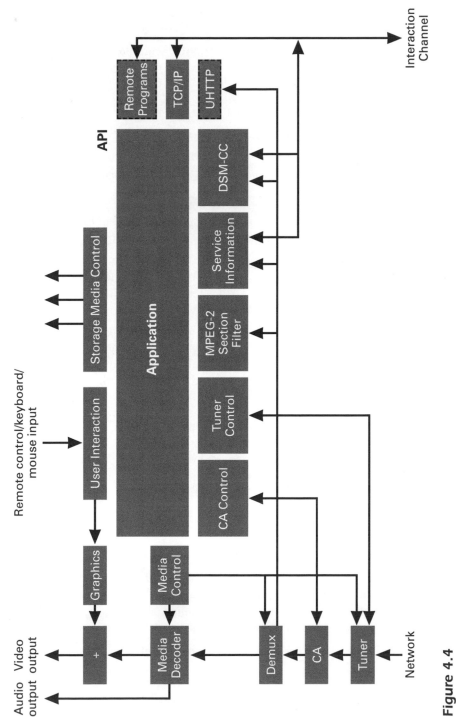

Figure 4.4
Interfaces between an MHP application and the MHP system Enhanced Broadcast or Interactive TV

Some of the main system functions are:

- application launch and control, session/event management;
- security and access;
- content loading;
- navigation and selection;
- declarative content and streams presentation control;
- communication and I/O control; and
- signaling, bit transport, driver and management functions.

The MHP API is actually constituted of a series of APIs addressing specific functionalities. According to the application format, low-level and/or high-level APIs will be used to deal, respectively, with procedural and declarative functions:

- *Low-level* APIs are more procedural and tend to access low-level procedural functions. The API interprets the application function or primitive but also knows how to activate the resources.
- *High-level* APIs are more declarative. The higher the level of abstraction declaration (i.e., the hiding of the system implementation), the stronger is the system independence. The API interprets the application function or primitive but does not need to know how the corresponding resources will be activated.

The DVB TAM group considered and evaluated a number of candidates for their API, including OpenTV, MediaHighway, MHEG-5, HTML, and Java. Each solution was examined for levels of openness, evolutionary capabilities, scalability, and flexibility. After a lot of debate and negotiations, MHP is working on the specification of a Java-based API to operate the MHP DVB-J platform. Any applications that are delivered to an MHP-based platform will comply with the Java VM byte code format.

Applications

DVB-TAM defines an application as a functional implementation of an interactive service that is realized as software modules. An application can also be seen as a set of organized functions that request activation of MHP hardware and software resources.

A DVB-J application is a set of Java classes that operate together.

DTV Application Software Environment (DASE)

A technical specialist subcommittee has been established by the ATSC to define a standard software environment for broadcast digital set-top boxes. The group is known as T3/S17 and is developing a reference architecture called the DTV Application Software Environment—commonly known as DASE. The new standard has been designed to support broadcast environments and embrace a variety of open Web standards. One of the main objectives of DASE is to minimize the complexity and hardware footprint of a digital set-top box. The reference software architecture developed by DASE is comprised of a virtual machine and engine for set-top applications and a presentation engine.

The T3/S17 group selected the P-Java Virtual Machine as the application virtual machine for all DASE compliant set-top boxes. Thus, TV applications written in Java and Personal Java programming languages will be able to execute on set-top boxes that comply with the final DASE specification.

With regards to the presentation engine, the TS/S17 were deeply divided between two HTML-based proposals and an MHEG proposal. Instead of supporting one specific component, the chairman of the T3/S17 subcommittee proposed an alternative called Broadcast HTML (BHTML). The new presentation engine is fully interoperable with the Java-based application engine. The chapter on set-tops enhanced TV will examine the new BHTML presentation language in more detail. At the time of this writing, DASE was continuing its work on BHTML. Ongoing projects included the refinement of elements, attributes, properties, and value parameters of the new language.

Advanced Television Enhancement Forum (ATVEF)

The ATVEF is a U.S.-based alliance comprised of companies from the IT industry, cable and satellite operators, consumer electronic companies, and individuals interested in defining standards for the convergence between PC, TV, and the Internet. The alliance is committed to making content production for digital television less expensive and more convenient for consumers by encouraging the open industry adoption of standards. The founding members of ATVEF include: Microsoft, Intel, Disney, NBC, CableLabs, Discovery, PBS, DirecTV, CNN, TCI, NCI, Sony Online, Tribune, and Warner Bros. The momentum of ATVEF in 1999 continued to increase with the signing of a number of new members.

Its main concentration of energies is on leveraging existing Internet standards to deliver an enhanced TV experience. ATVEF realized early on that without a standard specification, content developers would be reluctant to invest in tailoring content for different varieties of software platforms. Without the broad range of suitable TV content, consumers would not invest in set-top boxes. Consequently, the alliance defined protocols for HTML-based television, which allow content creators to deliver enhanced programming over all forms of transport (analog, digital, cable, MMDS, and satellite) to any intelligent receivers.

The group is committed to accelerating the creation and distribution of enhanced television programs so that consumers can receive enhanced television programs in the least expensive and most convenient way possible. The organization is actively working with the ATSC to define a standard presentation engine capable of displaying Internet content in a digital TV environment. The ATVEF group has created a specification, called Advanced Television Enhancement Forum Specification for Interactive Television 1.1, with guidelines for developing content and distributing to a variety of access devices such as digital set-top boxes. Chapter 12 provides a more detailed insight into how these guidelines, combined with other technologies, can be used to author enhanced TV content.

SET-TOP MIDDLEWARE CHOICES . . . .

Most technology analysts agree that no one particular middleware product will control the set-top market in the near future. The new computing paradigm has caught the attention of a number of software companies and has sparked the launch and deployment of several set-top middleware products. These companies have established reference designs and licensed them to various TV and set-top manufacturers. This section will focus on six of these candidates.

OpenTV

Thomson Multimedia and Sun Microsystems originally founded the OpenTV Company in 1994 when they formed a joint development and marketing alliance to produce software solutions for the expanding digital TV market. The alliance began shipping its flagship product line, OpenTV 1.0, in March 1996. In August 1996, the alliance was restructured into an independent operating company named Thomson Sun Interactive. In September 1997, the company changed its name to OpenTV Incorporated, after adding a new shareholder to its board. Currently, OpenTV is jointly owned by Myriad International Holdings, and Sun Microsystems. The company specializes in creating end-to-end digital TV software solutions for network operators across the world. The OpenTV software environment is particularly popular in Europe, with over 3 million homes using set-top boxes equipped with the OpenTV software environment. Business wins and deployments of the OpenTV platform include:

- In 1996 the French satellite broadcaster TPS (Television Par Satellite) chose the OpenTV platform to deliver a range of interactive TV applications. At the end of 1998, TPS's network comprised of 640,000 subscribers accessing advanced interactive services using OpenTV technology.

- In 1997, the Swedish network operator Telia Cable launched OpenTV-based services. Also in 1997, the company signed an agreement with British Interactive Broadcasting (BIB), a BskyB- and British Telecom-led consortium, to provide enhanced TV services to approximately 6 million subscribers in the U.K. At the time of this writing, OpenTV-enabled set-tops were being made available via retail stores to the general public in the U.K. and Ireland.

- Early in 1998, Tele Danmark Kabel TV (TDK) began offering a range of OpenTV-based interactive TV applications to their subscriber base. Also in 1998, OpenTV broke into the U.S. market, announcing a deployment with EchoStar.

The OpenTV customer base continued to expand in 1999 with digital cable companies, satellite providers, and terrestrial broadcasters across the globe continuing to select OpenTV as their choice of middleware.

Let's examine the OpenTV suite of interactive TV products in more detail. The OpenTV product family is comprised of a middleware product that is integrated with the set-top, a set of authoring tools, a suite of interactive TV applications, and utilities for integrating software applications into digital TV delivery environments.

Our next section takes a look at the architecture of the set-top middleware. On subsequent chapters we plan to look at the software applications and the head-end utilities in more detail.

The architecture of the OpenTV set-top system is comprised of a number of layers that fit into a footprint of between 350 and 560 KB of Flash memory.

At the core of the OpenTV client software platform is an adaptation layer that supports numerous embedded real-time kernels, including pSOS, VxWorks, Nucleus Plus, microTOS, and OS-9. One of the many benefits of OpenTV is its ability to shield upper-layer applications from differences in the set-top hardware platform. Hence, OpenTV applications can be executed on set-top boxes from different manufacturers.

To date, the company has licensed their technologies to 25 set-top box manufacturers. The shielding of applications from the hardware components within the set-top are made possible by the addition of an interpretive layer to the OS. This interpreter layer is responsible for translating OpenTV scripting language (called o-code) into native instructions for the host CPU. In addition to providing application developers with support for a range of hardware platforms, OpenTV has also developed a rich set of libraries. The libraries are logically located in the library layer and are comprised of a number of functions, including:

- graphics components for developing multimedia content;
- network communication stacks that enable full interactivity;

- manipulation of digital audio and video streams; and
- support for authentication and encryption technologies.

The final layer within the OpenTV set-top software architecture is needed to translate instructions issued by the set-top user to low-level commands that are understood by the set-top hardware devices, such as modems, high speed interface ports, and smart card readers. This is the driver layer and provides programmers with an API for developing drivers for specific hardware devices. This library of APIs can easily be extended to take advantage of new set-top multimedia technologies. The device layer is not included as part of the OpenTV operating environment, allowing manufacturers greater choice in terms of real-time OS and hardware platforms. OpenTV fully supports the downloading of updates via the TV operator's broadband network.

PowerTV

The architecture of the PowerTV client software is graphically illustrated in Figure 4.5.

Chapter 3 covered the features of the PowerTV real-time OS. This chapter takes a closer look at the middleware components of the PowerTV set-top platform. The resident application provides access to the digital television services through a standard

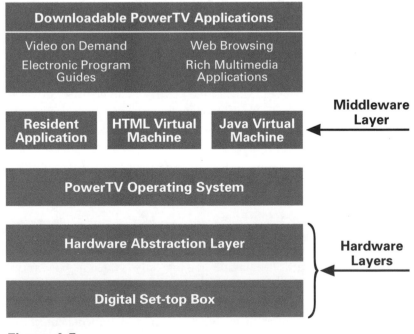

Figure 4.5
PowerTV client software

user interface and operates immediately on power-on of the set-top. At the time of going to press, PowerTV was not in the business of developing resident applications, but works closely with developers to provide optimized implementations to their customers. Next to the resident application, PowerTV has incorporated an HTML virtual machine. The incorporation of this component into the middleware layer allows PowerTV-enabled set-top boxes to process Web content that has been broadcasted over a TV network. Another important subsystem within the PowerTV middleware environment is the Java Virtual Machine. PowerTV was the first company to demonstrate Java applets executing on a set-top box over an RF broadband cable network in 1996. Since then, the company has worked very closely with Sun Microsystems in the requirements process for the Personal Java specification.

WebTV for Microsoft's TVPAK Platform

As described in Chapter 3, WebTV is a key part of Microsoft's digital television software platform. The company has integrated WebTV middleware technology into the Microsoft TV portion of TVPAK system. A layered structure of the Microsoft TV client software solution is shown in Figure 4.6.

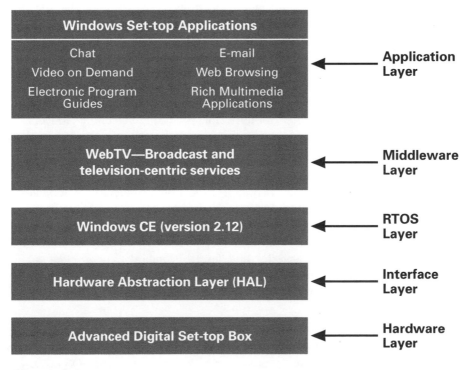

Figure 4.6
Microsoft TV platform

Essentially the Microsoft TV platform is comprised of five unique layers of protocols and services. At the bottom layer, we have the physical digital set-top boxes. More than 20 hardware manufacturers have already commenced on developing Microsoft TV-compatible set-top boxes. These hardware suppliers include: General Instrument Corp., Scientific-Atlanta, Thomson Multimedia, StellarOne, Pace Micro Technology, Vestel USA Inc., Philips Electronics, Sagem, Siemens, Matsushita Electric Industrial Co. Ltd., Hitachi Ltd., Sharp Corp., Sony Electronics Inc., Fujitsu Ltd., Tatung Co., The Acer Group, Trigem Computer Inc., and Samsung Electronics Company Ltd.

The layer above the hardware reference layer is commonly referred to as the hardware abstraction layer (HAL). The HAL presents a uniform interface to the layer above it. Apart from a few exceptions, the only way of interfacing with the set-top hardware components is through the HAL. As described in Chapter 3, version 2.12 of the Windows CE real-time OS is just above this layer. The next layer in the Microsoft TV client is the WebTV middleware layer. This layer utilizes the services of the Windows CE layer and includes a number of protocols and technologies that are used to control the TV-centric functions, such as electronic program guides, Pay Per View, channel tuning, and conditional access.

Finally, on top of these lower software layers, the actual subscriber applications, such as video-on-demand, the electronic program guide, Pay-Per-View, chat, e-commerce, e-mail, and multiplayer games are built.

MediaHighway

The French company Canal+ Technologies continues to amass support in the U.S., Europe, Israel, Brazil, and Asia for its flexible and open middleware product MediaHighway.

At the time of this writing, the platform had already been chosen by 20 international leading manufacturers and implemented in over 3 million set-top boxes and integrated television sets throughout the world. ONdigital, the world's first digital terrestrial operator, launched in the U.K. in November 1998, adopted MediaHighway as an integral part of its platform. The latest version of MediaHighway, MediaHighway+, is designed by Canal+ to quickly integrate with the open technical specifications of the DVB-MHP middleware standard as soon as the standard is finalized. Let's take a closer look at this powerful middleware standard that provides an open solution for providers who want to deploy a range of interactive TV applications. Pictured in Figure 4.7 is an overview of the MediaHighway software architecture that runs in a digital set-top box.

The MediaHighway software module is composed of only one layer. The set-top box manufacturer is responsible for developing the drivers for the various hardware components within the box. Above, driver and real-time OS layer, we meet the *device manager.* As the name suggests, its primary responsibility is to manage the various set-

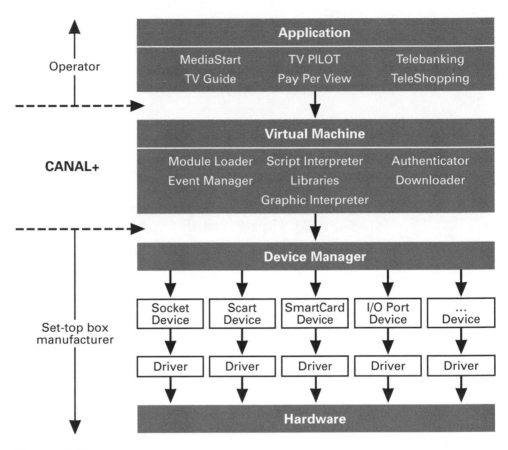

Figure 4.7
Architecture of MediaHighway system

top hardware devices. The layer above the device manager layer is called the MediaHighway middleware layer or Virtual Machine layer. Canal+ has written an API, called the device layer interface, which is used to pass data from one layer to another. This interface is currently available to set-top box manufacturers and has already been released to more than 10 licensed set-top box manufacturers. The middleware layer is made up of a number of different virtual machines that can be easily customized to meet the demands of customers. Earlier versions of MediaHighway only included a virtual machine based on a Canal+ proprietary programming language called PanTalk.

Nowadays, Canal+ have extended their middleware product by adding new virtual machines to support emerging standards such as Java, HTML, and MHEG.

The top layer in the MediaHighway software model is the *application layer*. This layer is made up of a myriad of Internet and TV-based applications. These applications can be written in different languages depending on the configuration of the virtual machines in the middleware layer.

Liberate eNavigator

Liberate Technologies is a U.S.-based company specializing in developing software telephone set-top boxes, phones, and other appliances to the Internet. The company was originally founded by Oracle and Netscape and was formerly known as Network Computers Incorporated (NCI). Today, investors in the company include ComCast, Cox Communications, Rogers Communications, Shaw Communications, and MediaOne Ventures; as well as General Instrument, Hambrecht & Quist Group, Sun Microsystems, Wind River Systems, Sony, Acer, Sega, Nintendo, NEC, and Marubeni. At the time of writing this chapter, the company had filed with the Securities and Exchange Commission to raise as much as $100 million through an initial public offering. Liberate is one of the chief rivals to Microsoft in the battle to provide software for advanced television set-top boxes.

It develops and markets software for three distinct audiences. The company's client solutions are targeted at Original Equipment Manufacturers of set-top boxes, game consoles, and personal digital assistants. Their server products (Liberate connect and applications) are sold to a variety of network service providers. For the TV content business, Liberate also provides a set of development tools that allow companies to create a myriad of applications for client devices running Liberate technologies. Chapter 6 examines how to develop content and applications for a Liberate-based platform. In this particular section of the book, we focus our energies on explaining Liberate's middleware solution that allows network operators to deliver applications, which integrate the Web's interactivity with the richness of TV-based content to its subscriber base. The company offers a product called eNavigator. Liberate eNavigator is a core client technology designed to be embedded in networked information devices such as point-of-sale credit card readers, PDAs, screen phones, digital set-top boxes, and other networked information appliances. eNavigator supports all major Internet and computing standards, including HTML, JavaScript, and HTTP. It is easily ported to multiple operating systems and low-cost hardware platforms. The client software can run on broadcast-only networks but requires a two-way network to provide fully interactive services. Liberate's middleware product is customizable and allows network operators to configure a set-top box with a range of settings.

PlanetWeb

PlanetWeb is a leading developer of Internet software products and services that integrate the Internet into consumer electronic devices. The company was founded in 1996 and has offices in Mountain View, California, and Toyko. The company provides a range of integrated software solutions that enable manufacturers to add Internet access

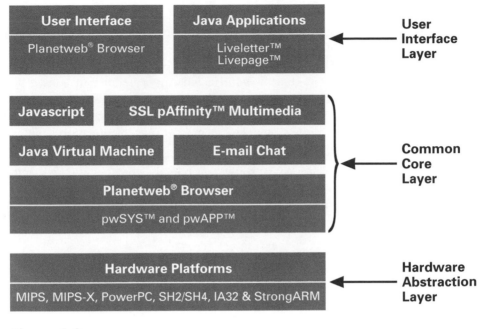

Figure 4.8
Architecture of PlanetWeb set-top solution

to products such as video game systems, screen phones, TV set-top boxes, video-phones, and DVD players, turning them into Internet advanced information appliances. Let's take a closer look at PlanetWeb's middleware environment. A graphical representation of the client software architecture is shown in Figure 4.8.

From the diagram we can see that the PlanetWeb set-top solution is comprised of three different layers: user Interface layer, common core layer, and hardware abstraction layer.

The User Interface Layer • The top layer of the PlanetWeb's software, it consists of user interface elements for the individual applications, including PlanetWeb's browser, e-mail, chat, and parental control as well as the HTML portions of the platform that are visible to the end-user. Such graphical and navigational elements include the company's patented magnifier; bump scrolling and command compass; and multimedia Java applications Liveletter and Livepage. All of these elements are fully customizable, using existing HTML and graphic development tools that are widely available. Display-quality issues are also handled on this top layer. Proprietary anti-aliased fonts, two-stage flicker reduction, and other sophisticated image-processing technologies were specifically developed to deal with the inherent "display" limitations of televisions and screen phones—appliances that are typically used as display monitors for Internet appliances.

The Common Core Layer • Interfaces with the hardware abstraction layer and does not need to be rewritten for each individual hardware platform. One of the main objectives of the common core layer is to support and handle various types of Internet protocols. This layer also contains HTML, Javascript, and Java virtual machines for processing Web content. Also included is a number of software modules that are responsible for generating PlanetWeb's own anti-aliased fonts, decompressing multiple image formats (including GIFs, JPEGs, etc.), and converting audio files for the sound system. File system and memory management is also handled at this layer.

The Hardware Abstraction Layer • It is the only layer that requires customization each time the software is ported, depending on the specific hardware. This layer is capable of supporting a number of TV-centric devices such as remote controls, wireless keyboards, and IR blasters.

SUMMARY . . . .

Middleware is used to isolate application programs from the details of the underlying broadband network. In a set-top environment, middleware consists of a number of components, commonly called virtual machines. Due to the explosive growth of the Web, HTML and JavaScript have become dominant standards in the world of publishing electronic documents. Subsequently, most set-top middleware products support HTML and JavaScript virtual machines.

The HTML engine supports the parsing and layout of web pages on a television screen. The JavaScript virtual machine is required to deliver high-quality interactive services to the digital set-top box. Support for virtual machines based on Internet standards gives service providers the ability to reuse existing Web content and services on their highspeed broadband networks.

Many companies are beginning to look at and embrace the power of Java technologies. Sun Microsystems have developed a lightweight implementation of Java, called Personal Java. Personal Java provides a robust programming language for software developers.

MHEG-5 is an ISO standard language which uses multimedia and hypermedia objects to build scenes within an interactive TV application. Terrestrial operators in the U.K. are currently broadcasting MHEG-5 content. The existing MHEG-5 player does not include a scripting engine, which limits the technology's interactive capabilities.

The current business model for digital TV services is comprised of a subscriber buying or leasing a set-top box running a proprietary middleware software system. With the move toward a retail model, the importance of open standards becomes key in ensuring that their set-top box investment is safe. The demand for open standards within the world of set-top middleware systems has resulted in the emergence of three groups in the United States and Europe: DVB—MHP, DASE, and ATVEF.

While the work continues on the definition of middleware standards a number of software vendors have launched interim solutions.

Table 4.1 summarizes some details about the leading suppliers of set-top middleware software products.

Table 4.1

Middleware product	Web site	Transition path to open standards
OpenTV	www.opentv.com	Yes
Microsoft TVPAK	www.microsoft.com/tv/	Yes
MediaHighway	www.canalplus-technologies.com/media/index2.html	Yes
eNavigator	www.liberate.com	Yes
PowerTV	www.powertv.com	Yes
PlanetWeb	www.planetweb.com	Yes

5 Set-top Specifications and Platforms

In this chapter...

Current set-top applications are still pretty limited in functionality and no one can predict what will eventually become the "killer" application in the world of digital television. The challenge for set-top box manufacturers and consumer electronic companies is to design different categories of set-top boxes to meet customer requirements. This chapter includes an overview of the three main categories of digital set-top boxes. Although the digital set-top business is relatively new, industry leaders and standard bodies in the United States and Europe have produced a number of reference hardware and software set-top specifications. These specifications act as references for manufacturers building digital boxes for various network operators.

This chapter discusses the major specifications to date and examines some of the implementations of these set-top standards, concluding with brief descriptions of set-top boxes that are being deployed on cable, terrestrial, MMDS, and satellite networks across the globe.

CATEGORIES OF DIGITAL SET-TOPS . . . .

Digital set-top boxes can be classified into three separate categories: broadcast TV, enhanced TV, and advanced services.

Broadcast TV • Broadcast TV set-top boxes are capable of providing traditional broadcast television that is complemented with a Pay Per View system and a very basic navigation tool. Broadcast TV-based set-tops have no return channel, and therefore do not imply interaction with computer servers located at the head-end. However, they are capable of receiving data contained within the digital MPEG stream. They are entry-level set-top boxes and come with limited quantities of memory, interface ports, and processing power. They have, however, been designed to evolve and support more advanced systems, such as near-video-on-demand and messaging services.

Enhanced TV • Enhanced TV set-top boxes include a return or back channel, which provides communication with a server located at a head-end. These set-tops are capable of providing e-commerce, video-on-demand services, Internet browsing, and near-video-on-demand services. The presence of a return channel further allows for broadcasts customized to the local viewing population and enables the set-top to support e-mail and local chat-style communication services. Such set-tops have double the processing power and memory capabilities of broadcast TV boxes.

Advanced Services • Set-tops from the advanced services category bare close resemblance to a multimedia desktop PC. They can contain more than 10 times the processing power of a low-level broadcast TV set-top box. Enhanced capabilities in conjunction with a high speed return path can be used to access a range of Internet and interactive services at very high speeds. Most of the set-tops in this category allow a subscriber to add a hard drive, if required. Such receivers come with a range of high speed interface ports, which allow them to be used as telecommunication centers in the homes of the future.

The set-top boxes described in these three categories are usually manufactured in compliance with a particular standard or reference hardware platform. Let's take a closer look at standards that have or are beginning to get finalized in Europe and the United States.

EUROBOX . . . .

The Eurobox specification was developed by the members of EuroCableLabs and is used by European cable operators as a reference model for designing and implementing advanced digital set-top boxes. EuroCableLabs is a working group within the ECCA organization focused on implementing the Eurobox and Euromodem projects. The concept of Eurobox is based on a common hardware platform with a common middleware and CA system for all European digital TV subscribers. The concept makes a lot of sense because standardization means manufacturers and TV operators can offer set-top boxes to their customers at low prices. Since its inception, Eurobox has become one of the largest and most advanced digital cable platforms in Europe. To date, the Eurobox set-top platform has been successfully implemented in a range of European countries including France, Sweden, Ireland, and Denmark. It has also been recently selected as a basis for the Nordic digital platform. Chances are by the time you read this book, many more new countries will have implemented the Eurobox set-top platform.

The Eurobox reference model supports a range of digital TV-based services, including: hundreds of digital TV channels, Pay Per View, and electronic program guides.

The Eurobox incorporates either a telephone or cable modem that can be used by digital TV subscribers to access a variety of Internet and interactive TV services. Two Smart card interfaces are located at the front of the box, one for the conditional access system and one for banking cards. Two Scart connectors are included to provide connectivity between the TV, the VCR, and the set-top box. The Eurobox design includes an RS-232 data interface and an IEEE 1284 interface, which can be installed as an optional extra. Viaccess from France Telecom has been selected as the default conditional access and ECCA has decided to use OpenTV as the standard middleware API for all implementations of the Eurobox standard (see Figure 5.1).

The set-top includes a facility to allow network operators to download and replace the entire software platform stored in Flash memory.

The Eurobox specification is updated on a regular basis. For more technical details of Eurobox-compliant set-tops, please download and review the complete specification from the following Web site: www.ecca.be.

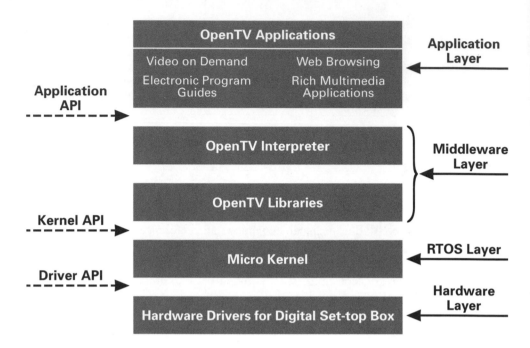

Figure 5.1
Layered structure of the OpenTV API used in Eurobox hardware implementations

Figure 5.2
Eurobox logo

Some people use this specification as a basis for writing requests for proposals to set-top box manufacturers. Set-top boxes complying with the Eurobox specification will be able to carry the Eurobox logo. The logo is shown in Figure 5.2.

OPENCABLE . . . .

OpenCable is a U.S. cable industry initiative, which seeks to obtain and deploy a family of interoperable advanced digital set-top boxes from multiple vendors. CableLabs is managing the OpenCable specification writing process on behalf of its cable operator members. The OpenCable specification process seeks to achieve the following goals:

1. Shall provide for integrated environments for broadcast services (analog and digital) and real-time interactive multimedia services, including IP data services (program synchronous and asynchronous), IP voice communications, video telephony, and on-demand interactive applications. Multiple models of set-top terminals are expected to coexist within any given system, allowing the network operator to offer various services.

2. Shall require openness and interoperability. OpenCable shall take advantage of "open" computing and network architectures, wherever possible, to minimize costs and maximize the ability to include new technologies as they become available and affordable. "Open" is defined as adherence to either international standard, North American standard, or de facto industry standard. In all cases, the acquisition of the necessary software, hardware, and intellectual must be achievable at fair and reasonable costs. All standard interfaces must be in the public domain or, if such technology standards are to be defined, they shall be available for license at a fair and reasonable cost. Closed proprietary systems are to be avoided.

3. Shall require portability. Retail availability of cable navigation devices is required in compliance with the FCC's 1996 Telecom Reform Act. The OpenCable system shall permit "point-of-deployment decisions" for network, security, and operator-programmed user interfaces for the variety of retail devices expected to be available.

4. Shall define a renewable and replaceable core encryption system (point-of-deployment [POD] module).

5. Shall provide cable Multiple System Operators (MSOs) the ability to provide information relating to the navigation and access of services (video, Internet, etc.) that they offer.

6. Shall present a migration path from unidirectional to bidirectional networks and from broadcast to real-time interactive applications. Media servers and the related hardware (e.g., disk storage, switch fabric, modulators) shall support the incremental addition of the required components to preserve any existing investment while taking advantage of more cost-effective solutions. In addition, the system software shall be designed to scale efficiently as more interactive applications are added and service

offerings expand. Of particular note are "authentication" and "name" services, database services, fault tolerance, and recovery mechanisms.

7. Shall allow efficient application and network design, by:
   • Reducing the absolute size of a digital stream through improved compression technologies; for example, by using improved MPEG-2 encoders and higher constellation digital modulation techniques.
   • Optimizing the use of network bandwidth, as it is a finite resource. During the broadcast applications phase, bandwidth is allocated to accommodate broadcast digital program streams. As systems migrate to real-time interactive applications, the system shall make efficient use of the network resources by dynamically allocating bandwidth.
   • Developing applications designed to use network resources efficiently, varying their behavior according to the network's resource availability.
   • Minimizing the network resources required when the consumer "turns on" the set-top terminal.

8. Shall maximize compatibility with existing and/or newly installed operational and customer support systems. All interfaces developed specifically for this effort shall be integrated into the current and/or newly installed billing support systems.

9. Shall coexist with the embedded base of existing set-top terminals.

The research team at CableLabs is extremely busy formulating a variety of different specifications to support the mass deployment of interactive TV-and Internet-based services. This chapter takes a closer look at an OpenCable specification for uni-directional set-top boxes.

The goals and objectives of this base-line OpenCable set-top box are:

1. To enable new digital broadcast services, and to support some on-demand services in the future.
2. To be developer-friendly.
3. To support nonscrambled analog services as well as new encrypted or nonencrypted digital services.
4. To be sold through retail channels directly to the customer.

An OpenCable unidirectional set-top box operates in a subscriber's home as follows. The box receives multimedia information by tuning to one of the many 6 MHz input channels available via the unidirectional cable connection. When the input channel is an analog channel, the signal is processed via the video decoder and the vertical blanking interval data decoder. When the input channel is a digital channel, it is processed via the QAM demodulator and then passed to the MPEG-2 Transport

Demultiplexer. Encrypted information is passed to the point of deployment (POD) module for security processing. The multimedia processor handles the synchronization and display of all audio-visual material, with the exception of high definition television programming, which is passed through the set-top box via the 1394 interface. The set-top terminal also receives control information and other data by tuning to an out-of-band (OOB) channel. This information is passed to the POD for processing, and relevant information is passed back to the set-top box.

In addition to defining a uniform hardware specification for the next generation of digital set-top boxes, CableLabs is also working on a specification for a common applications platform that is based on Internet technologies.

The following subsections provide you with some specific details about implementations based on the DVB and OpenCable standards. Please note that these specifications are subject to continual improvement and hence may change during the course of writing this book. There is a high probability that by the time you read this, many more digital set-top boxes will have hit retail stores around the globe.

IMPLEMENTATIONS ·

Sky Series 2200

Pace Micro Technology is one of the leaders in set-top technologies and is solely focused on the design, manufacture, and distribution of digital set-top boxes. Pace has manufactured set-tops for a number of network service providers around Europe, including ONdigital, BskyB, NTL, Canal+, and C&W (Cable and Wireless). It is beyond the scope of this chapter to evaluate all of their set-top products, but we will take a closer look at the set-top box that is being currently manufactured for BskyB.

It fully complies with standards defined on the DVB-S specification and has been designed to receive hundreds of digital channels, interactive services, and a limited number of Internet-based services. It supports an onscreen program guide, standard teletext data. It is running OpenTV software and can be easily upgraded through software downloads over the satellite network.

It comes with a QPSK demodulator and decoders that are capable of converting MPEG broadband signals back into a digital stream. The system is based on a reasonably high-powered processor with 4 MB of dynamic RAM, 4 MB of video RAM, and 16 KB of ROM. A V.34 modem is included with the set-top to allow the introduction of interactive services like TV banking and Web browsing. Other interfaces to the Sky box include:

- TV and video Scart connectors;
- two PCMCIA cards for security and e-commerce applications; and
- RS-232 for connecting the set-top box to a remote terminal or modem.

From a physical perspective, the box weighs in around 7.7 lbs. and measures 18.6 inches × 13.7 inches × 6.3 inches. It is pre-packaged with a remote control, a 3-meter cable for connecting the modem to the telephone port on the wall, batteries, and a detachable mains lead 1.5 meters long. At the beginning of May 1999, BskyB announced that they were giving away digital set-top boxes with accompanying satellite dishes to customers that sign up for its satellite digital service. The company also announced on the same day that they would switch off its analogue TV service by December 2002.

DCT–5000+

General Instruments (GI) is marketing the DCT-5000+ as the world's most advanced digital set-top box. GI signed an agreement with TCI and 12 other large U.S.-based cable companies in 1998 to supply 15 million set-top boxes over the next five years based on the DCT-5000 hardware architecture. The DCT-5000 set-top hardware design includes a high-powered MIPS processor that runs at a speed of 175 MHz, a 32-bit graphics chipset, and an Integrated DOCSIS cable modem. Another important aspect of the 5000's set-top design is the memory amounts used. The actual amounts of memory included with the box are dependent on the range of applications that are planned by the network operator. A typical entry-level DCT-5000 set-top comes with 2 MB of ROM, 4 MB of Flash, and 8 MB of DRAM, but these amounts can be easily upgraded. For example, it is possible to have DRAM amounts exceeding 32 MB. The DCT-5000 is capable of supporting several different operating systems and software applications.

One of the distinguishing features in the DCT-5000+ is its unique architecture, with three different tuners: one tuner dedicated to receiving video services and another to the DOCSIS channel for highspeed data services; the third tuner is used for the OOB control channel. With this architecture, users can simultaneously surf the Web at highspeed and hold a telephone conversation while continuing to watch traditional TV services. The consumer is never forced to choose between one or the other. This functionality provides the subscriber with a seamless interaction between data services such as Internet access and revenue-generating video services. To ensure system security of the various interactive digital services delivered to subscribers, the DCT-5000+ employs GI's DigiCipher II access control and encryption technology.

The DCT-5000 supports the latest video technologies. The MPEG-2 video decoder, for example, ensures that subscribers receive and view a high-quality picture on their TV set. It is also capable of supporting the decoding of High Definition Television (HDTV). In addition to supporting the latest and greatest video technologies, this GI set-top box also supports a variety of traditional analog and digital audio formats.

GI has partnered with a number of software vendors, including Microsoft, Liberate Technologies, Sun Microsystems, and Sony, to enhance the interactive capabilities of the DCT-5000+.

The powerful processing and graphics capability of the DCT-5000+ is complemented by a number of advanced digital networking interfaces. The entry-level model of the box comes with Ethernet and USB interfaces. Subscribers and network operators have the option to add FireWire and IEEE 1284 ports to facilitate highspeed data transfers between the set-top box and other consumer electronic devices within the household. The CA system is embedded inside the set-top box, therefore the box only contains one Smart card reader for e-commerce applications such as online shopping and home banking.

GI has also added an IDE hard drive interface to provide subscribers with the option of locally storing data. The DCT-5000+ hardware platform is compliant with OpenCable standards. GI is currently developing a DVB-compliant version of this set-top box for the European market, called the DVi5000+. Similar to its American counterpart, the DVi-5000+ has been designed to allow European subscribers access to a wide range of applications such as video-on-demand, Internet access, community networking, IP telephony, electronic program guides, and more. Expect to see this PC-like set-top box toward the middle of 2000.

Nokia MediaMaster T

Nokia's Mediamaster T has been designed especially for receiving a broad range of digital terrestrial programming and radio from the UK's terrestrial operator, OnDigital. It is an easy-to-use multimedia terminal that links together all electronic media. The MediaMaster T has a variety of powerful video and audio qualities. It is not only fully compliant with DVB standards, it is also capable of receiving free air channels and scrambled TV services. It also comes with an easy-to-use navigational tool that allows customers to review detailed information about favorite programs and shows.

The installation of the set-top is quite easy. Subscribers just follow the onscreen instructions and the set-top will automatically locate and sort out the various digital channels. Included with the set-top is an attractively designed remote control for controling TV viewing. The MediaMaster T is based on a 32-bit RISC processor and comes with the following memory configurations:

- 4 MB of DRAM;
- 4 MB of Flash; and
- 4 MB of video memory.

The tuner included in the set-top box is capable of demodulating COFDM terrestrial signals. To access terrestrial signals, the MediaMaster is connected to an antenna that is either located on your TV set or mounted on the roof of your house.

When the network operator introduces new functions and digital services, it is possible to upgrade the software resident in the MediaMaster. An attractively designed keyboard for both left- and right-handed persons accompanies the set-top box.

Motorola Streamaster

In September 1998, at the International Broadcasters Convention in Amsterdam, Motorola announced the launch of a TV set-top box for cable companies, code-named "Blackbird." The set-top box has since been renamed Streamaster and will provide digital TV subscribers with a variety of multimedia features, including Internet access, movie playbacks, and 3D games. The architecture of the box is based on a high speed PowerPC processor, an integrated decoder graphics processor, audio decoders, Smart card readers, and highspeed data interface ports.

Motorola's device is based on operating system software from MicroWare and uses Java-based applications. The company has, however, not ruled out the porting of other third-party real-time operating systems to the Streamaster platform.

In September 1998, Motorola also licensed a custom version of SpyGlass's Web browser technology, designed for television viewing as well as server software for controling and sending information to the digital set-top box. Both Spyglass products will be bundled with the new Streamaster set-top box platform. Motorola has already received orders for over 1 million Streamaster set-top boxes, so we can expect to see a number of derivatives of this product hitting the market in the near future. For a more detail, technical description of the Streamaster set-top box, visit the following address: http://mot-sps.com/ADC/DSTB.html

The Explorer Set-top Family from Scientific-Atlanta

At the 1999 National Cable Television Association trade show, Scientific Atlanta unveiled plans to expand its digital set-top product line with three new models that will complement its award-winning Explorer 2000 set-top.

Explorer 2000S

At the time of writing this book, the explorer 2000s had been shipped to 17 cable operators in the U.S. and Canada. This low-cost set-top allows cable operators to provide their customers with broadcast channels and interactive services such as Pay Per View and e-mail. The set-top has a limited number of highspeed interface ports and consequently is unsuitable for customers who require home networking capabilities. It is ideal for entry-level subscribers or a person who has multiple TV sets in their home.

Explorer 3000

The explorer 3000 set-top has double the processing power and memory capabilities of the explorer 2000 box. It incorporates a 108 MIPS processor and will come with an interface that allows customers to add a local storage device—a hard drive. This new model will be ideal for digital TV subscribers who want to simultaneously access a varied range of new multimedia and advanced Internet applications from the comfort of their homes. The explorer 3000 set-top is expected to be available in early 2000.

Explorer 6000

The explorer 6000 is the most powerful of the new models and will have more than five times as much processing power as the explorer 2000 currently being shipped. This advanced set-top box is expected to deliver more than 300 MIPS of processing power to customers. Cable customers will be able to use enhanced graphical capabilities within the box to receive high definition TV signals. In regards to software, the set-top box will use IP as a means of communicating with the head-end and customers are given a choice of either PowerTV or Microsoft TV software. This software in conjunction with the processing power of the box can be used to run a variety of advanced services such as video teleconferencing, home networking, IP telephony, video-on-demand, Internet TV services, and hundreds of digital channels. It will also be backward-compatible with applications that have been written for the explorer 2000 set-top box. A hard disk that allows subscribers to store popular musical CDs, such as those in the MP 3 file format, can also be added to this powerful set-top. In compliance with the OpenCable specification and FCC requirements, the box will also contain an interface option for a POD module. Expect to see this PC-like set-top box on the shelves toward the middle of 2000.

SUMMARY . . . .

The digital TV market of the future will be comprised of a large population of set-tops working busily on highspeed broadband networks. These set-tops will be composed of low-end boxes with limited capabilities as well as fully-featured set-top boxes.

To guarantee compatibility between set-top boxes, two standards bodies have defined high-level sets of specifications. In Europe, we have the Eurobox and in the United States, the OpenCable specification is nearing completion. Both initiatives are expected to lead to readily available set-top products that will address consumers huge appetites for new entertainment services.

Many companies are involved in the manufacture of digital set-top boxes. It is beyond the scope of this book to investigate all of these devices. We did, however, review a sample of set-tops that comply with emerging standards.

Before selecting and installing a new set-top box, you need to consider the types of services that you intend on accessing. If, for example, you're goal is to watch more channels, than a set-top box with a low CPU cost, a minimum amount of memory, and a low-speed return path is the obvious choice. If you need to access Internet-based services and connect to a home network, then a much more sophisticated box needs to be purchased.

6 Set-top Application Development

In this chapter...

Digital television presents many exciting possibilities and opportunities—interactivity, data broadcasting, electronic commerce, better pictures, HDTV, Internet services, improved audio quality and new applications that have not yet been dreamed about. Computer, IT, and software companies all over the world are buzzing about the new possibilities that digital television offers.

There is a wave of activity in the IT and broadcast industry right now centered on providing millions of people with a suite of set-top applications that will firmly establish the next computing paradigm. This new paradigm of developing programs for a set-top box instead of a standard PC will present software developers with a wealth of new and exciting opportunities.

It is very seldom nowadays to see TV network operators having their own development studios. Instead, operators are deciding to write down the application specifications and subcontract the development of applications to knowledgeable multimedia studios. The existing model of outsourcing set-top application development offers PC software companies with a multi-billion dollar growth opportunity. In this chapter, we briefly describe the main differences between developing for a set-top box versus a desktop PC. We then examine the development lifecycle of a typical interactive set-top application. The last part of our chapter talks about some of the software development kits that are available in the market today.

DEVELOPING FOR A SET-TOP ENVIRONMENT VERSUS A PC ENVIRONMENT . . . .

As the development of entertainment services for the digital TV market gathers pace, software engineers are being challenged to develop a variety of Internet- and TV-centric applications for the set-top box. Developing for a set-top environment is particularly challenging because they have limited memory and hardware resources when compared to a standard desktop PC.

Outlined below are some of the major issues that arise when developing a program for a set-top box instead of a desktop PC.

- The use of complex graphical interfaces is limited because television monitors have low resolution when compared to PC monitors.
- For a PC, software engineers architect a software interface based on the assumption that the end-user is only a foot or two away from the monitor. This paradigm is totally changed in a TV-centric environment because the viewer can be viewing information at distances exceeding 12 feet. This issue is overcome by increasing the quality and size of the fonts downloaded to the set-top.

- The normal method for navigating a PC application is to use a mouse to click and select particular functions. This method of navigation is impossible in a set-top and TV environment. Set-top software engineers will need to develop user interfaces that can be navigated using a simple infrared remote control. It is reasonably easy from a software perspective to develop a basic set-top application, however, consumer expectations for rich multimedia front-ends are growing by the day.

- The cost sensitivity of set-top boxes restricts the amount of memory and processing capabilities that can be added to a box. A typical configuration of a set-top box deployed in 1998 consisted of 2 MB of ROM for the operating system, 4 MB of Flash memory for resident applications, 4 MB of dynamic RAM for applications, and a processor running at 40 MIPS. To a set-top manufacturer and a TV operator, this type of box is considered reasonably powerful, however to a software engineer, who normally develops for a PC, the resources will appear very limited.

- In PC software development, the issue of application portability is not a huge issue since most desktops run the Microsoft Windows operating system. Due to the large number of set-top operating systems, the portability of applications between environments require a large amount of redevelopment work.

- Many television viewers have little or no computer experience.

SET-TOP APPLICATION DEVELOPMENT CYCLE . . . .

The gradual development of software for a digital set-top box from conception to retirement can be described as a life cycle. Each phase in the life cycle relates to a particular point in the development of the set-top application.

The idea of a life cycle makes the software development process predictable and controllable. It provides a formal structure within which the software development team can work. There are numerous models used by software development houses to produce software. Most of these models are structured into a cascade of phases, where one phase serves as the input to the next phase. And each phase constitutes a set of activities and results. Similar to developing a PC application, set-top applications need to be specified in detail by the customer—for set-tops this will likely be a TV or broadcast operator. Consequently, requirements analysis and specification is the first phase of the software development process. It is preceded by a feasibility study that evaluates the cost and benefits of the proposed software system to the company, and its technical feasibility. During this phase, the quality requirements of the proposed new software applications are determined and then documented. This phase results in the production of a detailed requirements specification document. Once the operator has broadly outlined the functional requirements of the application, the next stage of the development cycle is to choose a development platform. To ease the effort of developing applications, the platform that is selected needs to support several key features:

Portability • Applications portability refers to the ability of applications to run on more than one operating system.

Openness • Network operators, application developers, content providers, and broadcast developers do not want to be locked into a closed, proprietary development environment.

Networkability • Set-top applications will be deployed on two-way interactive networks, consequently the chosen platform will need to support all networking standards.

Scalability • The application development environment will need to be capable of scaling rapidly from a small number of set-top users to a very large subscriber base of several million set-top users.

Once a specific development platform has been chosen, the next step is to decide whether or not the application is programmed in native code and integrated with the set-top box or else stored at the head-end and broadcasted with the digital MPEG stream. If the network operator decides to embed the application into the set-top box, close cooperation between the manufacturer and set-top application developer is needed to ensure adequate hardware resources are available to run the application.

The TV operator may want to minimize set-top hardware costs and instead locate the application at the head-end. This being the case, a set-top application developer will work on:

- integrating with the operator's network architecture;
- localizing the application for a particular country; and
- modifying the look and feel of the application to match the operator's corporate image.

During the design and specification phase, the software engineers design a software application to meet the requirements set out in the requirement's specification document. The system is diluted into modules during the design and specification phase. And the software design usually progresses from a preliminary design to a detailed one. This phase produces a design specification document that outlines the architecture for the set-top software and the supporting servers in the head-end.

During the coding and testing phase, the software engineer uses one or more software development kits (SDKs) to write the programs for the advanced set-top boxes. Modules that have been coded in this phase are tested to verify whether each module meets its original specification. Once the coding and testing phase has been completed the software is integrated and tested in a lab environment. This is commonly referred to as alpha testing. The next stage of the cycle is the delivery of the full

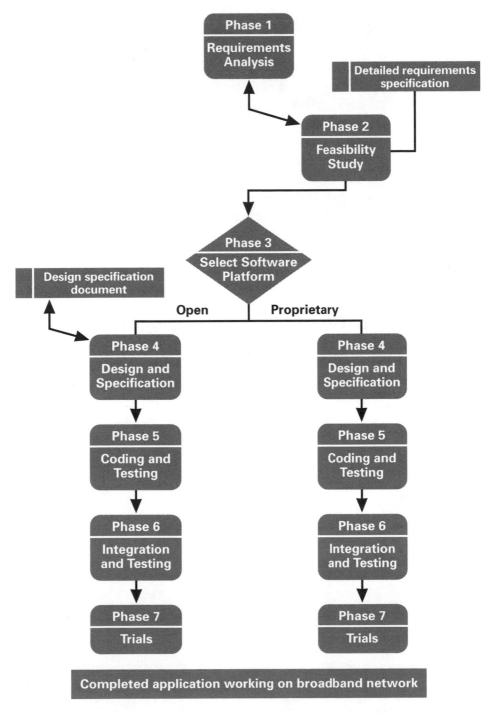

Figure 6.1
Phases of a set-top application development cycle

application to the network operator and put into use on the broadband TV network. It is normal practice to test the application on a broadband network with a few subscribers and make some modifications to the software, if required.

Regarding ownership of the application, it is normal practice for the operator to retain the rights to the application. The diagram in Figure 6.1 displays a structured approach to developing a set-top application.

Several programming technologies and platforms have been developed that allow developers to create exciting new applications for digital set-tops.

APPLICATION DEVELOPMENT ENVIRONMENTS . . . . . .

To facilitate and speed up the development of these compelling services for consumers, a number of set-top software development kits (SDKs) have been commercialized and are available for purchase.

OpenTV Application Development

OpenTV offers established developers and newcomers to the world of interactive TV applications a partnership program called OpenAdvantage. It is a special co-marketing program designed to encourage software developers to create services—using OpenTV tools—for affiliated OpenTV television networks, worldwide. In addition to joining the OpenAdvantage program, people who want to start developing applications or services for OpenTV set-top clients should purchase one or both of the following products.

OpenTV SDK

The OpenTV Software Development Kit is a complete content development environment for C-programmers who want to create interactive television services that are high in graphic content and have the look and feel of television. This SDK allows for very robust applications to be built using OpenTV's application programming interface. Applications developed with the OpenTV SDK require very little memory and processing power in digital set-top boxes, yet produce broadcast-quality television images.

Software programmers benefit from this SDK because it provides full access to the modular OpenTV architecture. It allows C-programmers to develop applications that use devices such as a remote control to navigate through the application. This SDK provides graphical and command-line tools along with application programming interfaces (APIs). These APIs can be used to create compelling new interactive applications, including advertising, gaming, shopping, banking, and information services.

Once created, these applications may be downloaded and executed on any digital set-top box running the OpenTV middleware system. In order to provide C-programmers with a method of testing and previewing applications in a native television environment, OpenTV can provide a specially modified, target digital set-top box. This SDK is backed by a complete programmer's tutorial, including step-by-step instructions and source code examples with electronic and hard copy documentation. Five-day training courses are available for developers at either the OpenTV headquarters in Mountain View, California, or at their European office in Paris, France.

OpenAuthor

In the previous section, we covered OpenTV's SDK, which was aimed specifically at the technical and software development communities. Realizing that a large market existed for people with no programming experience to develop interactive TV applications, the company launched a tool called OpenAuthor.

OpenAuthor enables nonprogrammers to design, implement, and test an OpenTV application without writing a single line of code. The building of a fully functional OpenTV application is made easy for OpenAuthor users through the use of prebuilt components called *gadgets.*

These gadgets are normally created by experienced programmers and integrated with OpenAuthor. The existing version of OpenAuthor comes with a rich library of gadgets. A gadget is fully customizable and is comprised of two distinct elements:

1. the editor element, which is run by the OpenAuthor application; and
2. the run-time element, which has been designed to run in the set-top.

OpenAuthor is extensible allowing third parties to develop new gadgets and plug-ins. A *plug-in* is a software module that adds a particular feature to the OpenAuthor application. For example a gadget may be created to add e-business capabilities to a TV application. There is also a professional edition of the product, which provides content developers and engineers with the features required to create new gadgets themselves.

While software developers may prefer the OpenTV SDK for writing advanced applications, it is expected that the OpenAuthor product will be the tool of choice for people who want to quickly deploy set-top applications.

Windows CE Application Development

From a developers perspective, the Windows CE real-time OS is a compelling platform. It offers a familiar development environment to anyone experienced in Windows development and it offers the existing base of 5 million Windows programmers a new paradigm for developing interactive TV applications. Analysts are predicting that over the next 10 years the marketplace for set-tops will grow significantly larger than the existing PC market.

All applications developed for a Windows environment must communicate with the operating system through the Windows API. The Windows API is an essential component and consists of a large set of functions that facilitate an application's requests for operating system services.

Most applications now being developed for the Windows operating system are 32-bit applications. A layer called the Win32 API defines the 32-bit functions of the Windows API. The Win32 API was initially developed for the Windows NT operating system.

Windows CE supports a rich set of Win32 APIs enabling experienced Windows programmers to port PC applications (such as word processors, spreadsheets, and games) to the set-top environment.

The existence of a vast developer community that already knows how to author programs for the Windows environment is expected to lower the costs and reduce time involved with deploying advanced set-top applications. Because Windows CE supports the Win32 API, application developers can use familiar development tools contained within the Microsoft Visual Studio product to create applications for digital set-top boxes.

Microsoft Visual Studio

Microsoft Visual Studio is a complete suite of development tools for building complete end-to-end data-centric solutions. The professional edition of the suite is comprised of Microsoft Visual J++, Microsoft Visual Basic, the Microsoft Visual C++ development system, the Microsoft Visual InterDev Web development system, and the Visual FoxPro database development system. Microsoft also offers an enterprise version of their studio product, which contains additional development tools for building end-to-end software solutions.

Our main focus in this chapter will be to give you an overview of specific Microsoft Visual Studio development products, which may be used by software engineers to author advanced set-top box applications.

Microsoft Visual Basic

Microsoft Visual Basic (VB) is a member of the Microsoft Visual Studio development tools suite that is based on the world's most popular programming language—BASIC.

The application itself provides PC developers with a wide range of preloaded controls that significantly reduce coding and design time. To complement the large library of controls, VB also comes with a variety of intuitive tools for editing, testing, and debugging desktop applications. It is available either as a stand-alone product or as part of the Visual Studio suite of development tools.

Some key features of the latest version of VB include:

- Full support for object linking and embedding (OLE), a technology available in nearly all Microsoft products, allowing developers to manipulate objects such as charts or documents on your desktop.
- Facilitates the integration of client applications with a variety of remote databases including SQL server and Oracle.
- Embraces Internet standards such as Dynamic HTML (DHTML), allowing PC software engineers to create Web-centric applications. DHTML is a uniform language for creating applications across browsers, operating systems, and hardware configurations.
- Facilitates the rapid deployment of Web applications and components.
- Integrates very tightly with the Microsoft BackOffice suite of products.

VB 6.0, the current version of the product, is available in three different editions:

1. The learning edition of VB 6.0 assumes no previous programming experience. It is designed for anyone who wants to learn how to start creating Windows-based applications.
2. The professional edition has been designed for more advanced developers who need to create complex client/server and Internet-based applications.
3. The enterprise edition has been designed for teams of developers who are involved with creating distributed applications.

To commence development of powerful and robust client applications for the TVPAK platform, programmers will need to also purchase the Windows CE toolkit. The toolkit is an add-on to the VB 6.0 development environment and includes emulation technology that enables programmers to develop interactive TV applications on their desktops without the need for a digital set-top box. Once the testing and debugging of the program has been completed, it is then uploaded to the set-top box using standard data connectors.

The toolkit integrates very tightly with VB 6.0, making it easy for VB developers to rapidly build set-top applications for the Windows CE real-time OS.

To get started with the VB toolkit for Windows CE you will need a Windows NT machine running the VB 6.0 application and at least 60 MB of hard disk space.

Microsoft Visual C++

To understand the importance of the C++ programming languages in a set-top development environment, it is first necessary to look at a brief history of its predecessor—C. C is a structured programming language that has been around for over 25 years. Initially its success was linked to that of the UNIX operating system. UNIX and its associated shell tools were all written in C. In 1983, C was revised to ANSI C, which is an internationally standardized version of C.

It has been implemented on all types of computer systems, from the smallest PCs to the biggest supercomputers. C has been used to write some of the most complex applications ever developed. It is not known for its user-friendliness, but it is an extremely reliable language.

C++ is the successor to the C programming language. In fact, it is likely that C will no longer be considered as a language in its own right, but as a subset of the language capabilities provided by C++. C++ is also backward compatible with C.

The C++ language was born as a result of extending the C programming language to incorporate the principles of Object Orientated Programming (OOP). OOP is a method of software development that has been adopted by a large number of companies in the IT industry to produce high quality, low-cost software components. OOP allows programmers to divide real-world problems into a number of logical reusable components or objects.

The reuse of objects to build new applications has proved to be highly cost-effective and has resulted in a migration of developers from traditional programming languages to OOP-based languages such as C++.

In OOP, an object can be thought of as a representation of a real-world object. Cars, televisions, and computers can all be thought of as objects. Each of these objects has a particular set of attributes. For example, a car has a particular color, engine size, and is capable of reaching a certain speed under certain conditions. An OOP-based language like C++ allows software engineers to build an application based on these object attributes. A C++ development environment will generally consist of several parts or modules:

- a text editor for writing the code;
- a C++ compiler that translates the C++ program into machine code;
- a linker for connecting C++ programs to various data sources;

- a standard C library of reusable code;
- class libraries; and
- a debugger needed to identify program errors and trace bugs.

Microsoft has integrated all these components into a single development tool called Microsoft Visual C++.

Microsoft Visual C++ provides application developers with an integrated environment for developing C++ programs and end-to-end software solutions for digital set-top boxes. Included with the tool is the Microsoft Foundation Class (MFC) library. MFC is essentially an application framework for developing Windows programs in the C++ language.

In order to develop C++ applications for a Windows CE set-top box, developers will need to purchase an add-on product to Visual C++ called Windows CE Toolkit for Visual C++. As with the toolkits for Visual Basic, the Visual C++ kit lets programmers use their existing Win32 API expertise to build a variety of applications for Windows CE-based products. Other features of the toolkit include:

- Full support for desktop emulation software.
- An extensive suite of sample applications.
- Allows developers to take advantage of Internet technologies through the TCP/IP protocol.
- Takes advantage of the over 1,400 Win32 API functions that are available on the latest version of Windows CE.

Microsoft recommends that the Visual C++ product and the toolkit are run on a machine preloaded with Windows NT 4.0 and service pack 3.0.

To date, development of programs for Windows CE-enabled set-top boxes has been slow. However, this is expected to change with the imminent launch of a version of Windows CE specifically customized for digital set-tops. All the indications at present suggest that the IT industry is poised for an explosive growth in developing Windows CE applications for the set-top computing platform.

You can find more information about Visual C++ at http://msdn.microsoft.com/visualc/

Personal Java Application Development

To understand the benefits of using Personal Java as a language for developing interactive TV applications, it is first necessary that we look at its parents—the Java programming language.

Overview of Java Technology

In 1990, a small group of engineers at Sun Microsystems were given the task of developing a programming language that could control a wide variety of consumer electronic devices. Existing languages such as Pascal, C, and C++ were not considered suitable for this purpose. The design team decided that a new approach was necessary and began developing the Java language.

For Java to be successful, the language needed to be portable. For example, if a developer wrote a program for a toaster, then this program would need to be easily adapted for use in a thermostat. In addition to being able to run on a variety of processors, the Java programs needed to be small and efficient. The first application of the new Java language was used to control handheld PCs and TV set-top boxes.

For a variety of reasons in the early 1990s, the deployment of this first generation of Java applications never became a commercial reality. It looked as if the full benefits of the Java programming language would never be realized until use of the World Wide Web exploded in 1995. The development team realized that Java would be an ideal language for developing applications and content for the Web. Coincidentally, many of the features of the Java programming language fit perfectly into the Internet environment. For example, the Internet is a heterogeneous collection of different computers, including IBM-compatible PCs, UNIX servers and workstations, and Macintoshes. Many of the computers connected to the Internet have limited memory and processing capabilities. Therefore a small, efficient, and platform-independent language like Java is ideal for developing programs for the World Wide Web.

The first Java program developed by the development team was a browser called HotJava. The browser was unique in its capacity to run Java programs. In 1995, Netscape announced that its Navigator browser would support the Java language. This announcement, combined with Microsoft's commitment to supporting Java in their browser, has meant that millions of people are not able to use their browsers to run Java applications.

During the early development of the Web, all pages were written in HTML, which were essentially static documents. To add interactivity to Web pages required the use of Common Gateway Interface (CGI) scripting. The CGI script receives data from the user, acts on it, and if required returns the results to the browser. This scripting language facilitated the addition of two-way interactivity to web pages. However, CGI had two big disadvantages: they increased workload on the web server; and they required large amounts of bandwidth, which was not readily available on the Internet.

In contrast to CGI, Java programs consume small amounts of bandwidth and can be quickly downloaded to a variety of computers connected to the Internet. For this reason, many of the interactive pages created nowadays incorporate Java programs.

Java Applets

An applet is a small program that is embedded into web pages and perform a range of useful functions such as:

- Accepting input from online forms and interrogating backend databases;
- Performing complex calculations at the client level;
- Enhancing the user interface and improving the overall Web experience; and
- Validating user responses.

Applets are executed within a Java-enabled browser such as Spyglass or Netscape Navigator. In line with the object-oriented nature of the Java language, an applet is itself an object.

Because they are reasonably small, applets can be downloaded from the Internet quite quickly. An applet is integrated with a standard page using the <APPLET> HTML tag and using at least five attributes:

1. Code—The name of the file.
2. Codebase—The location of the Java applet.
3. Alt—Provides browsers who do not have Java enabled with a text alternative.
4. Width and height—in pixels, give the initial applet display area size.
5. ALIGN attribute—specifies the alignment of the applet within the displayed page.

For example, lets examine how the news ticker was incorporated into the home page of the www.set-tops.com portal site. The HTML code reads as follows:

```
<applet code="fader.class" codebase="http://www.set-tops.com/"
alt="Java applet for latest set-top news" width="116"
height="107">
```

We can see that the file is called fader.class and it is located at http://www.set-tops.com/. The web designer has put in a text description for browsers who do not support Java and the dimensions of 116 by 107 have also been defined. The .class file extension indicates that the browser is executing a Java class. A *class* is a template that is used to create objects with the same or similar features. When a program is written in Java, a set of classes is normally created.

As you can see, the applet has been used in a practical way to enhance the Web page. Other ways of enhancing Web pages with Java applets include animations and generating various types of sound effects.

Java applets are often downloaded from the Internet, therefore they can pose a security risk to your local computer and internal network resources. The designers of Java were very conscious of the types of security risk that could be posed. Hence, to minimize security risks a number of restrictions have been placed on the functionality of an applet. When the applet is executing within a browser, it does not have access to any resources, including the local file system.

If the designers of Java allowed applets to read and write to files, it would make life very easy for hackers to write malicious code that has the ability to corrupt data on your hard disk. In addition to restricting access to local resources, applets are also unable to initiate network connections with foreign hosts. The only host the applet is capable of communicating with is the server from which it was downloaded. Most set-top browsers include full support for Java applets.

Java Language

The Java language itself is extremely powerful and incorporates many of the benefits of the C and C++ languages. If you are an experienced programmer, you will notice that the syntax of the Java language is very similar to the syntax of both these languages. If you have done some programming with C or C++ before, then you will find it relatively easy to move to Java.

Java is highly object-oriented—everything in the language is an object, apart from the simple data types. Unlike C++, which is an object-oriented derivative of the C programming language, Java was designed from the ground up using object-orientated technologies.

To complement the various objects, the language also contains a variety of data types, which have been categorized into numeric, character, or boolean data types. When we speak about data types, we are talking about the classification of a particular type of information.

Another important feature for developing applications is the management of memory resources. Traditionally, the onus was on the programmer to complete the memory management tasks. In a Java environment, the task of memory management is removed from the programmer and is automatically executed by the Java language instead.

The Java environment comes with a rich collection of classes that deal with standard computing functions such as I/O, networking, and graphics. Programs written in the Java programming language are platform independent.

When a program is first written, the source code is compiled into a language that is very similar to machine instructions called *bytecodes*. The main difference between bytecodes and machine code is that bytecodes are not specific to any particular processor. The use of bytecodes allows software engineers to write once and execute the program on a variety of different platforms including network computers, thermostats, mobile phones, toasters, and digital set-top boxes.

Once the program has been translated into bytecode, it can be transferred across the network and executed by the Java virtual machine, which is embedded in the client application. Bytecode files are easily recognized by their .class file extensions.

Java is a secure language because the virtual machine verifies the bytecodes before executing the program. In addition to verifying the integrity of bytecodes, the Java program is unable to access system resources such as hard disk drives.

Java Development Tools

Although Java is a reasonably young language, more than 1 million developers around the world have already embraced the Java platform. Java technologies has opened up an entirely new world of opportunities for building fully portable network-aware applications. Java offers programmers the ability to write applications once and have them execute on any platform that supports the Java environment.

To accelerate the deployment of these Java applications, a number of important tools have already been created to drastically cut the overall development cycle. Most of them have graphical user interfaces and normally include a library of ready-made Java components for reuse by developers.

Let's have a quick look at the main features of some of these development environments, which may be used by Java programmers to develop applications for advanced digital set-top boxes.

The tools we will discuss are Java Development Kit (version 1.2), IBM's Visual Age, Symantec's Visual Café, and Borland's Jbuilder2.

Java Development Kit (version 1.2)

To speed the development of Java applications for network-centric devices, Sun Microsystems has launched the Java Development Kit (JDK) to help software developers write and compile Java programs. The latest release of the JDK, currently at 1.2, can be downloaded from Sun's Web site at http://java.sun.com

The Java Development Kit contains the software and tools that developers need to compile, debug, and run applets that have been written using the Java programming language. The toolkit is currently available for the following platforms: SPARC Solaris 2.4–2.6, Intel x86 Solaris 2.5–2.6, and Windows 95/NT 4.

The most recent version, 1.2, includes the support for the JavaBeans middleware architecture and Java Database Connectivity (JDBC). JDBC is a standard database access interface, providing uniform access to a wide variety of relational databases. JDBC makes it possible for programmers to write a single database application that can be run on multiple platforms. It also provides a common base on which higher level tools and interfaces can be built. JDBC was developed by JavaSoft, a subsidiary of Sun Microsystems.

IBM's VisualAge

IBM's VisualAge for Java tool is an award-winning Java application development environment for building Java applications, applets, and JavaBean components. VisualAge for Java lets you take advantage of the most up-to-date, component-based development and visual programming technologies.

The tool places great emphasis on connecting enterprise applications with backend databases through its support for the JDBC standard.

You use the design tool within VisualAge to define the visual aspects of the set-top application, and then generate code around it. VisualAge for Java can also be used to build Java-based business productivity applications using components from Lotus eSuite.

The product comes in three different editions—entry, professional, and enterprise. All three editions can be run on the following platforms: Windows 95, Windows NT 4.0 with service pack 3, and Windows 98. A full version can be purchased online or at local retail stores. For more information about VisualAge, visit IBM's web site at http://www.software.ibm.com/ad/vajava.

Symantec's Visual Café

The Symantec Visual Café product is available in three editions:

Standard edition • The standard edition of Visual Café is a suitable tool for people who are beginning to learn the Java language. It provides developers with an extensive library of wizards that enable the rapid creation of sophisticated applications. In addition to wizards, the standard edition also comes with a library of over 100 JavaBeans.

Professional edition • The professional edition of Visual Café is a more advanced development tool. The professional edition contains all the features of the standard edition plus an expanded library of professionally developed JavaBeans. The professional edition also allows you to rapidly develop complex servlets. Servlets can be thought of as server-side versions of applets that extend the functionality of Web servers in the same way that CGI scripts do. However, servlets offer a substantial performance improvements over CGI and are truly portable across platforms. Hence, servlets are becoming increasingly popular as alternatives to CGI programs.

Database edition • The database edition builds on the standard and professional editions of the Café product. It includes new wizards and is used to accelerate database-enabled Java application development. For more information about Visual Café, see http://www.symantec.com/domain/cafe/deved/.

Borland's Jbuilder

Borland JBuilder is a family of highly productive, visual development tools for creating high-performance, platform-independent applications using the Java programming language from Sun Microsystems. With JBuilder, you can develop set-top applications quickly by using any of the JavaBeans components included in the product, purchased from third parties, or create your own reusable JavaBeans components using

JBuilder's visual design tools and wizards. JBuilder is designed for all levels of development projects, ranging from applets and applications that require networked database connectivity to client/server and enterprise-wide, distributed multi-tier computing solutions. It supports a range of Java technologies, including JavaBeans, servlets, JDK 1.1, applets, JDBC, and all the major corporate database servers. For more information, go to http://www.borland.com/jbuilder/.

Developing Personal Java Set-top Applications

The growing popularity of consumer appliances, such as digital set-top boxes running the Personal Java Application Environment (PJAE), represents an important new opportunity for Java programmers. As with any software development project, you need to determine the hardware configuration and requirements of your target device. Sun recommends the following set-top hardware configuration for running the PJAE:

- 32-bit processor running at 50 Mhz;
- 2 MB of Flash ROM;
- greater than 2 MB of RAM; and
- a wireless keyboard.

To start developing P-Java set-top applications, the first step that needs to be completed is the downloading of the JDK and the Personal Java compatibility classes. These compatibility classes are available for free on Sun's web site at: http://java.sun.com/products/personaljava/pj-cc.html.

Alternatively, you may want to use one of the other popular Java development tools such as Symantec's Visual Cafe for Java, Borland's Jbuilder, or Sun's Java Workshop. Once you have decided on a development platform, the next step is to write the interactive set-top application using the Java programming language. Once the application is written, you need to verify that the code conforms to the Personal Java API specification, using a product called JavaCheck. It does this by testing whether Java class files used by the set-top application are compatible with a particular API specification. The most recent version of the Personal Java Specification is version 1.1.1. JavaCheck is very easy to use and works side-by-side with popular third party Java development tools. Version 3.0 of JavaCheck is now available for free on Sun's web site at: http://java.sun.com/products/personaljava/javacheck.html.

The last stage of the development process is to test your set-top application with the Personal Java emulation environment. This is a software development environment used for verifying that the applets and applications you develop using a variety of Java development tools will run on devices running the Personal Java environment. For example, this software tool will allow you to test applets that will run in set-top browsers that support the PJAE.

The Personal Java emulation environment is available for download at the following Internet address: http://java.sun.com/products/personaljava/pj-emulation.html.

Developing DVB Java Applications

The MHP platform has a number of requirements that make it different from many of the existing computing environments that currently support the Java platform. In particular, most television viewers already have a perception of how a television should operate. An application written for television should improve the viewer's experience, not hinder it. Each application that is developed will need to comply sufficiently with the MHP reference model to ensure cross-platform interoperability in a competitive environment. This should result in host platforms where the integrity of the application is protected, and its behavior is stable and predictable (thus resulting in a high quality of service).

An interactive application is basically built around:

- *application script* (which can be declarative and/or procedural); and
- *content/scenes* (declarative interface and media streams).

The declarative interface is the representation of the man-machine interface. It can consist of graphics such as a background design, selection buttons, still pictures, text, and the like. Each scene can comprise a set of other scenes, application objects, and attributes. The pipes implement the interconnections between the scenes and concatenated functions.

Procedural applications, based on low-level functions and primitives, are used when very strong optimization is required at the host level (e.g., to minimize the platform footprint and maximize the use of the transmission resources). Procedural applications are generally platform-dependent and, hence, each one must be verified on the different host platforms.

Declarative applications use high-level functions and primitives. This allows DVB to define a platform-independent reference model which can verify whether such applications comply in terms of cross-platform compatibility and performance accuracy.

In reality, applications are neither fully declarative nor fully procedural. As an example, declarative applications can make use of procedural enhancements to improve their performance. This allows DVB to reduce the size of the application and to reduce its execution time by using routines written in executable code. Platform-independence is ensured by relying on embedded RTOS, virtual machines or other interactive engines. It is more difficult to achieve compliance of the compiled code routine libraries for different platforms, if they are not taken into account at the time of the platform design.

Applications are identified and signalled to indicate their availability, and an appropriate mode of access is presented to the user. Applications are launched automatically or by request. The application presentation can be nominal or downsized (if scalable), thus maximizing the use of the available resources. Application management encompasses: identification, activation, interruption, failure management, priority modes and dynamic resource allocation. Application Manager manages both DVB-J applications and non-DVB-J applications (through their respective plug-ins).

The overall application control procedures are described as part of the DVB MHP lifecycle. The DVB MHP application lifecycle model has been defined to design digital television applications with low start-up latencies that permit responsive user interaction. It includes a simple and well-defined state machine, a concise definition of the application's states and an API to signal changes between the states. Standard Java authoring tools may be used to design DVB-J set-top applications.

Developing MediaHighway Applications

To design, create, test, and debug interactive TV applications for a digital set-top box using Canal+ technologies, developers need to purchase the MediaHighway application workshop. This application workshop is a software package that is comprised of:

A user interface generator • As the name suggests, this tool provides developers with a number of graphical functions that are used to design the look and feel of an application's user interface.

An icon and image editor • This tool contains a number of utilities, which may be used to create and modify TV icons. The image editor is used to create and modify image files. For example, it could be used to convert a 256-bit color image in BMP format to a 16-bit JPEG image for improved viewing on a television screen.

A palette editor • Software developers use this tool to modify different palettes of colors.

A compiler • Applications for a MediaHighway-based set-top box can be written in a number of structured programming languages, including Pantalk and Java. Subsequently, Canal+ included a compiler in their workshop. The compiler checks the programming code for errors and optimizes the size of the code for downloading purposes.

A volume editor • This tool is used to create a group of modules that have been outputted from the compiler.

A set-top debugger • The debugger tool is used to define, control, and monitor the execution of a set-top interactive application.

Documentation • The documentation utility provides developers with easy access to a description of all the functions that are contained within the workshop application.

At the beginning of 1999, Canal+ decided to make its API specifications freely available to developers and software houses who want to develop interactive applications for set-top boxes that are running the MediaHighway client middleware system (over 3 million at the time of going to press). With this decision, Canal+ has taken the lead over their competitors in the digital television industry by being the first company to release its API specifications for interactive and multimedia applications. Canal+ is a strong supporter of Java technologies, and consequently parts of the specifications that are downloadable to the general public are based on the Java programming language. Table 6.1 summarizes the components that can be used with the MediaHighway application workshop to create a wealth of new TV-based applications.

Table 6.1   Details of Open MediaHighway API

Java Packages	DAVIC and DVB Packages	Mediahighway Packages
• java.awt	• org.davic.mpeg	• mhw.ca
• java.awt.datatransfer	• org.davic.mpeg.dvb	• mhw.card
• java.awt.event	• org.davic.mpeg.sections	• mhw.com
• java.awt.net	• org.davic.net.dvb	• mhw.dsmcc
• java.io	• org.davic.net.tuning	• mhw.event
• java.lang	• org.davic.resources	• mhw.media
• java.net	• org.davic.net	• mhw.modem
• java.text (partially)		• mhw.netstack
• java.util.zip		• mhw.si.database
• java.util		• mhw.si.information
• java.awt.image		• mhw.si.eventbrowser
		• mhw.si.installedservices
		• mhw.si.player
		• mhw.si.selection
		• mhw.toolbox
		• mhw.tvgraphics

Developing PowerTV Applications

Since the company's inception, the PowerTV software platform was designed to allow a rich set of interactive applications to be built and deployed into digital interactive cable systems using open Internet and computer-based standards. PowerTV continues to expand its set of tools and technologies to support the creation of compelling new interactive TV programs.

PowerTV provides a partnership program for application designers who want to reach one of the largest media outlets in the world—television. The PowerPartners support program gives developers all the tools necessary to successfully create enhanced TV applications and content for the PowerTV platform. All PowerPartners receive a copy of the PowerTV development kit. It includes everything you need to connect to your existing Windows-based PC and standard TV set:

- a Scientific-Atlanta Explorer 2000 set-top box;
- an external SCSI hard drive;
- 2 SCSI cables;
- video cables;
- an Ethernet cable;
- serial cables; and
- a software developers kit (SDK) CD.

To become a PowerPartner member and start developing two-way interactive digital applications for PowerTV-enabled set-top boxes, contact PowerTV at 1-888-696-8676.

Developing MHEG-5 Applications

MHEG applications need only be authored once and then run on any platform that is compliant to MHEG. The so-called MHEG *Interpreter* or *Engine* is in charge of performing interpretation and presentation of MHEG applications. To begin development of MHEG-5-based applications, we recommend you use some or all of the following tools:

MHEGDitor • An MHEG-5 development tool based on Macromedia Director, a third-party product that is one of the leading development environments for creating rich multimedia content. Director's intuitive and easy-to-use visual development environment makes it easy for MHEG-5 software engineers to create, import, animate, and control a wide variety of compelling interactive TV content. MHEGDitor is composed of Authoring Xtra, to create and edit MHEG-5 applications, and Converter Xtra, to convert resulting movies into MHEG-5 applications. It is worth noting that the two

MHEGDitor Xtras work separately. MHEGDitor is available for both Macintosh and Windows environments.

MHEGWrite • A textual editor, which may be used to manually create and manipulate native MHEG-5 programming code. The editor is based on a free software application called VIM, which is available for download on the Internet. Suitable for developers who have a strong understanding of the MHEG-5 programming environment.

MHEGPlayer • This is a software component that is used to interpret and execute applications that have been developed with the MHEGDitor authoring tool. The player is fully compliant with ISO and DAVIC standards.

MHEG Convertor • A tool used by software developers to check and optimize code for an MHEG-5 application. Similar to the previous tools, the convertor supports the complete functionality of the MHEG-5 international standard.

To download evaluation copies of the tools that have been described above, please visit the following Web address: http://www.mhegcentre.com/tools/download/list.htm.

Developing Liberate Applications

Liberate Technologies provides a content development kit (CDK) for manufacturers, network operators, and software developers who want to develop interactive TV applications for set-top boxes that run the eNavigator middleware system. The CDK contains information, tools, and examples to help you create powerful TV- and Internet-based applications.

The CDK that is delivered to you consists of the following items:

- a manual that documents how Liberate Technologies has extended HTML and JavaScript to embrace the world of TV-based content. Contains numerous tips on how to design Web pages specifically for a television screen;
- sample pages that illustrate the techniques used to create content that works well on a standard TV monitor; and
- samples of using the JavaScript language to create set-top-centric applications.

The entire CDK is delivered as a Web site, which needs to be installed on a standard Web server on your network. To get a copy of the CDK and become a member of their development community, visit the following URL for more detailed information: http://developers.liberate.com/become_a_developer/index.html.

SUMMARY . . . .

The evolution of digital television is beginning to open doors for the worldwide creative software development community. It acts as a springboard for people to imagine and develop a new wealth of entertainment applications. As computing devices such as digital set-top boxes continue to proliferate, the ability to write applications for these devices opens up new opportunities. Applications yet to be conceived are on the horizon.

As with everything in life, for every opportunity comes an equal and opposite challenge. Software designers who want to begin creating advanced applications for this new computing paradigm will need to understand that some techniques that are used to develop PC-based applications may not be appropriate in the world of set-top software development. The fundamentals are, however, the same, and each process requires a structured approach. From a developers point of view, it is important to be able to get interactive TV applications to market quickly. This depends on the quality of the software development tools.

At the moment, we have a number of development environments that are specific to the various middleware platforms we described in Chapter 4. OpenTV supplies a development environment for C-programmers and a basic tool (OpenAuthor) for nonprogrammers who want to create interactive TV applications. Programmers can use familiar tools such as Visual Studio to build Windows-based applications for Microsoft's new TVPAK software platform. As the market for Java-enabled set-top boxes grows, so too will the opportunities for Java programmers to build a wealth of new applications for the TV world. Developing interactive TV applications for the PJAE environment allows programmers to capitalize on their knowledge of existing Java development tools. Prospective MediaHighway developers need to purchase an applications workshop from Canal+ in France. The company has publicly demonstrated its support for open source set-top software through its posting of the MediaHighway API specifications on their web site at the beginning of 1999. PowerTV has developed a partnership program to assist software engineers that are active in the arena of developing applications for PowerTV-enabled set-tops. A number of specialized tools based on Macromedia's director technologies are required to develop MHEG-5 applications. Finally, if you plan to commence development for the Liberate platform, you need to contact the company directly and purchase their content development kit, version 1.1, at the time of going to press.

7

Set-top Internet Applications

In this chapter...

As the Internet has grown exponentially over the years, certain conventions and technologies around Internet have evolved. This chapter will familiarize you with several important Web concepts such as IP addresses, URLs, subnets, DNS, security policies, firewalls, proxy servers, and many more.

According to research work completed by Datamonitor, TV-based Internet access will grow by 45 percent over the next five years. This provides network operators with an opportunity to deliver a range of new Internet-based services. In this chapter, you will find out about the technologies that allow subscribers to access Web content at high speeds, participate in online chat rooms, and use e-mail on their television screens. The chapter concludes with a detailed description of Webcasting on a broadband digital network.

ABOUT THE INTERNET . . . .

The Internet is a massive collection of public and private networks that connect millions of companies, research institutions, databases, libraries, and individuals spread around the world. It allows a diverse range of computer users to connect with each other for business, educational, and recreational purposes. The Internet is not centrally organized and no one person or organization owns it.

The number of users accessing the Internet for work, study, or pleasure has increased phenomenally, and now amounts to many millions world-wide. Use of the Internet is growing at a phenomenal rate—from 40 to 50 percent a year by some estimates. There are now several million host computers on the Internet, and the number of users is measured in tens of millions. It has become a household word in most countries around the globe.

At the same time, the number and types of services available on the Internet has grown in line with demand. Depending on their particular needs and perspective, users see the Internet as:

1. a global electronic mail system;
2. a valuable research tool;
3. an archive of virtual communities and bulletin boards;
4. an online entertainment service; or
5. an electronic marketplace.

The Internet is a valuable research tool, containing masses of information on any number of subjects. Increasingly sophisticated search engines provide quick and easy access to this information from the home or the office. The Internet is also an extremely valuable source of online technical support and advice. Many companies nowadays are providing marketing information, software updates, and technical advice on the Internet. Companies and individuals that use the Internet potentially have a huge global audience in more than 190 countries for their products and services. Although the Internet has become a global and publicly accessible networked system, it was not originally conceived as such.

In fact, the Internet started out as an experimental network sponsored by the U.S. Department of Defense in the 1960s. The original purpose of this new network was to encourage communication and collaboration between people working in government and academic institutions. In 1969, the Advanced Research Projects Agency (ARPA), a group within the Department, established ARPANET. The first ARPANET nodes were installed in 1971 in four American universities. From this base, the ARPANET expanded during the 1970s as a number of research and educational institutions connected their local area networks to it.

Also at this time, a set of protocols known as TCP/IP became established as the standard communication protocol for linking computers together. TCP/IP is still the standard protocol used by computers to communicate on the Internet. It forms the basis of many data transfer applications still in use, such as the File Transfer Protocol (FTP), Telnet, and Gopher.

In the early 1980s, a high-speed data network supported by the U.S. National Science Foundation (NSF) replaced ARPANET. At the same time, the military site split from the new NSF data network to form their own closed network, known as MILNET. Large numbers of companies and other organizations connected their networks to the NSF network throughout the 1980s to form a backbone network. These networks belong largely to universities, commercial organizations, and government departments.

Other networks can connect directly to this Internet backbone by installing a high-speed gateway. However, this type of gateway connection is very expensive, and is beyond the means of most organizations and individuals. Users who cannot afford such a connection can access the Internet by subscribing to an Internet service provider (ISP). ISPs are companies who have established their own gateway to the Internet backbone and charge a fee for accessing the Internet through their gateway.

It is a heterogeneous network, meaning that many different types of computers are connected to it. Among the computers connected to the Internet are:

- mainframes;
- UNIX workstations and servers;
- IBM-compatible PCs;
- Apple Macintoshes; and
- handheld PCs.

This list is expected to expand dramatically in 1999 with the proliferation of digital set-tops, Web-enabled phones, and PCs for automobiles.

UNDERSTANDING TCP/IP . . . .

Simply plugging a set-top box into a cable TV network does not guarantee successful communications between the subscriber's home and the service provider's head-end system. For example, the set-top box needs to be told when and how to transmit signals across a digital TV network. The box needs network communication software to instruct the set-top how to transmit signals across a cable, MMDS, terrestrial, or satellite network. To help you understand how a set-top box operates and communicates on a broadband network, we first need to examine the Transmission Control Protocol/Internet Protocol (TCP/IP) suite of communication protocols. This suite describes how information from a software application running on a computer located at the operator's head-end moves through a network medium to a software application running on a subscriber's set-top box. As the name suggests, TCP and IP are two separate protocols that have been tightly woven together for the purpose of transmitting data in an efficient manner. The TCP protocol's main responsibility is to break the data into packets. The IP protocol delivers these packets to the correct location and the TCP protocol reassembles the packets on the receiving end. It was originally developed in the early 1980s by the ARPA group in the U.S. Since its inception, TCP/IP has become the de-facto communications protocol for the Internet. The widespread adoption of TCP/IP on the Internet has helped TV broadcasters and cable operators to use the protocol as a fundamental building block in delivering advanced entertainment services to their customers.

The TCP/IP communications model is a conceptual model composed of four layers that are stacked on top of each other, each specifying particular network functions (see Figure 7.1). Data is passed down the model from one layer to the next on the sending device, until it is transmitted over the broadband network by the network access layer protocols. Each layer in the communications model adds control information (such as destination address and error correction digits) to ensure proper delivery. At the remote end, the data is passed up the communications model to the receiving application.

The four layers of the TCP/IP model are as follows: the network access layer, the internetwork layer, the transport layer, and the application layer.

The *network access layer* relates to topics that coordinate the rules for transmitting digital bits on a broadband network. It is concerned with getting data across a specific type of physical network (such as HFC, satellite, terrestrial, or MMDS). It defines physical network structures (topologies), mechanical, and electrical specifications for using the transmission medium. The following network connectivity hardware is nor-

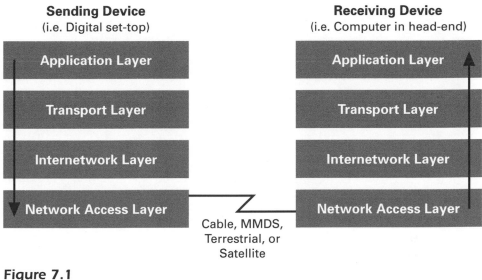

Figure 7.1
TCP/IP Communications Model

mally associated with the network access layer: telephone and cable modems; amplifiers and repeaters on an HFC network; and connectors.

The layer above the network access layer is called the *internetwork layer.* Its primary objective is to move data to specific network locations over multiple, interconnected, independent networks called internetworks. This layer is used to send data over specific routes to its destination. IP is the best-known protocol located at the internetwork layer, which provides the basic packet delivery service for all TCP/IP networks. The IP protocol implements a system of logical host addresses called *IP addresses.* We will explore the various addressing systems used by TCP/IP later.

The protocol layer just above the internetwork layer is the *transport layer.* It has been designed to hide the intricacies of the digital TV network structure from the upper-layer processes. Standards at this layer provide for the reliability and integrity of the end-to-end communication link.

Obviously, if a cable breaks, for example, the transport layer cannot ensure delivery of the data. If data is not delivered to the receiving device correctly, the transport layer can initiate retransmission. Alternatively, it can inform the upper layers, which can then take the necessary corrective action. TCP is the most important protocol employed at this layer of the TCP/IP communications stack.

The top layer in the TCP/IP communications model is the *application layer.* This layer provides the services that subscriber applications use to communicate over the digital TV network. These services include file transfers, access control, TV navigation, and printing capabilities.

About Internet Addresses

In a TCP/IP environment, networked devices use IP addresses and domain names to identify each other. There are two distinctive address systems used on the Internet, the Domain Name System (DNS) and the Internet Protocol (IP) address system. An IP address is a series of four numbers separated by dots that identifies the exact physical location of a host computer on the Internet, similar to your own home address identifying your place of residence. An IP address is a 32-bit binary number. This binary number is divided into 4 groups of 8 bits (octets), each of which is represented by a decimal number in the range 0 to 255. The octets are separated by decimal points. An example of an IP address is 190.100.5.54. In binary notation, this would be 10111110.01100100.00000101.00110110. The IP address is hosted in two sections: the network section, which is called the *netid* and the host section, called the *hostid*.

For ease of use and administration, the IP addresses are broken up into the following classes.

Class A • This describes a network whose first number in the IP address has a value of between 0 and 127. The remaining three numbers are used to identify a computer or set-top box within the network. For example, a set-top assigned IP address of 40.3.100.100 would be a class A address, with 40 being the broadband network number, or netid, and 3.100.100 being the identifier for a particular digital subscriber, or hostid.

There are 127 class A addresses in the world and each one of these networks has enough IP addresses to support more than 16 million unique network devices. All of these class A IP addresses have been licensed from InterNIC many years ago. InterNIC is a cooperative activity between the U.S. government and a company called Network Solutions Inc. InterNIC provides networking information services, such as directory services, to the Internet community. It is also responsible for the registration of new domain names and the allocation of IP addresses.

Class B • A class B network has an address whose first number has a value of between 128 and 191. There are approximately 16,000 networks on the Internet, each having the capability to support 64,000 unique network devices. Large organizations and Internet Service Providers have licensed most or nearly all of these addresses. For instance, in the class B address 132.6.2.24, 132.6 identifies the network, and 2.24 identifies the host.

Class C • A class C network has an address whose first number has a value of between 192 and 223. There are approximately two million class C addresses, each capable of supporting 254 addressable network devices. This is very suitable for a small company, however, these networks are of little use to large multinational organizations.

Class D and E • The first portion of the address containing a value of between 224 and 239 is known as a class D address. These IP addresses are used for multicasting purposes. An IP multicast is a special form of broadcast where copies of the data packet are delivered only to a subset of all possible destinations. Every receiver that is listening for that particular IP address then receives the data packets. This keeps bandwidth consumption relatively low and reduces the processing burden on the server to a small fraction of that found under conventional TCP/IP one-to-one communication.

Class E addresses range from 240 to 247 and are reserved for future use.

Subnetting an IP broadband Network

In large cable broadband networks with thousands of digital set-top boxes spread across a large geographical area, IP-based networks need to be subdivided into logical units called *subnets*. Subnetting a broadband network allows operators to identify and monitor individual sections of the organization's network without having to obtain new IP addresses. Operators also use subnet addressing to hide their internal network structure from Internet users.

Network administrators use special numbers called *subnet masks* to create subnets within a digital TV environment. Subnet masks are also a 32-bit IP address. The built-in default numbers for Class A, B, and C addresses are as follows:

Class A—255.0.0.0

Class B—255.255.0.0

Class C—255.255.255.0

The subnetting process is implemented using hardware devices called *routers*. A router connects to more than one network and makes a decision on where to send information. It takes the assigned subnet mask and applies the number against the IP number of the digital set-top.

Applying in this context basically means that the router moves the demarcation line between netid and the hostid sections of the IP address. The result of this operation is a new number, which helps the router send information to the correct set-top box.

The easiest way to understand how a cable operator would subnet a broadband network is to look at an example. Suppose a network operator located in Ireland owns a class B network whose IP address is 145.94.0.0. From the address we can determine that the netid is 145.94 and the hostid is 0.0.

The company has been licensed to deliver high-speed video and interactive services to the four provinces. To improve manageability of these regions, four new subnets are created using the first digit of the hostid to identify each subnet. So the subnets are identified as follows:

Subnet 1   145.94.1.0   Munster

Subnet 2   145.94.2.0   Leinster

Subnet 3   145.94.3.0   Connaught

Subnet 4   145.94.4.0   Ulster

The diagram in Figure 7.2 shows how this might look.

Hence, digital TV subscribers that avail of Internet services in the Munster region are assigned addresses of 145.94.1.1, 145.94.1.2, 145.94.1.3, and so on.

This sounds very easy, however, the Internet does not recognize addresses like 145.94.1.3 and 145.94.1.4 because they have been assigned locally by the network

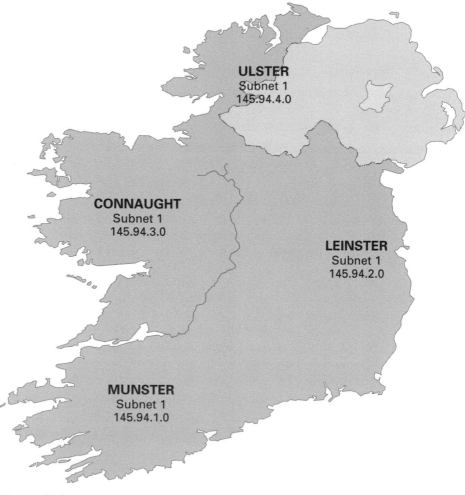

Figure 7.2
Subnetting an IP Broadband network in Ireland

administrator. To overcome this problem, a subnet mask of 255.255.240.0 is used in concert with the hostid section of the set-top IP address to ensure that the routers within the broadband network route TCP/IP traffic to the correct subnet on the Internet.

Subnetting also ensures that users on the Internet see the Irish digital TV network as a single entity rather than a series of logical sub-networks.

Future of IP Addressing

When the Internet's IP address structure was originally developed in the early 1980s, it was intended to meet the needs of current and future users.

The 32-bit addresses used by the current version of IP (IPV4) can enumerate over 4 billion hosts on a possible 16.7 million different networks. The recent phenomenal growth of the Internet is rapidly exhausting the existing pool of IP addresses provided for by IPV4. The scale and speed of growth experienced by the Internet in recent years could not have been foreseen by the original developers of the TCP/IP protocol. The number of networks connected to the Internet grows on a monthly basis. New network management tools demand that every item on these networks run the Simple Network Management Protocol (SNMP), a system which basically means each new device is assigned a new IP address. Future developments in the consumer entertainment market promise to make this problem much worse.

Digital television, home banking, home shopping, and a variety of information services currently under development could make every set-top box on the planet an Internet device with an IP address.

To find a solution to the limitations of the existing IP address scheme, the Internet Engineering Task Force launched IPV6 (Internet Protocol Version 6). IPV6 defines a 128-bit IP address that is compatible with current implementations of TCP/IP. This makes the transition to IPV6 an evolutionary rather than a revolutionary step. This means that we don't have to worry about waking up one morning and finding that we have to reconfigure every IP device on the planet. We can make the transition gradually because the protocol should be able to co-exist in most cases with IPV4 implementations.

In addition to backward compatibility, IPV6 greatly increases the available address space. In fact, the number of addresses possible under IPV6 will be 4 billion times 4 billion, which is a phenomenal amount of IP addresses. IPV6 also includes capabilities that will provide support for authentication, integrity, encryption, and confidentiality.

Domain Name System

It would be impossible for digital TV subscribers to remember these numeric IP addresses when sending e-mails or accessing web sites. The solution to this problem has been the introduction of the *domain name*. Domain names are devised to allow subscribers to enter friendly descriptions of Internet addresses. Besides being easier to use and remember, domain names increase productivity because users make fewer mistakes.

All computers connected to the Internet have a domain name and a corresponding IP address. All of these computers are part of a hierarchical naming system for the Internet called the Domain Name System (DNS).

Domain names and IP addresses are stored and managed on a computer known as domain name servers. If, for example, a subscriber enters a friendly domain name like www.set-tops.com, this address is sent to the domain name server and mapped to an equivalent address, in this case, the value would be 10.16.0.1.

Let's take a quick look at how DNS is used as a foundation block for Internet-based e-mail applications.

An Internet e-mail address is made up of two sections separated by an @ symbol. The section of the address to the left of the @ symbol is the username. The second part of the address on the right hand side of the @ symbol is the domain name, which defines where the person has the e-mail account. Contained within the domain name section of the IP address is an identifier, which describes the type of institution where the computer is located.

Common domain name identifiers on the Internet include:

.com　　commercial organizations such as www.set-tops.com

.net　　network organizations such as the domain registration company internic.net

.edu　　academic institutions such as http://www.trinity.edu/

.gov　　U.S. governmental departments such as www.nasa.gov

.mil　　military networks which are not normally connected to the public Internet

.org　　organizations such as www.dvb.org

In addition to these general domains, a naming scheme for different geographical areas has also been developed. This system uses two letters to identify a specific country. The .ie extension in a Web address would indicate that the site is Irish-based.

Internic is the global registrar of .com, .net, .org, and .edu names and has registered more than 3.4 million .com Web addresses since 1993. Network domain names are crucial for doing business on the Internet and popular names such as internet.com are extremely valuable pieces of online real estate. A variety of new top level domain names are expected to increase the number of Internet names available to entrepreneurs and online businesses.

For example, the .TV corporation in Canada has become the exclusive worldwide registrar for all .TV top level domain names. The .TV domain works like other domain names such as .ie, .com, and .org. This name will give great intrinsic benefits for those offering services to set-top users. For example, which e-mail address do you think your subscribers would prefer: subscriber@brand.tv or subscriber@brand.com? As you can see, the placing of the .TV symbol next to your corporate name extends brand awareness to the Internet and clearly identifies your company as a supplier of high-quality digital TV services. To promote our vision of convergence between PC, Internet, and TV, set-tops.com has partnered with the .TV Corporation and is offering site visitors the opportunity to extend their corporate identity to the world of television. Visit the following URL for more detail: http://www.set-tops.com/TVdomain.html

Assigning IP Addresses to Set-tops

Suppose a network operator wants to allow their customers access to various Internet services such as Web browsing, online chat, and e-mail. To deploy these types of services, every digital set-top will need to be assigned a unique address to enable them to communicate on a TCP/IP network.

The manual configuration of TCP/IP on every set-top box on the network is a painful process and is extremely time-consuming. The answer for network operators is the deployment of the Dynamic Host Configuration Protocol (DHCP) on their networks. DHCP is a protocol that automatically assigns each set-top on the network with a unique network number.

The use of this system simplifies network administration because the software keeps track of IP addresses rather than employing IT personnel to manage the task. This means that new subscribers can be added to a network without the hassle and time of manually assigning new addresses. The software that is required to dynamically lease IP addresses to digital TV subscribers is stored on a server in the head-end.

It should also be noted that a set-top box may have a different IP address every time it is power-cycled and connected to the broadband network.

DHCP offers network operators many advantages:

- By using DHCP, all the necessary configuration details for the set-top box are fixed without the subscriber having to know about the details.
- DHCP offers centralized management of set-top IP addresses.
- Quick and easy server set-up and administration.
- Administrators in the head-end can specify a range of available IP addresses for specific geographical areas.
- Automatically configuring TCP/IP reduces the possibility of assigning duplicate IP addresses and of mistyping other configuration information.

Once the network has been deployed, then a system is needed to manage the thousands of set-top boxes. Most of the popular network management systems are based on the SNMP management protocol.

The management software periodically sends requests and retrieves data from the set-top boxes on the network. Network management systems typically include a user interface to display data retrieved from the set-tops. Chapter 10 examines network management technologies in more detail.

SECURITY POLICIES AND FIREWALLS . . . .

Today, more and more cable companies, satellite providers, MMDS operators, and terrestrial broadcasters are aiming to take advantage of the business opportunities afforded by the Internet. This makes a lot of business sense, however, once these organizations connect with the Internet, they are automatically exposing their private TV networks to a variety of security risks. Breaches on a TV operator's network could result in any of the following:

- introduction of viruses;
- loss or damage of data stored on SMS, CA, content, application, proxy, and e-mail servers;
- breach of personal privacy of subscribers;
- attempts by hackers to break into local systems;
- huge financial loss; and
- pirating and distribution of sensitive information to unauthorized recipients.

For TV operators connecting to the Internet, they should always treat it as a potentially hostile environment. There are, however, a number of steps that may be taken by network operators to minimize the security risk of connecting a private digital TV network to the public Internet. The implementation of a tight security policy incorporating a secure firewall is a key step in the deployment of interactive TV services.

Using a firewall is the most popular method of protecting cable networks from outside intruders. An Internet *firewall* is a hardware or software system that implements a security policy between two computer networks.

Firewalls can consist of a single router or it may be comprised of a combination of components such as routers, computers, networks, and security software. A firewall is normally located at the interface between the TV operator's private network and the leased line, which connects TV subscribers to a variety of Internet services. The company's security policy should stipulate that all data and voice traffic between these two networks is examined by the firewall.

A firewall impedes the ability of outsiders to gain access to the operator's internal broadband network. It is designed to protect the TV operator's digital network against unauthorized access. A standard firewall normally consists of a variety of hardware and software components. The exact combination of components chosen to build your firewall depends on the level of security required.

A common entity of most firewalls is a router, which is capable of examining each data packet that passes through the firewall and filters according to a set of authorization rules. The router will check the header of each packet and examine the services and addresses contained within each packet. This information is compared with a set of criteria, which have been defined by the cable operator. If the packet of data is acceptable, then it is forwarded onto its destination point. Otherwise, it is discarded and the set-top user will receive a service-disallowed message on their TV screens.

This method of protecting your internal digital TV network has certain limits. For example, the router will only examine the header of the packet and does not look at the actual contents of the data packet. This system would leave the operator's network open to certain types of attacks. To overcome this shortcoming, TV operators are beginning to install application-level gateways or proxy services that restrict access to particular applications such as newsgroups or incoming file transfers.

A TV operator would install a proxy service for each application that set-top users are allowed access. For example, access to e-mail services would require the installation of a proxy e-mail service within the firewall. This service could then be configured to support specific features of the e-mail system. This type of firewall is extremely effective in enforcing security policies, however, they can be expensive to install and often has slow performance for the set-top user.

It is up to the TV operator to decide which services on the Internet are accessible to the company's subscribers. For example, some TV operators may want to block the FTP service because it has the potential to consume large sections of available bandwidth capacity. Although this method of prohibiting certain services limits the functionality of the set-top box, it does, however, improve the overall security of the system.

It should be noted that the presence of a firewall alone does not always guarantee the protection of a TV operator's network. The technical components within a firewall need to be used in conjunction with other security measures such as virus protection, educating employees on security risks, and a lot of plain old common sense. For example, it is pointless having a firewall in place if the company has not already implemented basic security measures such as locating servers in a physically secure location. The benefits of implementing a firewall include:

- controlled access to internal systems;
- protecting digital TV customers from the hazards and dangers of the Internet; and
- centralized security administration for the digital TV system.

The firewall market has matured in the past few years, with software companies offering customers a variety of sophisticated security products. Table 7.1 gives details of some of the more popular firewall products currently available.

Table 7.1

Firewall product	Brief overview	Vendor
PIX Firewall	Cisco PIX Firewall is the dedicated firewall appliance in Cisco's firewall family. The PIX Firewall provides full firewall protection that completely conceals the architecture of an internal digital TV network from the outside world.	Cisco Systems is headquartered in San Jose, California. For cable companies who require more details on this firewall product, please visit: www.cisco.com
Check Point FireWall-1	The Check Point FireWall-1 product suite delivers an enterprise-wide security system for digital TV network operators.	Check Point has its U.S. headquarters in California and its international headquarters is located in Israel. Detailed product information is available at www.checkpoint.com/products/index.html
SecureZone	This is Secure Computing's latest firewall product offering and is a successor to Secure's Borderware Unix firewall. A suitable product for managing enterprise security policies in a digital TV environment.	Secure Computing Corporation is Headquartered in San Jose, California. For cable companies who require more details on this firewall product, please visit: www.secure-computing.com/products.html
Novell's BorderManager	A high-performance Internet security management suite that includes integrated firewall, virtual private networking, authentication, and caching services for networks leveraging Novell Directory Services.	Novell was established in 1983 and has its corporate headquarters in California. For cable companies who require more details on this firewall product, please visit: www.novell.com/bordermanager/index.html
Gauntlet	The Gauntlet Firewall allows companies to enforce their security policies by enabling only those services specifically configured by the firewall administrator.	Network Associates is headquartered in California. Details of their Gauntlet FireWall product are available at www.nai.com/products/security/security2.asp

INTRODUCTION TO WEB BROWSING . . . .

The World Wide Web is a distributed information system created by researchers at CERN (the European Laboratory for Particle Physics) in Switzerland. The Internet is the physical carrier network for the World Wide Web. The World Wide Web is also known as the Web, WWW, and W3, and was introduced in 1990. The Web was originally designed to allow scientists to collaborate on research projects by sharing documents. It has since evolved to become the ideal medium for publishing information on the Internet. The Web is currently the most popular and fastest-growing part of the Internet.

The Web uses an electronic publishing technology known as hypermedia. Information published on a hypermedia system is broken into smaller graphically rich documents known as Web *pages*. Each of these pages or documents contain connections called *hyperlinks* to other related documents on the Web. A hyperlink can be a word, a phrase, or a graphic, distinguished in some way from the surrounding material, for instance, having a different color or by being underlined.

When a user clicks on a hyperlink, the Web page it refers to is displayed on screen.

This hypermedia technology allows users to view or "surf" documents that are stored on computers in different parts of the world. Users find the point-and-click method of navigating through a Web document intuitive and easy to use.

The resources available on the Web can include text, graphics, video, audio, and animation. People can access these resources using a software program called a browser, which provides a graphical, point-and-click interface to Web pages. This easy and transparent access to information is one of the reasons for the Web's explosive growth in recent years. Popular browsers for the PC environment include Netscape Communicator and Microsoft's Internet Explorer. It is possible to access web resources by inputting a unique location address, known as a Uniform Resource Locator (URL) into the browser. This flexibility and ease of access has made the Web an ideal environment for publishing information on the Internet. And has contributed enormously to the explosion in popularity of the Internet in the home, education, and business sectors.

Set-top Browsers

The new era of digital TV presents cable operators, and satellite and wireless providers with an opportunity to deliver profitable Internet-centric services to their subscribers. Cable companies are able to offer an Internet access service to its subscribers at a much higher rate than traditional and specialized Internet Service Providers (ISPs).

Subscribers will be impressed with receiving multimedia content from a digital broadband network at blazing speeds—up to 1,000 times faster than traditional telephone dial-up connections. With the recent explosion of the Web, a lot of focus has been given to delivering this rich consumer-orientated multimedia content to a range of non-PC devices including televisions, mobile phones, and personal organizers. In a television environment, the delivery of this rich content has proven problematic due to a number of reasons. These include: set-tops have limited memory, processor, and data storage capabilities; and the screen resolution of a TV screen varies greatly from a PC monitor.

In other words, Web content, which was originally designed for a PC environment, may not be legible when displayed on a television. The problem could be resolved if Web site developers created special versions of their sites. However, this approach is unlikely to happen in the near future because developing new versions of Web sites is a complex and time-consuming process. Chapter 12 examines in more detail the techniques and tools involved in authoring content for a TV environment.

The set-top browser provides a solution to this problem by organizing Web content in a format that is viewable on a television. These types of browsers are normally downloaded from the network and operate in conjunction with a proxy server. This combination of software technologies offers digital TV subscribers a powerful platform for browsing the Web.

FUNCTIONAL OVERVIEW ....

Before presenting you with specific details about set-top browsers, it is necessary that we review the architecture in which the browser resides.

Described below is a generic infrastructure, which may be used by TV operators to deliver high-speed Web access to their subscribers. When delivering Internet access to set-top users, it is imperative that the TV operator chooses a software platform designed around open Internet standards. A graphical overview of a network topology used for set-top browsing is presented in Figure 7.3.

As you can see, the underlying technology platform has four major components with a number of subcomponents.

Set-top Web Browser Application

Browsers built for the new generation of digital set-tops need the same robust functionality found in desktops, but with access to a fraction of the memory. Due to these constrained memory restrictions, it is impossible for set-top browsers to support all forms of content utilized on the Web. Subsequently, all browsers support HTML, standard text, and the following types of images:

GIF • GIF stands for Graphical Interchange Format. It was originally developed by Compuserve and was released to the public in 1987 as a free and open specification. It is a standard that defines a mechanism for storing and transmitting images over the Web.

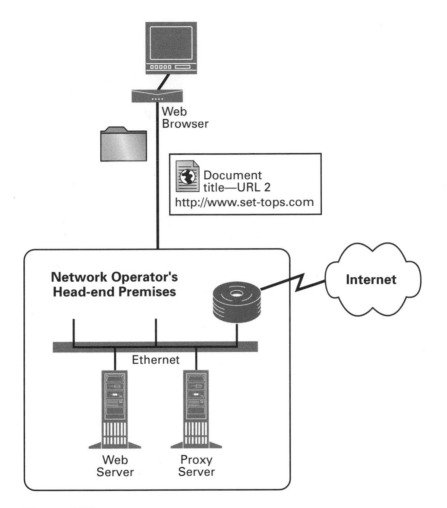

Web
Browser

Document
title—URL 2
http://www.set-tops.com

**Network Operator's
Head-end Premises**

Internet

Ethernet

Web
Server

Proxy
Server

Figure 7.3
End-to-end set-top browsing environment

The GIF format compresses images to reduce the size of a particular file. Compression is used to squeeze data into a size that can be easily stored, so that it takes as little time as possible for the viewer to download them. The technique used to compress the GIF image data is called LZW (after Lempel-Ziv-Welch). Compression of GIF images is very effective because none of the original image is lost during the process. GIF has an 8-bit color map, which means that it only supports 256 colors. Due to this limitation, GIF is not the best format for photographs and video stills. However, it is ideal for designing various Web components such as icons, buttons, animations, and navigational bars.

JPEG • Pronounced "jay-peg," it stands for Joint Photographic Experts Group. JPEG uses a "lossy" compression mechanism that loses a portion of the image data to make it more compressible. In other words, to save space it just throws away parts of an image. Using this technique, JPEG compression technologies can reduce file sizes to about 5 percent of their normal size. JPEG has a 24-bit color format that can handle a wide range of colors (up to 16,777,216), which makes it an excellent format for multicolor images and photographs that need to be compressed.

PNG • PNG is short for Portable Network Graphics (pronounced ping), and is very similar to the GIF format. In actual fact, PNG was approved as a standard by the W3 consortium to replace the older and simpler GIF format. The most recent versions of digital set-top Web browsers support the PNG format. PNG's compression is among the best techniques currently available for reducing file size without losing image quality. For example, PNG compresses an image around 5 percent to 25 percent better than GIF in almost every case.

Additional support for animations and multimedia components may be incorporated into the set-top browser through the use of *plug-ins*. A plug-in is a software module that adds a specific feature or service to the set-top browser. For example, a new plug-in could enable the set-top browser to display 3-dimensional graphics, RealAudio, or QuickTime movies.

When a digital TV subscriber starts their set-top browser application, the program automatically loads a home page. A *home page* is the customer's gateway to the Internet that contains introductory information and a collection of links to other related resources. Home pages can be personalized to meet individual customer's information demands. The network operator is able to configure specific home pages on a per household basis. The home page can be customized to include specific logos and other branding elements. This page represents an opportunity for the operator to present targeted information such as advertising to the customer. For Web browsing systems on the television to be a success, they need to be very easy to use. With this in mind, all of the set-top browsers currently on the market use navigation controls on the television screen that are accessible from a remote control or a wireless keyboard. The user interfaces for set-top browsers are customizable and easy to use. Subscribers use the arrow keys (up, down, left, and right) on their remote control or wireless keyboard to highlight buttons and menu options on the TV screen. A colored box usually indicates a selected option. Pressing any one of the navigation buttons moves the colored box to the nearest selectable option. If this selectable option is a hyperlink and the subscriber also selects the enter key, then the browser will display the Web page associated with that particular link.

From a subscriber's perspective, the amount of memory in the set-top will affect the performance of the browsing experience. When less memory is available, fewer pages are cached locally. Let's examine in more detail the main features and navigation controls provided by a typical set-top browser.

Back

Takes subscribers from the page currently displayed within the browser to the previous page. For example, if you mistakenly click a hyperlink on a web page. You can return to the previous page by simply selecting the back control button on your television screen.

Forward

If you want to move forward again, you simply click the forward control button and the requested page appears on the television screen.

Address bar

When selected, subscribers can use their wireless keyboards to enter the URL of a Web site. With some of the newer versions, you don't even need to type the entire Web site address to go to that page. Just start typing, and the AutoComplete feature suggests a match based on Web sites you visited previously. For example, a TV viewer can type in www.se to go to the http://www.set-tops.com portal site.

Favorites or bookmark list

This feature allows subscribers to record details of their favorite sites on the Web. Let's say a set-top user has been browsing the Web and has found a Web site that contains useful information on a particular topic. As the Web site is updated regularly, the user wants to be able to return to this site at any time.

The easiest way to return to Web sites quickly is by using the Favorites control button. When a customer adds a Web site to the favorites list, the browser stores the URLs of the sites on a server at the network operator's head-end. As set-top users add more and more pages to their list of favorite sites, people will find that their list becomes unmanageable. To solve this problem, newer versions of set-top browsers allow digital TV customers to organize Web pages into folders.

Search

To help subscribers find a particular site on the World Wide Web, or information on a particular topic, set-top browsers allow customers to conduct a search for that site or topic. Suppose you want to find out information about restaurants in Ireland. You simply use the remote control to select the Search option on the television screen and the browser retrieves a search engine page. Network operators can specify any page as the default search engine page.

Once the page is retrieved, you now type in the search keywords using a wireless keyboard into the Find field. The search engine displays the first 10 search results of all the matches found. Each result consists of the title and a short summary of each item. You scroll down the page on your television set until you find an item that interests you. Note most set-top browsers support some type of vertical scrolling. To read the item, click its title, which is a hyperlink to the actual document.

History list

The history list automatically keeps a complete record of all sites that the set-top user has visited within a specific time period. This feature is useful for people who want to quickly navigate to a page they viewed earlier in the session. The history list for a set-top browser only stores the addresses of pages for a browsing session.

Once the browsing session has been completed and normal TV viewing is resumed, the list is cleared from memory. For customers who want to revisit a particular site at a later date, the favorites list should be used for bookmarking particular Web sites.

Stop

The Stop control button is used to terminate the transfer of information downloading to the set-top box. Suppose you click a hyperlink to access a particular Web page and the page is taking a long time to download to the television set. You can terminate transfer of the page by simply clicking the Stop control button.

Print

The Print control button enables subscribers to print information currently displayed onscreen to a printer connected to the parallel port on the set-top box.

Refresh

This control button instructs the browser program to start reloading the current Web page again. This function is useful if, for instance, you are looking at a Web page that changes constantly, such as a video file.

Save

If a subscriber purchased a set-top with a hard drive, then this option will allow you to locally save a range of useful Web pages.

Help

This control button retrieves HTML-based help pages from the servers located at the network provider's head-end.

Advanced features

- Some modern versions of set-top browsers also include an in-built chat system. This enables subscribers to exchange comments in real time.
- Status bars pop up on a subscriber's TV screen when the browser is fetching a Web page. The bar indicates the status and progress of the fetching process.
- Support for 3D graphics and virtual reality content.
- Errors are issued to the subscriber if the HTML page and its components are too large for the memory contained within the digital set-top.

The RAM and ROM usage of a set-top browser is dependent on the number and types of Internet standards that are supported by the browser. Web browsers are available for a variety of middleware platforms, such as OpenTV, Windows TVPAK, PlanetWeb, PowerTV, and Liberate Technologies.

Web Server

A Web server is basically a file server. A Web server's main function is to listen for and respond to HTTP (Hypertext Transfer Protocol) requests from Web browser clients. Web servers were originally developed for UNIX systems, and most Internet servers still use a flavor of UNIX. Nowadays, however, it is possible to run a Web server on many other platforms, including Windows 98, Windows NT, and Macintosh servers. Web servers are sometimes called HTTP servers. This is a communications protocol that was developed specifically for the World Wide Web. When a request is received, the server opens a connection to the browser and sends the requested file. After servicing the request, the server returns to its listening state, waiting for the next HTTP request. HTTP is extremely rapid. According to Tim Berners-Lee, the developer of HTTP, the request is made and the response is given in a cycle of 100 milliseconds. The delays experienced are usually the result of congestion on the network. The files stored on a Web server are usually encoded in HTML format.

A Web server can also be seen as a software program that answers requests for documents from browser clients over the Internet. In addition to responding to requests from browsers, Web servers are also responsible for completing more tasks, including:

- logging activity on the network;
- protecting Web pages from unauthorized users; and
- sending requests to peer Web servers on the Internet.

The hardware requirements for a Web server will vary according to the level of interaction between the set-top box and the Web server.

For cable operators providing an Internet service, it is important that they install a server that provides for future growth. The typical configuration of a computing platform required to support 1,000 set-top customers availing of a high-speed Internet service is comprised of the following hardware components:

- Dual Pentium II processors.
- RAM increases set-top user performance, a minimum of 256 MB of RAM is required.
- The Web server requires expansion interfaces, such as Enhanced Integrated Device Electronics EISA or PCI bus standards, to transfer data at high speeds.
- The server will also need at least six 6-GB SCSI hard drives for storage purposes.
- A 24-speed CD-ROM drive provides ease in installing software.
- A high quality network card to allow the server to communicate with the Internet.

In addition to hardware components, the server also needs a multiple user network operating system, such as Windows NT, Windows 2000, OS/2, or UNIX, to support network activity. Also, the network card needs to be loaded with TCP/IP software and configured so that the server becomes a node on the Internet.

A Web server program then needs to be installed to facilitate communication between the set-top browser and the Internet. Choosing a Web server is an important part of building your set-top browsing network architecture.

There is a wide range of Web server software packages currently available, both as commercial products and as public domain shareware. The difficulty lies in choosing the right Web server because each server has its own strengths and weaknesses.

Table 7.2 gives details of some of the more popular Web server products.

Table 7.2

Web server product	Brief overview	More detailed information
Microsoft Internet Information Server (IIS)	A file and application server that is fully integrated with the Windows NT network operating system. The combination of Web and operating system services makes it possible for broadband network operators to deploy scalable and reliable Web-based applications.	www.microsoft.com/ ntserver/web/default.asp
Netscape Enterprise Server	High-performance, highly scalable Web server software for deploying large-scale Web sites.	www.netscape.com/ enterprise/v3.6/index.html
Lotus Domino Web Server	A Web application server from Lotus with developments that embrace open Internet standards and programming models.	www.lotus.com
Oracle Web Application Server	An HTTP and a transactional server that enables organizations to create and deploy powerful Web-based systems.	www.oracle.com
Apache Web Server	Apache has been the most popular Web server on the Internet since April of 1996. A 1999 survey found that over 53% of the Web sites on the Internet are using Apache, thus making it more widely used than all other Web servers combined.	www.apache.org/

Set-top Proxy Server Software

When using a resource-constrained device such as a set-top box to browse the Web, it makes sense to incorporate an optimized proxy server within the overall system architecture. A *proxy server* is a computer running a software program that acts as a gateway between a digital TV network and the public Internet. It allows a TV operator to designate members of its subscriber base who can access the Internet and which services they can use. In other words, the proxy server program vents all requests, deciding which ones can be passed on and which need to be discarded. From the perspective of a digital TV customer, the process is invisible. The proxy server, on behalf of the set-top Web browser, communicates any requests to the Internet that have been approved. A proxy server is used to speed up subscribers' access to the World Wide

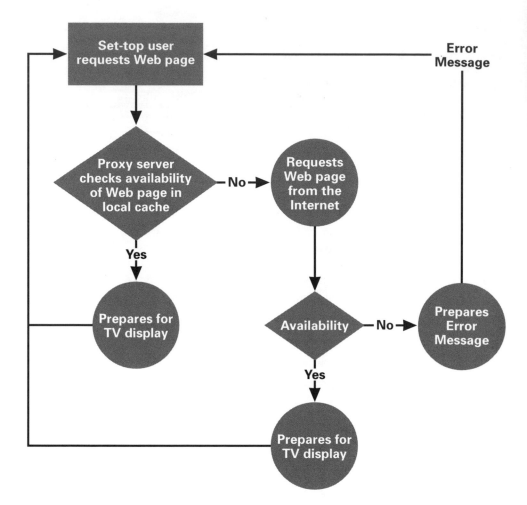

Figure 7.4
Data flow diagram of set-top requesting and retrieving pages from proxy server

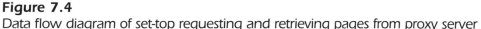

Web by caching frequently accessed Web pages. Caching is a technique used by proxy servers to locally store popular Web pages. The procedure is illustrated in Figure 7.4.

When a subscriber requests a Web page, the set-top browser first checks the proxy server in the head-end to see if a copy of the page is stored locally. If it is, the proxy server prepares the page for TV display and sends the Web page back to the set-top box. Once received, it is rendered by the set-top browser and displayed on the subscriber's television set. This is appreciably faster than downloading the page from a remote Web site on the public Internet. For TV network operators paying for leased lines per megabyte, this caching technology will dramatically reduce the costs associated with offering a set-top browsing service.

If, however, a copy of the requested Web page does not exist at the proxy server, or if the page has gone out of date, the proxy server then requests the page from the remote Internet site. The extra request from the proxy server to the remote Web site can cause slight delays, however, it is relatively small compared to the time taken to download the actual page. If the page is available, it is returned to the subscriber, but if the page has been removed from the remote Web server, then an error message is displayed on the subscriber's TV screen.

As you can see, caching of Internet content improves user performance and reduces bandwidth consumption on an organization's Internet connection. Many of the modern versions of set-top proxy servers are also capable of automatically retrieving and caching commonly requested pages during periods of low activity, without increasing the server load. This type of automated caching allows the proxy server to anticipate the Internet requests that set-top users are likely to make.

Browser clients need to be set up or configured by the software vendor to use the proxy server. In addition to caching Web pages, proxy servers have several other features, which are outlined in the following categories.

Security

Security is an important consideration for digital TV subscribers. They should never have direct contact with resources on the Internet. A Web proxy server can act as a gateway connecting the broadband TV network to the public Internet. When used in conjunction with a firewall system, it provides an easy and secure way of bringing Internet access to every digital TV subscriber on a high-speed broadband network.

In addition to security risks on the public Internet, there also remains the possibility of hackers manipulating data while in transit between the set-top box and the proxy server. The most common method of protecting sensitive information on a broadband digital TV network is encryption. When information is encrypted, it is altered so that it appears as meaningless garble to anyone other than the intended recipient of the information. Currently, the most popular protocol for encrypting data between a set-top box and a proxy server is SSL, or Secure Sockets Layer. This protocol was originally developed by Netscape Communications for transmitting private documents over the public Internet. SSL verifies the merchant's identity to the customer, encrypts the data in transit, and in some cases verifies the customer's identity to the merchant. This process makes it very difficult to tamper with or eavesdrop on transactions. SSL support encryption of data using 40-bit and 128-bit keys. The greater the number of bits in a key, the more difficult it is for a snooper to crack an encrypted message. Currently, U.S. law does not allow the export of keys greater than 40 bits long. Although a message can be encrypted with a 128-bit key in the U.S., it is illegal to do this internationally.

SSL operates as follows. The proxy server and set-top user each possess a public key and a private key for use in encrypting and decrypting messages. The public key is made available to anyone who wants to access it and the user retains the private key secret. If, for example, a subscriber wants to send a message or document to someone else, the subscriber would encrypt it using his or her public key. Data encrypted using the public key can only be decrypted using the private key, and only the intended recipient has access to their private key. Therefore, the subscriber can be sure that only they can decrypt the message. This means that even if the message is intercepted during transmission, it cannot be understood. SSL also supports digital signatures. These certificates allow the recipient of a message to verify user authentication. User authentication means ensuring that a user is actually who they say they are. Most modern set-top browsers support SSL and many e-commerce sites use the protocol to obtain confidential user information, such as home addresses and credit card numbers.

By convention, the addresses of Web documents that require an SSL connection start with https: rather than the usual http: SSL supports the following security features:

- Encryption of information transferred between an e-commerce site on the Internet and set-top clients.
- Validation that information was not tampered with en route over the broadband TV network.
- Server authentication through the use of digital certificates.

Certificates are an important client security feature offered by most major set-top Web browsers. A certificate is a file attached to an electronic message that confirms the identity of the sender. Organizations called certification service providers, act as trusted third parties, are responsible for issuing valid digital certificates. This certificate guarantees the identity of a particular person.

Certification service providers also develop certificate revocation lists. These lists detail certificates that are no longer valid. A certificate may be declared invalid if it is stolen. There are now a number of companies providing third-party certification. VeriSign is probably the most widely known service provider.

A basic certificate used by set-top browsers will contain the following items of information:

- the name and address of the subscriber;
- a public key that matches the subscriber's private key;
- a digital signature unique to the subscriber;
- a signature from the CA that issued the certificate;
- expiration date; and
- the certificate number.

They can hold other items of information, such as an e-mail address or telephone numbers. Once a security system of this nature is implemented on a broadband network, the chances of a hacker intercepting details about the subscriber are almost nonexistent.

Filtering content and parental control

Some proxy servers include filtering systems that allow operators and subscribers to restrict access to certain Internet sites containing inappropriate content. Every address requested by a digital TV subscriber is checked against a database of objectionable sites on the Internet. If the proxy server finds that the addresses are from objectionable sites, it won't allow that information to be passed on to the set-top user. Since the Internet is growing at a phenomenal rate, the database of inappropriate Web sites could become outdated very quickly. To solve this problem, the TV network operator needs to update the database every month.

Transcoding

The display characteristics and processing power of a digital set-top box vary greatly in comparison to a standard multimedia PC. For example, some set-top browsers are able to display bitmap and GIF files but are unable to display JPEG files on your TV screen. The proxy server uses a process called *transcoding* to convert and format Web content into a simpler format, which is suitable for display on a standard television. Transcoding can be divided into two broad categories: HTML transcoding and Image transcoding.

The parsing and layout of HTML programming code requires a good deal of set-top processing power. Lightweight set-top clients are unable to perform all of this processing, so the transcoding feature within the proxy server preprocesses the HTML content before delivering to the set-top box. The preprocessing of HTML content includes checking the code for any errors. An example of an HTML error would be the absence of a `</html>` tag on a standard Web page. Transcoding filters these errors and produces a version of HTML that can be easily rendered by the set-top box. In addition to checking for errors, the HTML transcoding element is also capable of changing the layout to a TV-centric format. For example, the default font size for a Web browser is normally 10 points. If this font size were to be displayed on a television screen, then it would be very difficult to read. Consequently, the proxy server will automatically increase the size of the font to 20 or 22 points. This approach means that less text can be displayed on a TV screen than in a comparable area of a computer monitor. However, the text is legible for subscribers that are viewing the page from a distance of 4 to 5 feet away from the television. In addition to automatically adjusting font sizes, proxy server software is also capable of adjusting the size of a page to fit within the width and height of a TV screen. Image transcoding is responsible for converting the many image formats used on the Internet to a format that is suitable for a set-top environment. So, for example, when a user requests a Web document that contains JPEG images, the proxy server retrieves the data from the Internet and automatically converts the images to GIF or bitmap format. Once the Web document has been converted to a format suitable for viewing on a TV screen, it is sent back to the set-top box. In addition to translating the file format, some set-top proxy servers are capable of formatting and scaling the content for a television screen. This could involve adjusting color maps or sizing images on Web pages to fit the resolution of the TV screen.

Digital TV subscribers that participate in full Web browsing exert severe demands on the transcoding element of the proxy server. The number of simultaneous set-top users that can be supported by the transcoding element is a function of a number of parameters, including:

- percentage of cache hits and misses;
- the processing power of the hardware platform; and the
- speed at which the subscriber is selecting Web pages.

The process of defining how Web content is converted to set-top format is controlled by the network operator. This approach to displaying HTML content in a TV environment ensures that Web professionals do not need to modify the content of existing sites.

Integration with head-end equipment

The set-top proxy server also needs to be capable of interoperating with the existing digital TV network infrastructure.

Logging Internet activity

The ability of a proxy server to monitor and track Internet traffic is an extremely important part of a set-top end-to-end browser system. The logging function records sites visited by digital TV subscribers, and any problems that users have had with accessing certain sites. The system administrator then uses this information to design and build better access services for customers.

Support for Internet standards

All set-top proxy servers provide protocol support for Internet protocols.

Planning a set-top proxy server deployment

For TV network operators planning a set-top proxy server installation, it's good practice to begin by performing a site analysis of the organization's requirements. The first step is to determine how many digital TV customers will require access to the public Internet and what type of access they will need. For example, some customers may require constant access, while others may only need occasional access. In addition to access habits, a service provider needs to determine what applications will run across the broadband network and what elements of the proxy server are needed to support these applications.

For example, most set-top users will need the HTTP protocol to browse Internet documents, hence the proxy server needs to run the Web proxy service to meet these demands. The next stage of planning is to estimate the capacity requirements of the proxy server based on the anticipated volume of traffic across your network. For example, a group of 1,000 users downloading multimedia-intensive files across a broadband network requires much more server capacity than the same number of users downloading plain HTML documents. In this case, the service provider may need to consider the installation of more than one proxy server to balance the overload of traffic on the network. Once the TV operator has decided the requirements of customers, the proxy server will then need to be introduced into the TV environment in stages. It's a good idea initially to run a beta test using a limited number of digital TV customers and monitor performances over a set period of time. This gives the operator an opportunity to tune the configuration while only having to provide support to a limited number of users.

Once this has proved successful, the service provider will then be in a position to add more subscribers to the set-top browser system.

High-speed Internet Connection

The proxy server supports all traffic to the Internet using a single high capacity line. Instead of each user having a separate line to the Internet, a common connection is used. This high capacity connection to the Internet must be available 24 hours a day, 7 days a week, as subscribers will want to be able to browse and send e-mails at any time. To meet these commercial and technical demands, a permanent leased-line connection needs to be established between the head-end and the Internet.

This is usually installed jointly by the Internet service provider (ISP) and a local telephone company. An ISP is a company that provides access to the Internet. The ISP usually charges a monthly or annual membership fee, plus a charge for the number of hours spent online. ISPs have a gateway that they share between many users, allowing them to access the Internet. ISPs can be split into four distinct categories:

1. *Local.* Local providers provide access to users within a limited geographical area. They usually obtain network access from larger regional providers and resell the bandwidth. The cost of accessing the Internet through a local provider is relatively low for customers because access is gained via a local dial-up telephone call.

2. *Regional.* Connecting to a regional provider offers companies more advanced Internet services such as hosting e-commerce sites. The membership costs for these types of ISPs are generally higher.

3. *Backbone carriers.* Backbone carriers are capable of delivering a full range of high-speed, dedicated access options using the latest in cutting-edge Internet products to large organizations.

4. *Cable ISPs.* This type of ISP provides high-speed Internet access to digital subscribers over cable TV networks. The two best-known ISPs in North America that are focussing on the cable industry are RoadRunner and Excite@Home.

The first step in establishing an Internet connection is to estimate the amount of expected bandwidth required from the new Internet connection to support customers accessing set-top Internet services. Bandwidth refers to the amount of information that can be carried over a dedicated communications link. Bandwidth is usually listed in kilobits per second (Kbps) or megabits per second (Mbps). If you have a good idea of the size of the Web documents to be transferred and the estimated number of connections there are likely to be in one day, companies can use the following formula to estimate the amount of bandwidth required to support full set-top Web browsing.

(Average Internet connections per day/number of seconds per day) × average document size in kilobits.

Let's take an example of an MMDS and cable operator who is currently providing digital TV services to 400,000 customers. The company plans to offer a full Internet browsing service to its customer base and needs to determine the capacity of a leased line between their own digital TV network and the Internet. The company is making the following assumptions:

1. The company is predicting a 25 percent take rate for the new service.
2. All customers will connect at least once a day.
3. The average size of a typical Web page is 25 KB.
4. The company is predicting that caching pages at their head-end will fulfill 60 percent of requests.
5. A browsing session will last one hour per day and a digital TV viewer will view 20 pages of Web content.

The formula for calculating the bandwidth capacity would look like this:

The file size of 25 KB must be multiplied by 1024 to establish the number of bytes (1024 bytes = 1 KB) and this figure is then multiplied by 8 to calculate the number of bits. This calculation gives us a figure of 204,800 bits of information. To convert to kilobits we again need to divide this figure by 1024, which gives us an average document size of 200 Kbps. This figure then needs to be multiplied by 20 to give the total amount of data downloaded per day/per user to the set-top box. The next parameter we need to investigate is the average number of browsing sessions in a day. To arrive at this figure, we need to calculate 25 percent of 400,000 subscribers, which is 100,000 people. The number of seconds in a day is 86,400. The company's bandwidth calculations are then calculated by inserting these values into our formula:

$$100,000/86,400 \times 4000 \text{ Kbits} = 4629 \text{ Kbits.}$$

To establish the number of Mbits required, this figure is divided by 1024 to give an overall bandwidth requirement of 4.5 Mbps. According to one of the network operator's assumptions, at least 60 percent of Internet requests will be serviced using proxy server caching. Therefore, the actual quantity of bandwidth required is 40 percent of 4.5 Mbps, which is 1.8 Mbps. These calculations can then be used to determine the type of leased line needed to deliver high-speed set-top Internet services.

The two basic types of leased line available to network operators are analog and digital. An *analog* line is simply a standard telephone line that is permanently open. Implementing an analog leased-line solution requires the installation of modems at both ends of the connection.

A modem (modulator/demodulator) converts the digital signals from the operator's broadband network into the analog signals used by the telephone line (and vice versa).

The data transfer rate of an analog line depends on the speed of these modems. Currently, the fastest modems available on the marketplace have a data transfer rate of 56.6 Kbps. As you can probably see by now, an analog leased line is not a suitable solution for network operators who want to offer high-speed Internet applications to their set-top subscribers.

Many of the digital leased lines are based around the Integrated Services Digital Networks (ISDN) standard. ISDN is a worldwide digital communications network that has emerged from the Public Switched Telephone Network. It is much faster and safer for data transfer than an analog dial-up connection because it uses digital phone lines. A basic rate interface (BRI) ISDN line is logically divided into two 64 Kbps data channels and one 16 Kbps control channel. These channels can then be combined into one 128 Kbps leased line.

A Primary Rate Interface (PRI) ISDN line has a much higher capacity and is the more popular option for large organizations who want to connect their internal broadband networks to the public Internet. This type of line is typically comprised of 30 data channels and one control channel. In the United States, the PRI ISDN is called a

T1 connection. A T1 has a bandwidth capacity of 1.544 Mbps. In Europe, the equivalent connection is called an E1 and is able to support the transfer of data at 2.048 Mbps. E1 and T1 lines are much more expensive to run than ISDN or dial-up lines, but costs are gradually coming down.

Frame relay is another technology that is being offered by an increasing number of ISPs. As described earlier, a leased line is between the head-end and the ISP. Frame relay, on the other hand, is installed between the head-end and the nearest frame-relay access point. This method of communication is cheaper than a standard leased-line connection because the telephone company does not need to run the digital line all the way to the ISP. At the frame-relay access point, the data to and from the digital TV subscribers are combined with that of other frame-relay clients and transmitted via a high-speed link to the ISP. So you are essentially "sharing" the cost of the high-speed leased line with several other customers. It can support transfer speeds of up to 45 Mbps.

Frame relay is quite popular in the U.S. because it is relatively inexpensive. However, it is being replaced in some areas by faster technologies, such as asynchronous transfer mode (ATM). ATM is a developing technology that provides networks with high bandwidth speeds. ATM networks generally use fiber optic cable that can reach speeds of up to 155 Mbps.

Inadequate quantities of bandwidth would result in frustrating digital TV subscribers and defeat the purpose of launching set-top Internet applications. Bandwidth is, however, a very expensive commodity. Hence, network operators need to make a compromise between available finance and requirements of the needs of their subscriber base.

Another important consideration for operators offering Internet services to their subscribers is the overall reliability of the service. For example, if there was only a single connection to the Internet, then a failure on this link would result in subscribers being unable to access e-mail or browsing services.

To minimize this risk, operators normally install backup links, which improve the overall reliability of the service.

HOW SET-TOP WEB BROWSING WORKS . . . .

Every item of information on the Internet has a unique address called a Uniform Resource Locator (URL). An example of a URL is as follows: http://www.set-tops.com/etail.htm. This particular URL addresses the online software store at set-tops.com. All URLs have two main parts: the protocol identifier and the resource name.

In the example above, HTTP is the protocol identifier and www.set-tops.com/etail.html is the resource name. You will notice a colon is used to separate the two components. HTTP is a very simple request/response protocol. The request/response paradigm of a set-top browser is illustrated in Figure 7.5. When a

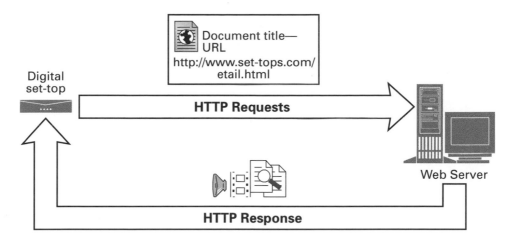

Figure 7.5
HTTP Request/Response paradigm

digital TV subscriber wants to request an HTML page from a Web server on the Internet, it uses HTTP to request the page. Once the Web server receives the request, it processes the HTTP commands. If the subscriber has a valid username and password, the Web server will respond by sending the requested Web page back to the set-top browser.

If the server is unable to authenticate the set-top user, then a message is displayed on the TV screen indicating that the page is restricted.

The HTTP standard is evolving very quickly. The first version was called HTTP/0.9 and included very simple commands. This version of HTTP was soon superseded by HTTP/1.0 and version 1.1 is now beginning to become the standard communication protocol between clients and servers on the Web.

Choosing a Set-top Browser Platform

The factors, that may influence your final decision about purchasing a browser for your digital set-top box include:

1. How quickly it loads Web pages.
2. What are the minimum hardware requirements.
3. What network transport protocols are supported.
4. What, if any, bugs (errors) it has.
5. List of features it has.
6. How well it is supported.

7. Level of security.

8. Level of support for Internet graphics standards.

9. Level of support for Internet audio standards.

10. Level of support for Internet animation standards.

Some of the most popular browsers used by network operators to deliver Web content to consumers' TV sets are detailed in each of the following subsections.

Personal WebAccess

Personal WebAccess is a Web browser that has been developed by Sun Microsystems and Spyglass for set-top boxes that run the Personal Java operating environment. At the time of going to press, Sun had launched version 2.0 of the application. As to be expected from Sun, the browser was entirely written in the Java programming language. At present, it is mainly targeted at set-top box manufacturers who want to provide their customers (network service providers) with a browsing solution for their subscriber base. Personal WebAccess uses JavaBeans as part of its architectural design, allowing set-top manufacturers to choose the level of functionality needed by the service providers. Sun's strategy of using JavaBeans enables Personal WebAccess to be integrated easily with other set-top Internet services such as TV chat and TV mail. Typical of most set-top browsers, Personal WebAccess supports Internet standards, including HTML (version 3.2), frames, tables, Java applets, cookies, and version 1.1 of the HTTP communications protocol. All of these browser technologies can be stored in approximately 950K of set-top memory. At the moment, Sun is licensing Personal WebAccess to consumer device manufacturers and telecommunications and RTOS vendors. For more information on becoming a licensee for this new and exciting product, please visit Sun's licensing page at http://java.sun.com/nav/business/index.html.

Spyglass

Spylass is one of the leading providers of expertise and software applications for Web-centric devices such as digital set-top boxes, personal digital assistants, and mobile phones. The company's central office is located in Illinois and has a number of regional offices in Asia and Europe. Spyglass is very active in the interactive TV arena and licenses a core set of technologies to a wide range of software companies including Microsoft, Sony Corporation, and General Instruments. In this section of our book, we take a closer look at their Device Mosaic browser, which allows manufacturers to add Web functionality to digital set-top boxes.

Similar to other set-top browsers, Spyglass designed the Device Mosaic application to run within a memory footprint of less than 850 KB. Similar to Personal

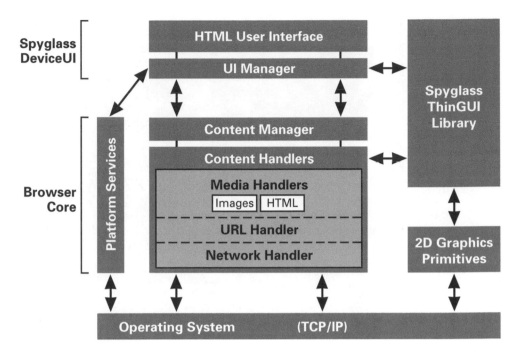

Figure 7.6
Architecture of Device Mosaic platform

WebAccess, the Spyglass browser supports HTML 3.2, a number of image formats, authentication technologies, and a variety of other browser-like features.

As we can see from the architectural diagram in Figure 7.6, the Device Mosaic comes with an HTML-based user interface. This allows network service providers to add their own look and brand identity to the browser. As we can see from the diagram, the core of the browser consists of a number of handlers or subsystems that are used to process the various types of multimedia content that are found on the Internet. Also shown on the diagram is the interfacing between the core browser and the ThinGUI library. This is a library that occupies less than 300 KB of memory and contains a number of graphics that are used to enhance the overall functionality of the browser. The browser is very portable and has been optimized to run on many of the real-time operating systems we covered in Chapter 3, including VxWorks, pSOS, Windows CE, OS-9, PowerTV OS, and many others.

PlanetWeb

The PlanetWeb browser offers original equipment manufacturers (OEMs), a cost-effective and proven solution for adding Internet capabilities to their digital set-top boxes. The browser has already been ported to a number of hardware platforms and

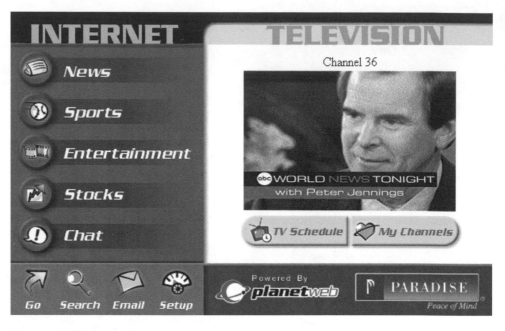

Figure 7.7
Screen capture of PlanetWeb user interface

supports a wide range of real-time operating systems, including VxWorks, pSOS, and others. The display quality of PlanetWebs' browser is excellent because of their sophisticated image processing technologies and proprietary anti-aliased fonts, which improve text readability. The browser has been localized for Europe, South America, Japan, Asia, and China. In addition, the browser supports Latin-1 fonts. PlanetWeb user interfaces are easy-to-use and intuitive (see Figure 7.7). Innovations include a patented magnifier, an onscreen navigator called command compass, and bump scrolling technology, which eliminates the need for scroll bars.

The browser also contains an easy-to-use parental control filtering system that connects to an online database of over 90,000 rated Web sites and millions of Web pages. The minimum hardware requirements for this browser include a 32-bit processor running at 33 MIPS, 500 KB of Flash memory, and 2 MB of ROM. The browser fully supports networking protocols such as HTTP and TCP/IP.

INTRODUCTION TO SET-TOP E-MAIL . . . .

From the earliest days of society, people have used various systems and technologies to communicate with each other. With the recent explosion of the Internet, the most popular means of communicating between computers is electronic mail (e-mail). It is a fast and economical method for anyone with a PC and modem to stay up to date with friends and relatives around the world. E-mail can be defined as the sending and receiving of electronic messages.

Back in the early 1980s, e-mail was restricted to a small number of academic and research environments. Nowadays, e-mail is beginning to gain widespread acceptance and is being used as a standard method of communication.

E-mail has many benefits:

- It facilitates communication between organizations and individuals around the globe.
- People can attach video, sound, spreadsheets, word processing documents, and executables to their e-mail messages.
- It is faster than conventional communication systems.
- It is possible to send e-mail to many people at once instead of having to place multiple phone calls or leave multiple messages.
- It promotes the whole concept of a virtual office, where people work from home and use e-mail to communicate with the office.
- E-mail is cheaper than sending faxes or making phone calls.

E-mail is by far the most popular of all the Internet applications, boasting a user base of approximately 50 million people worldwide. With the advent of digital TV, this figure is expected to increase to 1 billion users by the year 2003. To gain a greater understanding of this application, lets examine how e-mail will work in a set-top and digital TV environment.

How Set-top E-mail Works

The subscriber will not need to worry about the technical details of how e-mail works, however, a deep understanding of the subject is required of the network operator to ensure the subscriber receives a high level of reliability.

Before we describe the process of using an e-mail application on your TV screen, it is important to mention the fact that e-mail is a fast method of communicating. However, it is not a real-time application. In other words, you do not have a direct link with the person with whom you are communicating. Systems like set-top chat and set-top video conferencing provide TV viewers with this functionality. These applications will be discussed later.

E-mail operates very similar to a postal system. Once you write your letter, it is presented to the postal company and delivered to a specific address. Once the letter is physically located at the recipient's address, the letter can be opened and read any time. With set-top e-mail, a similar approach is adopted. The e-mail application is launched from local memory on the set-top box. A user types a message on their TV screen and it is sent to a mail server that is located at the network operator's premises.

If the recipient is located on the local network, then the message is forwarded to the recipients mailbox. Otherwise the TV mail is sent out onto the public Internet. To enable subscribers to send e-mails over the Internet, the TV operator needs to have a high-speed connection to the Internet.

The Internet will find the fastest route to the recipient's mailbox. Once in the mailbox, the recipient is free to access and download the new message. The main advantages of using set-top e-mail versus the traditional postal system is ease of use, low costs, and a much faster method of communicating with friends and business colleagues around the world.

The diagram in Figure 7.8 shows how an end-to-end set-top e-mail solution might look.

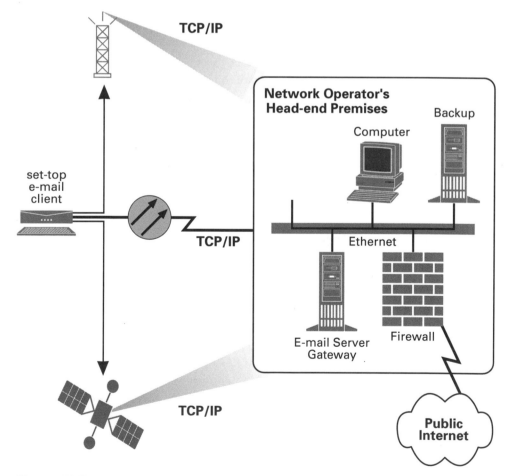

Figure 7.8
End-to-end set-top e-mail solution

From a technical perspective, every subscriber that avails of the set-top e-mail service will receive a unique e-mail address and a mailbox. The mailboxes are stored and managed on mail server gateways at the network operator's head-end. These servers are connected to the Internet and also interface with the subscriber management system for billing purposes. The gateway is a software program that runs on a mail server and links an internal cable, satellite, MMDS, or terrestrial network through a firewall to the Internet. In addition to connectivity, the software also converts e-mail from an internal system into Internet-compatible SMTP format.

E-mail messages are always transmitted in the American Standard Code for Information Interchange (ASCII) format. ASCII files are text-only files.

The transfer of e-mail messages in a digital TV environment are normally based on Internet mail standards such as SMTP, IMAP, S/MIME and POP.

SMTP • SMTP stands for Simple Message Transfer Protocol. It is used to transfer set-top mail from the mail server located at the head-end to another e-mail server on the Internet. It is designed for reliable and efficient mail transfer. SMTP forms part of the TCP/IP protocol stack. SMTP does not specify how the mail system accepts mail from a user or how the user interface on the set-top presents the mail. It is simply a protocol, which specifies how messages should be passed from transmitting to receiving hosts. SMTP will establish credentials about the sender and make sure that the mail arrives in the recipient's mailbox. It is important to bear in mind that SMTP can only handle the transfer of plain text files and is unable to carry binary files such as spreadsheets, word documents, and video clips. To overcome this obstacle, the mail server at the head-end will encode the file, convert it to a text message, and transmit it to the recipient's mailbox.

S/MIME • **S/MIME** stands for Secure Multipurpose Internet Mail Extensions. MIME is a new Internet standard that lets set-top e-mail clients automatically encode and decode binary files from their original format into a format that is viewable on your TV set. It specifies how non-ASCII messages should be formatted so that they can be sent over the public Internet. Examples of non-ASCII messages include graphic, audio, and video files. Popular set-top e-mail clients and web browsers support MIME.

This means the e-mail clients running on a digital set-top box can send much more than just text messages. There are many predefined MIME formats, including JPEG file graphics and PostScript files. You can also define your own MIME types. Secure/MIME, or S/MIME, is a more secure version of MIME. It allows MIME types to be encrypted.

POP3 • POP stands for Post Office Protocol. The set-top user can use this protocol to access messages on the mail server at the head-end.

IMAP • IMAP stands for Internet Message Access Protocol. The latest version of this protocol, IMAP4, has similar functionality to POP3, but supports some additional features, which are very useful for customers of digital TV.

For example, a subscriber can search through their e-mail using keywords while the e-mail remains on the server. Subscribers will then be able to select specific messages and download to the set-top.

As previous chapters in the book probably made obvious, the expectations of digital TV subscribers are very high. To meet these customers' demands, e-mail operations need to run smoothly at the head-end and support personnel need to perform a variety of maintenance tasks, including:

- *Backing up subscriber's e-mail accounts.* One of the most important jobs of the person managing a set-top mail system is to manage and maintain backups.

- *Monitoring the space occupied by subscribers' e-mail accounts.* Subscribers who send and receive large amounts of e-mail with attachments need to be monitored closely; otherwise, the hard disk space on the e-mail server will become depleted.

- *Managing the e-mail server's connection to the Internet.* If costs are a factor in selecting a dedicated digital connection, TV operators should bear in mind that most e-mail messages are relatively small and don't need a high bandwidth connection. Depending on the customer base, it may be acceptable to send mail in batches every couple of hours. These are business decisions, which are specific to each network operator.

Set-top E-mail Clients

The set-top box, with its interactive capability, is seen by many as a natural environment for e-mail in the home. The client e-mail application is normally integrated with the digital set-top box and uses the TCP/IP protocol to communicate with the operator's head-end. Modern set-top e-mail applications fulfill a wide range of functions and let subscribers do more than just send or receive mail. With some products currently available in the marketplace, set-top users will be able to attach documents. It is even possible to capture a number of pictures using a digital camera and send these images as attachments using the set-top e-mail client. As mentioned earlier, e-mail is transmitted across the Internet in ASCII format, hence all attached files will need to be formatted according to this specific format. Most of these attachments are encoded in binary format, which is an unsuitable format for transmitting data. To resolve this issue, the set-top e-mail system will encode the attachment into ASCII format using the MIME standard.

To enable a set-top box to open and view an attachment that has been received from another source, the box will need to be running a program that is equivalent to the one the file was written in. For example, if a subscriber receives mail with a Microsoft Excel spreadsheet attached, the set-top box will not be able to display this file on your TV set. To overcome this problem, many TV operators are converting proprietary file formats to HTML and using the set-top browser to open, view, and save these files. In addition to attaching files, customers will be able to send one or more copies of messages to other people using the carbon copy (cc) and blind carbon copy (bcc) options. Most set-top e-mail programs are very user-friendly and allow you to send a copy of the message you are answering along with the reply.

Another popular feature for modern set-top e-mail applications is the presence of a personal address book, where subscribers can store and retrieve all types of information about friends and relatives such as street addresses, telephone numbers, e-mail addresses, and fax phone numbers. If subscribers are able to connect their PCs to the set-top box, it may also be possible to import an address book and store it on the e-mail server at the TV operator's head-end. Network providers can also configure an e-mail client to notify customers of new mail arrivals.

Although the actual format of a message is dependent on the set-top e-mail application you're using, all of these programs will have the same basic format. The top section of the message will always consist of a date, the name of the sender, and the recipient. The next section of the e-mail is called the subject line and describes the contents of the e-mail message. The final part of the message is the main body of the e-mail and consists of standard text characters.

Advanced versions of set-top e-mail applications will allow subscribers to:

- preview mail;
- organize e-mail in their mailboxes;
- print e-mail;
- attach a URL for a Web site to an e-mail message;
- capture a voicemail and send it as an attached file; and
- use a camcorder to catch 20 or 30 seconds of live video and send as an attachment.

E-mail can be sent both within the TV operator's network and over the Internet. It is usually quicker to send messages over the TV operator's network to another set-top user who is using the same e-mail system than it is for sending an e-mail to a recipient on the Internet who is using a totally different e-mail system.

Set-top E-mail Security

It is vital that e-mail data is safeguarded against unauthorized access to prevent loss of revenues. All set-top e-mail systems currently embrace some form of security system based on passwords. Most of the systems will allow TV operators to set up five user accounts per household. Each of these accounts will have a unique password and it will be the responsibility of the TV operator to define a set of rules relating to password security.

People often create passwords that can easily be guessed. Many people, for example, use passwords made up of their first name and last name. Other popular passwords include date of birth, names of pets, and ages of children. This is acceptable for set-top users who do not require a huge amount of privacy when accessing their set-top e-mail accounts, however, there will always be a certain percentage of the population who do not want other members of their family reading their TV mail. As mentioned, one system that may be used by TV operators to reduce the risk of passwords being compromised is to establish a set of password rules. For example, the e-mail server used to store set-top user accounts may be configured to ensure all passwords for a particular family be a minimum length of eight characters. This type of functionality exists now and is an appropriate security system for subscribers who are using set-top e-mail to send or receive messages that contain sensitive or private information.

It should be noted that if a password and e-mail message is transmitted over the network as a clear text message, then there is a possibility that determined people could potentially access and read this information. To reduce this risk, many of the set-top security clients will support encryption. The main purpose of encryption is to scramble the contents of an e-mail message so that only the intended recipient is capable of reading it. The level of encryption available to a set-top user will depend on the e-mail application that is running on the device.

Although not widely deployed in a set-top and digital TV environment, the use of public-key cryptography is expected to become available to set-top users in the year 2000. In public-key cryptography, a public and a private key are involved in securing e-mail messages. Everybody on the operator's network will have a public key and a private key. Suppose, for example, a subscriber sitting at home wants to use their set-top box to send a message that contains sensitive information to a colleague at work. For this to happen in a secure manner, the set-top user will need to forward their public key to the intended recipient. Once the recipient has a copy of the public key, the message can be encrypted using the private key and forwarded across the TV network. The recipient can then use the public key to descramble and read the confidential e-mail. For this type of encryption system to work properly, set-top users will need to make their public keys freely available while the private keys are not revealed and remain exclusive to each individual.

These public and private keys can also be used to generate digital electronic signatures. A digital signature is an authentication technique that proves without a doubt that a user of the set-top e-mail system wrote a particular message at a particular time. These digital signatures are very similar to electronic ID cards.

Digital signatures are based on complex mathematical algorithms and are increasingly being used in financial transactions conducted across the Internet. Digital signatures are usually quite short, consisting of a few hundred bytes and may be used as evidence in a court of law. The next generation of set-top e-mail applications will incorporate digital signature technologies. This move by set-top software suppliers is seen as key to the development of electronic commerce in a digital TV environment.

The Set-top E-mail Marketplace

The increasing popularity of using a digital set-top box and a TV set as a medium for sending and receiving e-mail has led to the development of a number of set-top e-mail applications.

PowerTV, PlanetWeb, and Spyglass are examples of applications that allow you to use a digital set-top box and a TV set to send e-mail over the Internet.

ONLINE CHAT . . . .

This application allows subscribers to use their televisions to participate in interactive chat rooms. The network service provider decides on the types of chat rooms that are available to their customer base. Some providers, for example, do not allow subscribers to access public Internet-based chat rooms. From a technical perspective, the TV operator needs to install a powerful community chat server in the head-end. Chat servers are easily customizable and seamlessly integrate with advertisement banners. The client application has very low memory and processor requirements and makes it very suitable for use in digital set-top boxes. Most set-top chat programs offer one-to-one and one-to-many communication channels.

WEBCASTING . . . .

The ability of the Web to deliver graphical and multimedia content has encouraged millions of users around the world to join the Internet community.

The very success of the Internet and the Web has, however, brought problems for consumers. Content developers are developing multimedia-rich Web sites that consume large amounts of bandwidth. This can make downloading a time-consuming and frustrating process. In addition, Internet users spend a lot of time browsing within a site to find relevant and recently updated information. It is time-consuming to repeatedly search the same site in order to find small pieces of updated information on topics that concern you. The use of a set-top Webcasting application can save a subscriber's time by allowing the service provider to deliver updates and new software to the set-top box.

How Webcasting Works?

Webcasting is a system used by service providers to distribute software updates and "push" content to a subscriber's set-top box over a broadband TV network. A set-top

Webcasting application can use the following methods of retrieving up-to-date information for a subscriber:

1. Basic webcasting—subscribing to a site on the Internet.
2. True webcasting—subscribing to channels located at the service provider's premises.

In basic Webcasting, a customer uses their set-top browser to subscribe to a frequently accessed web site. Once a subscription has been made, the set-top browser will monitor that particular Internet site on a regular basis and notify customers when new content is available. Subscribers can retain control over what kind of information is received, and how it is received. For instance, they can choose to store the updated information on a hard drive if it is available in the set-top box. For customers who use terrestrial and satellite set-top boxes, content can be downloaded while call rates are cheaper, and then viewed more quickly offline without the bandwidth limits of a telephone modem.

True Webcasting is a more complex method of sending information to the subscribed user and is comprised of the following components:

- channels;
- content agents;
- a scheduling tool;
- a channel transmitter; and
- a webcasting client application.

Figure 7.9 shows the logical components of an end-to-end set-top Webcasting solution.

A channel is essentially a collection of files. Channel contents consist of a main Web page, and any related pages. Pages within the channel can contain anything you would place in a normal Web page, such as HTML, Java class files, multimedia content, or JavaScript components.

Service providers also add images and logos to improve brand awareness. As long as the set-top box is connected to the broadband TV network, a channel updates itself automatically. So subscribers will always have the most recent version of the channel. The content agents are software programs that are responsible for aggregating information from sites on the Internet and storing this information on Web servers that are located at the digital head-end. They scan deep into sites and create an index of all words on the site. Content agent technologies are based on a standard called Channel Definition Format (CDF).

The W3C proposal that was developed by Microsoft describes CDF as an open specification that permits a Web publisher to offer frequently updated collections of

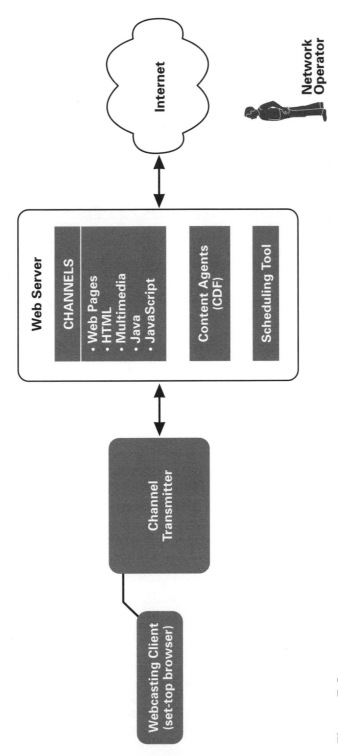

Figure 7.9
Set-top Webcasting technologies

information, or channels, from any Web server for automatic delivery to compatible receiver programs on PCs or other information appliances. The CDF file is used to establish the organization of the channel's content. It also provides an index or map of a Web site, which describes the type of information contained on the site.

The file is normally written in Extensible Markup Language (XML) and uses the same syntax as HTML files. XML is a new specification being developed by the W3 consortium. It enables Web designers to create their own customized tags to provide functionality not available with standard HTML. For example, XML supports links that point to multiple documents, as opposed to HTML links, which can reference just one destination each. A more comprehensive description of the XML standard is provided for you in Chapter 10. A CDF file basically contains a list of URLs, which point to content on the Internet. They are easy to create, and require no changes to existing Web pages. The scheduling tool is used for creating and maintaining information delivery schedules. Network operators use this tool to decide how often new channel information should be delivered to a subscriber's set-top box.

The channel transmitter runs on a server connected to the broadband TV network. It is mainly responsible for the management and distribution of channels over the TV network. It serves the channel files in response to a request from a browser, which resides on the customer's set-top box. Transmission of set-top channels is similar to the way in which a Web server delivers HTML files to a requesting PC browser. The Webcast content is normally delivered using DSM-CC broadcast carousels, which may be delivered in-band or out of band. DSM-CC is an acronym for Digital Storage Media Command and Control.

It is a standard that has been developed by the International Standardization Organization (ISO) with the International Engineering Consortium to deliver a range of rich multimedia services over a broadband network. DSM-CC is a collection of protocols that can be used in a standalone mode or in concert with other protocol areas, depending on the application(s) being addressed. For example, it provides Webcasting applications with a client download that allows a service operator to deliver IP data to its subscribers over an HFC network. Other features of the DSM-CC protocol include interfaces for VCR-like control of video streams and high-speed changing of TV channels. A more detailed description of the DSM-CC protocol is available at the following URL: http://www.cselt.stet.it/mpeg/documents/dsmcc.htm.

Other Webcasting innovations include the ability to customize and personalize the transmitter's output for each subscriber. It can, for example, modify all the channel's text to reflect the language preference of the subscriber. Finally, the Webcasting client application allows users to subscribe to a particular channel and receive the content from the Webcasting transmitter. When customers subscribe to channel sites, they no longer have to visit the sites to check if they have been updated, or if new content has been added. The Webcasting client automatically checks the site for new or updated content and notifies the user if there is additional information. The Webcasting client (set-top browsers are commonly used as Webcasting clients) also has a graphical interface that displays the installed channels, their status, and when they were last updated on the subscriber's television screen. Network operators can also use true Webcasting to download software upgrades over a broadband digital network to the set-top box.

SUMMARY . . . .

Over the past couple of years, the Internet has become an inescapable part of our lives. It has been around in one form or another since the late 1960s. In the last few years, it has caught the imagination of millions of people around the world with the number of people connecting to the Internet doubling every six months. To people involved in the digital TV business, the Internet is a huge opportunity. For any device such as a digital set-top box to be considered as Web connectable, it must use a protocol called Transmission Control Protocol/Internet Protocol (TCP/IP). The TCP/IP suite of communications protocols will be at the heart of the broadband networks of the future. TCP/IP is implemented on all types of computers and digital set-top boxes. Once you are connected to the Internet, you can access thousands of computers throughout the world. The Internet's best-known feature is the World Wide Web (the Web). The terms Internet and Web are sometimes used interchangeably, but they are not synonymous. The Web is a global hypertext system that uses the Internet as its transport system. The Web presents rich content, including text, graphics, and multimedia clips. Digital TV subscribers can view this wealth of information by using a set-top browser and a standard TV screen. There are four major components associated with an end-to-end TV browsing application:

1. a browser for displaying content on a television screen;
2. a Web server to listen and respond to requests;
3. a proxy server to improve performance and optimize for a television environment; and
4. a high-speed physical connection to the Internet.

E-mail is another Internet application, which has been adopted by the world of digital television. This application allows a subscriber to use his or her digital set-top box in conjunction with a wireless keyboard to send a message to anyone connected to the Internet. The message can contain a combination of text and embedded graphical images. For groups of people with similar interests, a set-top online application is an ideal and cheap communication system. It can exist as a standalone application or else can be integrated with the set-top browser. Webcasting is a generic term used in referring to the automated delivery of personalized and up-to-date information via a broadband TV network.

8 Set-top Intranet Applications

In this chapter...

Over the past few years, many organizations have been setting up their own world-wide networks to link remote offices. Some of these companies use a wide variety of expensive wide area networking technologies. Not only was this strategy very costly, it also had many limitations, such as users not being able to instantly share data. Companies tried to get around the problem using various strategies, but they were still locked into a closed and expensive set of proprietary technologies. The arrival of the World Wide Web changed everything, in particular, the way information could be distributed between people. This new model of distribution of data fueled the growth of a new type of network—an Intranet.

Intranets are private local networks with Web-based technology and access to the Internet. Although an Intranet has access to the Internet, the Intranet itself is accessible only to employees of the company or corporation where it resides. By now you are wondering what corporate Intranets have to do with digital set-top boxes and high speed TV networks. As in the world of information technology, we are seeing cable, MMDS, satellite, and terrestrial TV operators setting up the next generation of high speed Intranets. In this chapter, we will learn about the basic concepts of an Intranet and gain insight into the types of applications that can be deployed on these futuristic networks.

ABOUT INTRANETS . . . .

Intranets can be defined as private networks based on the following standard Web technologies and protocols:

1. TCP/IP for transferring information across the network.
2. HTML for publishing and viewing internal documents.
3. SMTP for sending and receiving e-mails.
4. HTTP for retrieving Web pages from Web servers.

Intranets are normally owned and controlled by organizations and are not accessible to users on the Internet. They make extensive use of Web servers and browsers to deliver mission-critical information between various departments. Intranets can be deployed quite quickly because they are based on open Internet standards. Broadcasters worldwide are looking to maximize the opportunities that a large digital broadband network can offer. The deployment of a variety of software applications and services on these high-speed networks provides a solution to their requests. In this book, we use the term "Intranet" to describe these networks because they are owned and controlled by a variety of network service providers.

CHOICE OF BROADBAND INTRANET APPLICATIONS . . . .

The types of applications running within a company's broadband Intranet can be broadly classified into two main categories: client-server interactive applications and TV broadcast services. These categories can be further divided into several subcategories (see Figure 8.1).

The set-top client-server applications are divided into home banking, e-commerce, education, gaming, weather, and services not yet dreamed about. From the diagram, we can see that TV broadcast services are divided into electronic program guides, Pay Per View, near video-on- demand, video-on-demand, teletext, and parental control.

Client/Server Computing

Once connected to the broadband network, set-tops interact with the head-end equipment using the client-server-computing model. Under this model, the processing tasks involved in running an interactive TV application are intelligently divided between a client set-top box and one or more servers. The bulk of back-end processing tasks, such as accessing databases and retrieving rich multimedia applications, are performed by the servers.

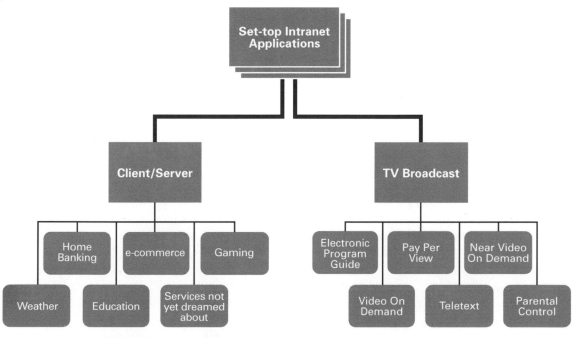

Figure 8.1
Categories of broadband Intranet applications

A *server* is a computer that provides a single service to a large group of users and manages network resources, such as file and application sharing. A computer used as a server is usually dedicated solely to this role, performing no other tasks. Consequently, servers need a lot of processing power, fast I/O systems, and large amounts of storage space. A server typically has several storage devices connected to it. These devices include hard drives, CD-ROM drives, and tape backup drives. Because a server's main function is to provide a service to clients, they don't need hardware components to support technologies such as multimedia. For that reason, many servers have only rudimentary sound and video capabilities. The memory, storage space, and processing power of servers varies greatly, depending on the needs of the network service provider. Entry-level servers, for example, are typically used for less resource-intensive applications. These servers can cope with low to medium levels of set-top user requests. However, they may become overloaded by high levels of customer requests, or by being used for processor-intensive set-top Intranet applications. An entry-level server will have one or two processors, depending on the application for which it's intended. Due to their limited hardware resources, entry-level servers can only be used in a digital environment with a subscriber base of less than 25,000 set-top users. If a service provider requires servers with greater processing abilities, then serious consideration needs to be given to the installation of mid-range servers at the head-end. Mid-range servers are more reliable than their entry-level counterparts because they include redundant components such as power supplies and hot-swappable hard drives. *Hot-swappable drives* are those that can be installed in or removed from a server in the head-end without having to shut it down. In addition, they typically have two processors and include support for dual processing. Support for dual processing basically means that running a program can be split across the available processors in the server. This improves the performance of both the TV-based applications and the system in general. Mid-range servers support a larger amount of disk storage than entry-level servers do. Their dual processing capabilities, combined with larger amounts of disk storage, makes them suitable for digital Intranets with between 25,000 and 100,000 digital TV subscribers.

For operators with a subscriber base greater than 100,000 subscribers, a high-end server is a more appropriate choice than its lower-specification counterparts. To deliver multimedia-rich set-top applications to a subscriber base of this size requires the installation of a server or a number of servers with very large disk capacities and vast amounts of memory and processing power. So a typical high-end server has at least four processors, at least one gigabyte of memory, and several terabytes of storage space for video-on-demand applications. A terabyte is approximately 1 trillion bytes. High-end servers have even greater reliability than that available with entry and mid-range servers. To achieve this, they support all the reliability techniques used by both types of servers. And they support a greater number of hot-swappable components.

Unlike a server, set-top clients don't need to provide the same high level of reliability as servers. Because many customers on a digital network depend on a server to carry out its functions, it should be practically 100 percent fault tolerant. If a set-top box fails, only one household is affected. As the demand for set-top applications increase over time, additional servers may be added to the broadband network. Spreading the processing of set-top requests among several servers ensures that all requests from customers will be performed in the most efficient manner possible.

Client set-top boxes handle the front-end processing tasks of a TV application, such as interacting with the customer. They rely on network connectivity and control because they have minimal or no local storage capabilities. As a result, data that would be normally stored on a client is more likely to be kept on the server. This applies to types of data such as favorite Web sites, e-mail, and personal financial information. Depending on the hardware capabilities of the set-top box, the client application can be resident in ROM or else dynamically downloaded over the network into RAM.

Among the most important applications run by client/server systems are database applications. In general, a database application system deployed in a digital TV environment has four distinct parts:

- a client program;
- database connectivity software;
- a database management system (DBMS); and
- a database.

The client program running in the set-top box acts as the front end to the customer. Traditionally, this client was constructed using vendor-specific proprietary languages, which meant the client program was dependent on a particular software platform. Today, network operators are beginning to deploy Intranet applications based on open Web standards. Consequently, proprietary-based clients are being replaced with standard set-top Web browsers. Browser-based clients will run without modification on different set-top real-time operating systems, thereby platform-independent.

The main purpose of the client program is to gather customer input. If the client set-top box is using a browser, then standard HTML forms are normally used to collect information. The client program then interacts with the head-end using the digital TV network as a means of connection. The database connectivity software is used to pass the data gathered by the client back to the physical database.

Simply put, a database is a collection of information organized in such a way that an individual or a software program can easily extract certain pieces of data. Databases organize data into fields, records, and files. A *field* is a single piece of information, such as a product description. A *record* is one complete set of fields, for example, the name, description, price, and code for a single product. A *file* is a collection of records, such as a video store's list of all products in stock.

A database can contain one record or millions of records. The amount and type of data involved is irrelevant, as long as the information is organized according to a strict predefined set of rules. Databases are sometimes described as electronic filing systems. Most database vendors nowadays support a variety of complex data types such as graphics, animations, and video clips. Databases are controlled via a database management system (DBMS), a collection of programs whose main function is to control and manipulate databases. Additionally, it allows application programs running on the set-top box to change, update, delete, and sort data records. A DBMS must also ensure the integrity of the data it stores.

The most popular kind of DBMS used in the commercial world is the relational database management system (RDBMS), often referred to as relational databases. The majority of databases used to support advanced Intranet set-top applications are based on RDBMS technologies. The term "relational" refers to the way a DBMS organizes information internally. The internal organization affects the speed and flexibility with which information can be retrieved. A relational database stores information in the form of multiple tables made up of rows, where each row represents a record. The format of records can vary from table to table.

Individual tables relate to one another through keywords or values. Programs accessing the database do not have to know about links between records and how and where the data is stored. Information stored in one particular table can be accessed through one or more of the other tables based on the "relationship" established within the database. RDBMS-based applications use a standard high-level language called Structured Query Language (SQL) for manipulating the database. SQL (pronounced "sequel") allows users to retrieve data by creating appropriate queries on the database. SQL is a powerful method of retrieving information from a database. Some well-known database technologies include:

- Microsoft SQL Server;
- Oracle 8i;
- Informix Workgroup Server; and
- Sybase Server.

We suggest thorough exploration of all these database products before making a selection. A typical digital TV client/server system includes one or more server-based database management systems (DBMSs) connected to a large number of set-top clients. The most popular client/server applications being currently developed and implemented by network operators are as follows.

Set-top Home Banking

For the past 10 years, evangelists have predicted that home banking would revolutionize the way we pay bills and access financial accounts. In fact, financial institutions were turning their attention to the concept of home banking as far back as the 1970s. The most popular approach to home banking was the use of the touch-tone telephone. This enabled customers to check account balances, transfer money funds, and pay bills. Despite the initial optimism about the system, home banking via the touch-tone phone never really took off. The main reasons for this included the lack of visual verification for the consumer, and the fact that many households did not have push-button phones in the 1970s.

Cable television (CATV) was the second medium to be considered. This also turned out to be a largely unsuccessful system for delivering home banking to the mass population because the networks lacked two-way communications. With the advent of the PC in the early 1980s, banks quickly turned their focus to developing expensive homegrown systems. The bank's proprietary software was installed on the customer's PC. This communicated with the bank's server through a standard modem and telephone line.

Virtually without exception, these proprietary systems failed to meet analyst's expectations and were either scaled back or abandoned entirely. The slow take-up of home banking using a PC in the 1980s and early 1990s has been attributed to the following reasons:

- Banks were unable to attract enough customers to break even.
- The software was cumbersome and difficult to use.
- The communications link between the PC and the mainframe was extremely slow.

In today's economic climate, home banking within the mass consumer market is finally becoming a reality because:

- People nowadays are working longer hours and are leading more diverse lifestyles than previous years. They are no longer satisfied with traditional methods of banking, buying and selling stocks, securing loans, and dealing with other financial necessities. Customers are demanding flexibility, service and convenience in dealing with their finances.
- Media attention is increasingly turning to the area of home banking. This makes consumers more aware of the alternatives to traditional methods of banking. The current high degree of awareness means that consumers are increasingly demanding more from their banks.
- Due to technology advances, an online banking solution can be designed and deployed more cost effectively than the proprietary systems of only a few years ago.

The delivery of online banking services is an extremely lucrative business, with competition intensifying in the following areas of home banking.

Home finance-based systems • To use off-the-shelf home finance products for online banking, the customer needs to install a dedicated financial software package on their PC. The leading competitors in the home finance software market are Intuit, with Quicken, and Microsoft, with Microsoft Money.

Web-based banking • Because many consumers today are familiar with the Internet, banking on the Web has a very good chance of success. Banking via the Web means customers can carry out transactions anywhere in the world, as long as they have access to a PC. They don't need any extra software, a Web browser is sufficient. Many traditional banks are now offering Web-based banking services. An Internet bank customer can enjoy 24-hour access to financial services, 365 days a year.

Set-top-based banking • The Cable and digital TV network operators are poised to become a major player in the home-banking arena this year. Entrance into this vast market will be facilitated through a number of revenue-sharing partnerships and the launch of set-top boxes capable of supporting easy-to-use home banking applications. The deployment of a set-top home banking system on a digital TV network poses enormous opportunities for subscribers and TV operators. The benefits for subscribers include the ability to use a digital set-top box in combination with a television set to carry out the following financial activities 24 hours a day, 7 days a week:

1. making loan repayments;
2. transferring money between bank accounts;
3. determining payment schedules;
4. completing credit card and loan applications;
5. safely paying bills;
6. reviewing statement activity;
7. accessing up-to-date account information; and
8. e-mailing banks.

From a network operator's perspective, the benefits include improved customer satisfaction and additional revenue streams through targeted marketing campaigns. One of the biggest concerns about home banking has always been the overall security of the system and the protection of sensitive transaction data. A set-top banking application addresses these security issues by combining various encryption technologies with digital certificates to ensure financial information transferred between the customer and the banking server is protected from prying eyes. The easiest way to understand how a set-top banking application operates on a broadband digital cable TV network is to look at an example. Suppose a cable company chooses to offer its customers a home banking service. The following steps follow the flow of information as it travels between the digital TV customer and the banking application (see Figure 8.2 for a graphical illustration):

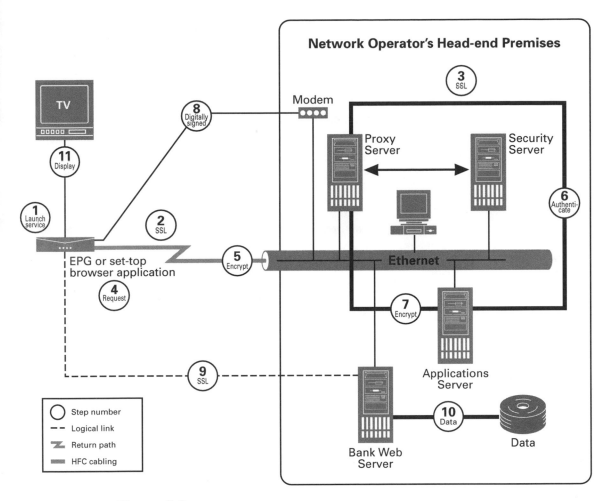

Figure 8.2
Flow of messages within a set-top banking application

1. The customer will normally use either their program guide or a set-top browser to launch the home banking service.

2. The set-top application opens a secure session with the head-end proxy and security servers based on the SSL cryptography standard.

3. The proxy server will then open an SSL session with the server hosting the network operator's applications.

4. The subscriber makes a request to run the banking application.

5. This request is encrypted and forwarded over the digital network to the proxy and security server.

6. The request is authenticated, re-encrypted, and forwarded directly to the operator's applications server.

7. The application server encrypts the banking application and forwards to the head-end proxy and security servers.

8. The head-end proxy and security servers decrypt the application, signs using the operator's digital certificate, and then sends back to the set-top client.

9. The set-top client decrypts the information and now opens a direct SSL connection to the bank Web server (such as Microsoft IIS or Lotus Domino).

10. The Web server retrieves the requested financial information from the local database and responds by sending the private data back to the set-top box.

11. The set-top interprets the requested data and displays it on the television set for customer viewing.

Set-top E-commerce

Electronic commerce (e-commerce) is the term used to define the process of buying and selling goods on the Internet. Conducting business in this manner means that an organization does not even need a physical retail outlet. A customer wishing to make a purchase on the Internet can simply access an organization's Web site. They can then browse through the products available or search for a particular product using various keywords. When a customer decides to buy a product or service, they fill out a purchasing form online and it is sent electronically back to the e-commerce store. Online shopping is one of the fastest-growing markets in modern business. Over the next several years, Internet-based e-commerce will undergo phenomenal growth. According to forecasts by independent research groups, electronic commerce will garner more than $300 billion worth of transactions annually by the year 2002, up from $8 billion in 1997. E-commerce not only makes shopping easy; it also drives prices down. In effect, customers are able to order directly from the source. This new model of purchasing goods and services presents network operators with a compelling new business opportunity. The main drivers behind the growth of e-commerce in the digital TV world include:

- Few cable operators, broadcasters, satellite, and MMDS providers can afford to pass up the opportunity of growing revenue streams and profits through the deployment of advanced e-commerce applications.

- Customer's attitudes are changing. Today, many consumers prefer online shopping because of the convenience, reach and availability of products and services.

- E-commerce improves advertising revenues and attracts new digital TV subscribers.
- The rising levels of expectations on the part of customers are beginning to put pressure on network operators to begin offering e-commerce services.
- The deployment of set-top e-commerce applications provides a competitive advantage and positions the company for future growth.

With a set-top e-commerce Intranet application, digital TV subscribers can use a standard remote control to browse, select, and securely purchase goods from various electronic storefronts through their televisions.

The building of an e-commerce store on a broadband TV network represents a significant investment in time and resources. Consequently, network operators are establishing revenue-sharing partnerships with existing online merchants. In this new e-commerce business model, the network operator is responsible for the underlying infrastructure and the merchant takes care of all the back-end order and payment processing requirements. Payment is at the heart of all transactions, and like conventional commerce, purchasing goods or services on a digital TV network has a variety of payment mechanisms. Subscribers can use electronic cash (e-cash) and credit cards.

E-Cash

Electronic cash, also known as e-cash or electronic purse, is a form of payment system that allows subscribers to perform large and small commercial transactions over the digital TV network. An effective e-cash system needs to have the following properties:

- It must be safe from counterfeiting and any unwanted forms of duplication.
- It allows subscribers to exchange digital cash when and wherever they want.
- It must be secure.
- E-cash systems need to incorporate measures to prevent and detect double spending. Double spending is similar to bouncing a check in the real world. It occurs when somebody tries to use the same e-cash to buy goods more than once.

At present, there are three main categories of e-cash initiatives, these are: anonymous cash, Micro-payments, and Smart cards.

Traditional methods of cash payment using cash is anonymous because a subscriber can spend cash anywhere in the world without having to provide any form of identification. Digital cash attempts to provide a level of anonymity to consumers who want to electronically purchase goods or services.

You would normally use coins when making small payments in the real world.

A *micro-payment* allows consumers to use small denominations of digital cash to make a small payment, similar to using coins in the real world. Micro-payments are generally less than $5 or $10. Payments that small are generally not economical for a merchant and service provider to handle via credit card.

In an interactive TV environment, micro-payments are ideal for online vending machines that provide such services as games, gambling, and entertainment, and require very low-cost and small denomination payments of digital cash. This method of payment is becoming popular for network operators because the transaction costs to both the operator and the subscriber are very low. In Europe, Smart cards are the most popular method of payment within a digital TV environment. They have a certain amount of cash stored electronically in them. And they contain silicon chips that deduct the amount needed for a particular purchase and transfer it to the merchant that sells the goods or services. Most digital set-top boxes include a Smart card reader that allows network operators to download cash over the broadband network to the card. Some well-known e-cash systems currently on the market include: Mondex, CyberCash, ECash, Millicent Micropayments, and OpenMarket.

Credit Cards

Using a credit card to make a purchase over a digital TV network is similar to credit card purchasing in the real world. There are three main categories of credit card payments:

1. plain, unencrypted credit card payments;
2. encrypted credit card payments; and
3. electronic wallets.

The most basic method of making a credit card payment is when a subscriber decides to purchase a particular product and submits raw payment details across the network to the merchant located at the head-end. Sending unencrypted credit card details across the digital network is not secure because any hacker can identify the subscriber's credit card number and bank account details and use them for their own purchases.

The second system of credit card payment uses encryption technology. The credit card details are encrypted when a consumer submits the information into the set-top e-commerce application. The details are then sent from the subscriber to the merchant as an encrypted message.

The third and final category of credit card payment involves the use of electronic wallets. The wallet is located on the set-top box, which sends the encrypted credit card details through the merchant to a trusted processor. The financial details are validated and authenticated by the online processor and are passed on to the subscriber's bank for authorized approval.

The easiest way to understand how a set-top e-commerce application operates on a broadband digital TV network is to look at an example. Let's take a simple consumer-to-business transaction, such as a subscriber using their credit card to order a CD from the e-commerce application. The purchasing process, illustrated in Figure 8.3, is described by the following steps:

1. The set-top box will need to be provisioned with an IP address.
2. The subscriber will normally use either their program guide or a set-top browser to launch the set-top's e-commerce application.
3. A full screen catalog containing text and multimedia information on every item is presented onscreen.
4. The user navigates the catalog of items and decides to order a particular item. In this example, the customer orders the latest U2 album.
5. The set-top client establishes an SSL connection with the merchant's server.
6. The subscriber uses the set-top wireless keyboard to enter payment and shipping information to initiate the purchase process.
7. The merchant's server, located in the network operator's head-end, receives the purchase request and returns a summary of the order to the set-top.
8. Details of the order, including the price of the CD, credit card number, shipping address, and order number are displayed on the television screen.
9. The subscriber verifies the information and uses the remote control to select the "PAY" button. Once this button is selected, the information is sent back to the merchant server.
10. Naturally, the merchant server will not have direct access to the subscriber's account details, so it requests the information from its financial institution.
11. Prior to forwarding the request, the merchant server carries out the following tasks:
    - strips away the order details;
    - encrypts the customer financial information;
    - digitally signs the data; and
    - reformats the data and sends it via a leased line to the financial institution.
12. At the financial institution, a transaction server receives the request and passes it on to a database server.
13. The database server accesses a database of credit card accounts, and retrieves data relating to that credit card number.

14. If the financial institution doesn't have direct access to a credit card database, it may send the information on to another institution or banking network such as Visa, Diner's Club, Access, American Express, or Mastercard.

15. The bank's database server then sends a request to the credit card database to debit the customer's account. Similarly, it sends a request to

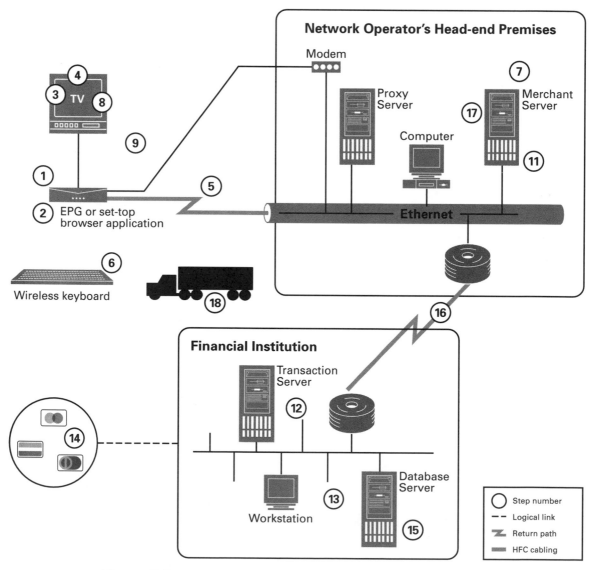

Figure 8.3
Example of set-top e-commerce transaction

its own customer account database to credit the CD store's account with the relevant amount.

16. Once the financial transactions are complete at the bank, an approval or denial code is returned to the merchant system located in the head-end.

17. Provided the subscriber's details are correct, the merchant server will activate the other necessary business processes such as inventory, accounting, and fulfillment.

18. When these are complete, the subscriber's order is processed, and the U2 CD is delivered.

This type of purchasing procedure ensures that the actual credit card number is never transmitted to the merchant, so there is no chance of credit card theft at the merchant's end. When described in such detail, the CD transaction may seem like a lengthy process, but remember, it takes place mainly without any form of human intervention. For the most part, the transaction is processed automatically by server applications, making it a speedy, reliable, and efficient way of doing business on a high-speed digital network. Many of the merchants end the transaction with a confirmation message that is returned to the subscriber as a page in their set-top browser. This helps to reassure the digital TV customer that their order has been received. Some merchants also send an e-mail of the order and give an expected delivery date.

Set-top Education

All areas of education, including, primary, secondary and third level education, will be moving into a new dimension in the twenty-first century. The ability of cable operators, terrestrial, satellite, and MMDS providers to deliver a wide range of multimedia content a thousand times faster than traditional telecommunication connections will dramatically alter the existing education model. Much of the change will be realized through the deployment of sophisticated set-top educational applications. These applications will help to create virtual classrooms, where students in different schools and countries interact and learn as naturally as if they were in the same room. The benefits to society of introducing a set-top educational service include equal access to education in rural and inner-city areas and the availability of a national curriculum to all parts of a country. This all seems to be a reasonably straightforward set-top application. It will appear very simple for consumers who use the application, but a great deal of planning and design must go into the head-end systems to bring this exciting application to life. Figure 8.4 shows the architecture of a typical end-to-end set-top educational application within an MMDS environment.

Essentially, the application is comprised of a browser or resident program running in the set-top box, a database server that stores the various educational programs, and a broadcast server for managing and injecting the requested data into the MPEG video stream.

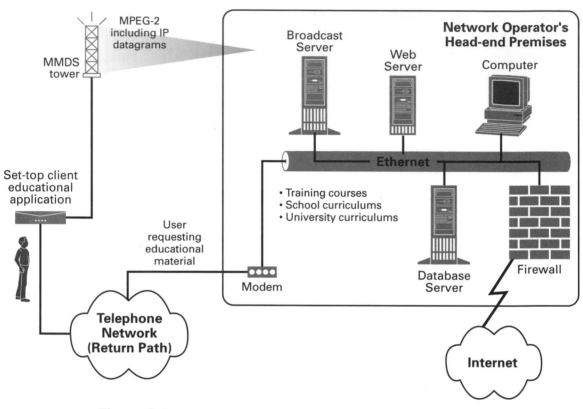

Figure 8.4
Architecture of set-tops educational application

In addition to moving toward offering a range of new educational services to digital TV subscribers, some network operators in Ireland are looking at the concept of expanding this educational model into areas like health and social care. For example, customers could use their set-tops and television monitors to pay a fee and access specialists anywhere in the world.

Set-top Gaming

Over the past couple of years, industry analysts have suggested that online interactive games would become the next killer application on the Internet. To a large extent, these predictions have never materialized due to bandwidth constraints.

With the deployment of high capacity digital networks, the promise of multi-user network games will finally become a reality for the critical mass market. The introduction of a video game service on a broadband network is relatively cheap and easy when compared to the implementation of an e-commerce or banking application.

Network operators can create a dedicated games channel. The lists of games contained within the channel are accessed using a standard set-top box and a remote control. Figure 8.5 illustrates the primary system components of a set-top gaming application.

The role of each one of these components is briefly outlined in the following paragraphs.

Broadcast server • This server is responsible for injecting or inserting the gaming application into the digital MPEG-2 transport stream.

Games application server • This server is used to store the programming code of the various games that are available to subscribers.

Set-top box with resident games application • Once the subscriber switches to the games channel, the application is downloaded by the server into the set-top box. If the set-top box has enough memory, the application can be stored locally. The gaming application graphically displays the list of games available on the channel. The subscriber can then select a favorite game by pressing a button on the remote control. The request is forwarded over the modem to the head-end servers. Once the request has been authorized, the set-top box is transformed into a powerful game console with the remote control acting like a wireless joystick. Some software companies optimize their gaming programs for set-top boxes so that 100 percent of hardware resources are devoted to playing the game. Such a design can enhance the overall customer experience of the gaming service.

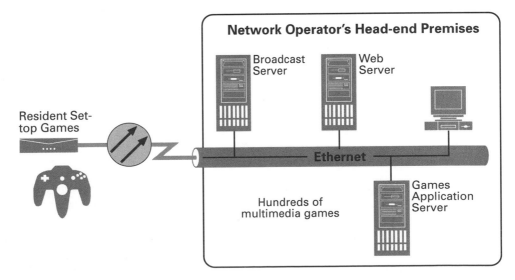

Figure 8.5
Set-top gaming application architecture

Set-top Weather

The weather application allows TV viewers to check the latest local or World weather conditions on a regular basis. The weather application normally works in conjunction with a dedicated weather channel. Once launched, the set-top weather application allows a subscriber to select a particular geographical region and view the following types of information:

- high and low temperatures for the day,
- expected rainfall levels,
- detailed weather maps,
- humidity levels,
- wind speeds, and
- times of sunrise and sunset.

TV BROADCAST SERVICES . . . .

Electronic Program Guides

Since digital television brings into the home many more channels and services than were previously available in the analog system, people need a way of navigating the myriad of choices. An application that does this is typically referred to as an electronic program guide (EPG). It is an onscreen navigation tool that gives the viewer easy access to TV programming information. An EPG's primary function is to provide the viewer with an overview of the programming currently available, as well the ability to browse upcoming television programs. They can include seven full days of program information for every channel and detailed descriptions of every program within each channel. In addition, subscribers are able to search by genre, programme title, channel, and even time. Viewers can use their EPG to prepurchase PPV events up to 14 days in advance of the broadcast. Some of the more powerful ones that are being developed by AT&T in the United States will incorporate Internet functions such as browsing, e-mail, and online chat.

An EPG is free of charge and when a customer turns on their digital set-top box, the opening page of the EPG appears on their television screen. This makes the space on an EPG screen a prime location for advertisers who want to sell products and services. Because the amount of TV real estate is slim, operators need to make the balance between promotional material and EPG data. Too many advertisements will only discourage subscribers of using the EPG. The EPG is the most popular application of all the TV broadcast services; consequently, we have decided to allocate our next chapter wholly to this complex subject.

Interactive Channel Browser

This TV browser application is a simple navigation tool that displays each broadcast channel within a small window (stamp size) on the TV screen. The subscriber is able to use the arrows on their remote control to move from one window to the next. Each time a window is selected, the set-top box will play the sound associated with the particular channel. In addition to sound, the set-top will also display channel information, including title and beginning and ending times. By simply pressing the OK or Enter button on their remote control, the window extends to the full length and width of the television screen. You need only to sit back and watch the channel in comfort.

Pay Per View (PPV)

A PPV system only allows authorized users to watch an event, such as a movie or a football game. Ordering a PPV event can only take place within a designated time window. The window deployed by most operators opens a couple of weeks before the event start time and ends 10 minutes after the event starts. Placing an order outside this window will result in either no event or the wrong event being ordered.

The PPV application is resident either in the ROM component of the set-top box or else is downloaded from the network into RAM. A relatively low-grade set-top box is needed to access and run PPV applications. It allows subscribers to view movies at scheduled start times. The viewer will normally use either their program guide or a set-top browser to launch the application. Operators can also configure the PPV application to start automatically when a PPV movie or event is detected on one of the PPV channels.

The viewer is then prompted for a secret Personal Identification Number (PIN). Once an accurate code has been entered, a new screen appears on the television and a secure connection is established between the set-top modem and a communications server located at the operator's head-end. The PPV screen contains different menus that allow the viewer to look for events on the current day, the week ahead, or two months ahead. The look and feel of the menu screen layout is customizable and is unique to each service provider.

Once an event is selected, an order is placed using the set-top modem and the rights to watch the event are returned to the viewer within 30 seconds of the request. The PPV application allows customers to pay for the event either, using a pre-arranged credit (electronic tokens) that are stored on the Smart card or else using a standard bankcard, located in the second Smart card reader. Advanced PPV set-top applications allow subscribers to preview events and movies.

PPV applications can operate in two different modes:

Impulse PPV (IPPV) • This mode of PPV operation allows digital TV subscribers to use their digital set-top boxes to purchase electronic tokens directly from the network provider. A section of the Smart card called the electronic wallet is used to store and manage the purchased tokens. The subscriber can then use these electronic tokens to impulsively purchase PPV events without using the return channel. Once an event is purchased, the quantity of tokens contained within the wallet will be decremented by the amount of tokens that are related to the purchased event. Some operators can also use this system to implement a type of credit system, whereby a customer would be able to purchase PPV events, even if the number of tokens stored in the wallet were not sufficient. Once the customer exceeds a predefined credit limit, the operator will accordingly bill the customer for the amount that is due. A simple telephone call to the local service provider is normally required to refresh the tokens stored on the Smart card. Most IPPV systems also support a report back or call back feature. This feature ensures that operators automatically receive accurate information about subscriber's IPPV purchases. The Smart card uses the modem built into the set-top box to send the information back to the operator at predefined times (i.e., at the end of every month).

Pre-booked PPV • This mode of PPV operation allows digital TV subscribers to book upcoming events in advance. A pre-book event can be placed not only for a single broadcast event, but also for multiple PPV events. Traditional methods of order-

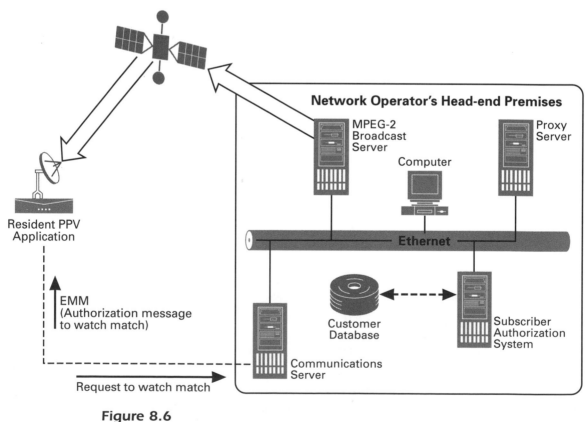

Figure 8.6
Pre-booked PPV system

ing a PPV event included calling the operator's customer service department or dialing an automated voice server using a touch-tone phone. This, however, is changing with demands coming from customers and subscribers to automate the order and payment process. Such a requirement is met through the use of the return path.

The easiest way to understand how a set-top PPV application operating in pre-booked mode uses the return path to order an upcoming PPV event is to look at an example (illustrated in Figure 8.6).

Suppose a digital TV subscriber wants to book an international soccer game a week in advance. He browses the PPV listings through the onscreen EPG and selects a soccer game, Ireland versus England, for example. The in-built modem will then establish a two-way connection between the communications server in the head-end and the set-top box. The PPV request is sent via the modem and communications server back to the Subscriber Authorization System (SAS). The SAS then forwards the request to the billing system for verification. Once verification has been received, the SAS will use the return path to send the entitlement (EMM) required by the subscriber to watch the game. When the game is about begin, a reminder will appear on the customer's television informing him that the game is about to commence.

As you can see from our example, a PPV application running in this mode is completely automated and requires no staff involvement. The mode of operation chosen by operators often depends on marketing strategies and the overall business model for the new digital TV services.

Video on demand

Video on demand (VOD) is a hot topic in the world of digital TV. A VOD system enables an individual customer to demand a program or movie when and where they want it. VOD obviates the need to make a trip to a video rental store. A highspeed network is required to deliver digital-quality programming and sophisticated multimedia content to subscribers in real-time. Cable companies, satellite providers, and wireless broadcasters are currently developing such networks across the globe.

The primary components of a VOD system is illustrated in Figure 8.7.

As we can see from the diagram, the VOD system is based on a client/server-computing model. At the head-end, a large database of movies is stored on a powerful video server. The size and capabilities of the video server varies from supplier to supplier, however, popular servers currently on the marketplace will support most of the following hardware features:

- Fault tolerant hard disk technology that is capable of storing up to 5,000 GB of on-demand movies.
- Multiple dedicated I/O processors.

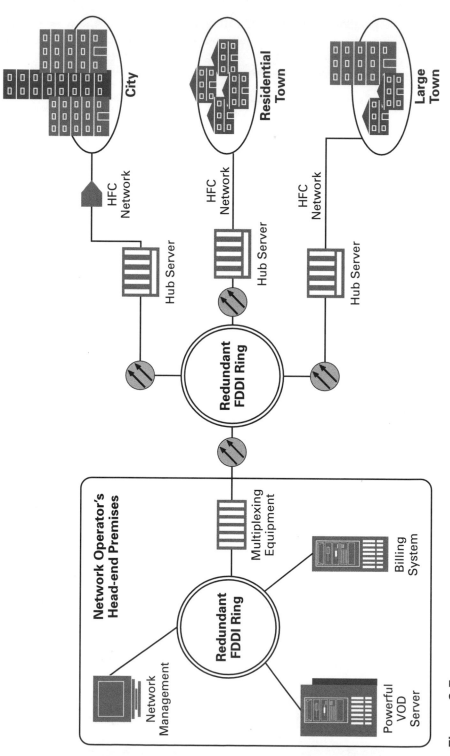

Figure 8.7
VOD system architecture

- Redundant PCI bus architecture.
- 2000 MPEG streams that allow a server to simultaneously serve up to 20,000 VOD customers.
- High capacity network interfaces that efficiently connect the server to remote hub sites.
- Scaleable hardware architecture to meet a growing customer base.

From the diagram we can also see that the video server located at the head-end is connected via a Fibre Distributed Data Interface (FDDI) ring to a number of hub servers located throughout the broadband cable network. These hub servers in turn use an HFC network to directly deliver multimedia-rich VOD titles to customers in towns and cities across a particular geographical area. Interfaces to the billing system are also needed to charge the customer for movie purchases. On the client side, the subscriber uses an eloquently simple VOD application to select and download specific movies. VCR-like controls, including pause, fast-forward, and rewind, are provided with the set-top application. Many of the VOD clients currently available have small hardware requirements and are customizable using the HTML programming language. The time between confirming a video purchase and video play is in the order of two to three seconds. If a hard drive is installed in the set-top box, the subscriber can store, play, fast forward, and rewind the movie at will.

Near Video on Demand

NVOD refers to a system that starts the same program on a different channel with a time interval between start times (e.g., every 15 minutes). A fully implemented NVOD system allows subscribers to easily choose the viewing time and day that suits them. With NVOD, cable subscribers have the convenience of renting a video without leaving their home. An end-to-end NVOD system is comprised of a number of powerful servers that are used to store, schedule, and deliver full motion video content. The subscriber then uses a simple onscreen menu to select a convenient viewing time to watch a particular TV event. At the specified time, the set-top box automatically tunes to the appropriate channel and begins decoding the TV event. The servers that are used to build NVOD systems are similar to the computers used in VOD systems.

Teletext

Teletext is the generic name for a system that broadcasts information as pages of text alongside the standard television signal. Although the use of the Web has increased rapidly over the past three years, there are many thousands of people who use teletext services to access the following types of information resources:

- Financial transactions—including budgets, interest rates, currencies and share prices.
- Sports—including results of football, soccer, golf, horse races, and tennis.
- Travel—information on flights, ferries, buses, special deals, and traffic reports.
- Weather—including local, national weather reports, humidity levels, temperatures, and rainfall levels.
- Entertainment—including cinemas, restaurants, music, and theater details.
- Jobs—including employment and contact details.
- News—including local, national, and international.

Teletext services are very popular in many countries. In the U.K. for example, almost 60 percent of homes have a TV that is capable of processing teletext services. Viewers are very familiar with the convenience of obtaining up-to-date information from teletext pages on their television screens. The teletext information is accommodated within the standard television signal. Teletext information is comprised of standard text combined with limited amounts of graphics.

The BBC and Oracle introduced the first teletext systems into the U.K. in the 1970s. A page on this teletext system used only 8 different colors and displayed 24 different lines of text on the television screen. The size of the page was only one kilobyte, therefore TVs only required a small amount of memory for each page. Even though the size of the teletext page is very small, accessing a page can be slow because the teletext information is transmitted in a sequential basis. A new version of this original system was launched in 1997 with improved graphics, more colors, and new features. Nowadays, broadcasters are planning to use digital TV technology to introduce enhanced teletext services. Teletext on digital TV offers 256 colors, scrollable menus, smoother graphics, and a range of new fonts. Teletext pages can be accessed faster than their analog predecessors and there will be more sophisticated links between pages. The new system will also have the ability to display multimedia images and text. Additionally, digital Teletext opens up the following range of possibilities for advertisers and network operators:

- The ability to broadcast in 256 colors with rich multimedia graphics means that advertisers are able to enhance the appearance of their banner adverts.
- The presence of a return path within a digital set-top box will encourage consumers to respond positively to a large number of advertisements.
- Digital interactive applications such as teletext offer network operators a powerful revenue opportunity.
- It will also encourage and develop brand loyalty.

In an analog teletext system, a viewer accesses information using a standard remote control to select a three-figure number on the screen. In a digital teletext environment, however, subscribers use a series of pop-up menus to jump within or between key sections of the service.

Once the section of the service has been selected, the digital set-top box will retrieve the selected teletext page from the incoming video signal. At the time of writing, the deployment of digital teletext services had not got off to a great start. Broadcasters began developing their own systems, which meant that set-top boxes were unable to receive teletext services from different companies. For example, the MHEG-5 hypermedia standard has been designated as the standard authoring language for coding teletext services on the digital terrestrial platform in the U.K. Only set-top boxes with an MHEG-5 virtual machine can process and format this teletext information. Analog teletext is popular in many European countries, although it did not take off in America. Only time will tell how popular this application becomes in the digital world.

Parental Control

In addition to parental control software located at the head-end, some set-top boxes provide a service, that allows subscribers to control which programs are watched in their homes. The parental control service is accessed using a secret (PIN) code. After the subscriber enters the correct number, the parental control screen is launched. This screen will let subscribers specify what categories of program can be viewed and how much money can be spent when ordering a particular PPV movie.

Restricting access to a certain category of television programs involves highlighting the category and pressing an onscreen restrict or disallow button. A cross mark or tick will then illustrate all categories that have been restricted. Members of the family can only view programs in restricted categories if they have first entered the correct PIN number. In addition to controlling access rights to channels and programs the parental control feature also allows customers to control spending limits. For example, if a customer sets a limit of $5, only members of the household with the correct PIN number can purchase movies that cost more than $5.

As you can see, the secrecy of a PIN number is extremely important, consequently subscribers of a service provider should be advised to take the following precautions when selecting and managing a PIN number:

- Keep the PIN number a secret.
- Choose a PIN number that can be easily remembered.
- Change the PIN number every three months.

SUMMARY . . . .

Simply put, an Intranet is a private network that utilizes Internet technologies as the underlying architecture. An Intranet is built using TCP/IP, HTML, SMTP, and HTTP technologies. Intranets make use of standard Web browsers to allow new types of communication and collaboration between people.

With the enormous growth of Intranets in the corporate world, it did not take long for people in the digital TV business to recognize that components that worked so well in the computing world could be extremely valuable internally. This is why applications based on a client/server-computing model are being deployed on broadband TV networks throughout the world. Under this model, powerful servers that are designed to scale up to millions of subscribers will deliver database applications to lightweight set-top boxes. Intranet technologies allow network service providers to offer their subscribers the following client/server services:

- Home banking—In the coming years, subscribers will expect to be able to use their digital set-top boxes in conjunction with their televisions to check account balances, pay bills, transfer funds, and review transactions.

- E-commerce—The phenomena of electronic commerce has the potential to fundamentally reshape the business models associated with the TV business. Service providers will establish revenue-sharing partnerships with dot-com businesses to provide their customer bases with the ability to purchase goods and services from the comfort of their homes. Two standard payment mechanisms are expected to emerge from this new TV commerce paradigm, credit cards and e-cash. Credit cards are familiar and will be used for the purchase of relatively expensive items; e-cash will be mainly used for small purchases.

- Education—Operators hold the keys to a world where people from all classes in society have equal access to rich multimedia-based educational content.

- Games—Set-top games applications exploit cable's unique advantages of real-time, two-way broadband functionality.

- Weather—A frequently used set-top application that provides subscribers with some useful information.

In addition to delivering advanced client/server applications to subscribers of digital television, broadband Intranets also include a number of TV-centric applications:

- EPGs and channel browsers are essential tools that accompany the implementation of digital TV. It enables viewers to browse from one channel to another.

- Pay Per View allows a subscriber to order and purchase one-time events and groups of events over the phone.
- Video-on-demand gives customers instant access to hundreds of the latest Hollywood movies. Additionally, the service offers fast-forward, pause, and rewind functionality to set-top users.
- Video rental stores make vast amounts of money in renting out movies to customers. A near video-on-demand system allows a network operator to tap into this lucrative market.
- Teletext is an analog data information service that is transmitted mainly in Europe. In the digital domain, companies like the BBC have developed a new multimedia text service based on the MHEG-5 middleware standard.
- Parents will feel more comfortable with digital services if they can block their children from viewing inappropriate content. Parental control is a small but an important TV-based application that allows adults to rate programs according to content.

9 Electronic Program Guides

In this chapter...

In a new digital TV landscape that could soon include 500 digital channels and potentially millions of Internet sites, consumers need help in navigating through the myriad of options when they turn on their digital set-top box. As mentioned in the previous chapter, the tool that is most widely used by consumers to browse digital TV services is the EPG. These tools have been around a long time before the advent of digital technologies. In the U.K., the teletext service allows customers to view TV listings and has been around for years. The proliferation of PPV channels in North America in the early 1970s prompted the development of onscreen guides, which kept subscribers informed of channel line-ups. In the eighties and early nineties EPG development was limited by technological and commercial constraints, thereby many of the products that were developed had limited functionality and were purely text-based. Today, with the advent of digital technologies, we are seeing the deployment of a new breed of EPG with advanced multimedia based user interfaces and endless strings of features.

In this chapter, we take a closer look at the types of EPGs that are being deployed on broadband networks across the globe. Once you understand the types of EPGs that are available, we then take a look at how the EPG has become a key to unlocking the broadband portals of the future.

BASIC EPGs . . . .

This version of an EPGdisplays program lineup and episode information for current and future broadcast programming choices, displays the current channel contents in a window, and allows you to select a particular broadcast channel. Subscribers use the arrow keys on their remote controls to highlight and select various options. The basic EPG application normally resides in the set-top's system memory and is developed using full scale programming languages like C or C++ by the manufacturer of the box. This speeds up response times for the customer because it launches and operates immediately once the set-top is powered on. The service information (SI) within the MPEG stream is used as the data source. SI data is a standard used by broadcasters to describe the content of present and future program events. Additionally, the set-top box uses the SI data to configure and synchronize itself with the network. The SI data is always structured in table format. For network operators deploying this type of EPG, it is important to know that the speed at which customers can "zap" from program to program is related to the quality of these SI tables. For digital broadcasters, the transmission of the basic SI data stream is a mandatory requirement. The basic EPG will analyze the incoming SI stream and informs the customer about services, that can be accessed. This type of EPG is suitable for operators that are leaning toward rolling out digital services in the form of broadcast and "simple" interactive systems, and migrating to fully interactive systems at a later date.

ADVANCED EPGs ....

In addition to the features contained within the basic version, advanced EPGs can be configured to alert subscribers about the arrival of new e-mail, keep track of favorite channels, preview particular programs, and personalize TV viewing. They can also give viewers a detailed description in multiple languages of programs on offer. They could also include such features as:

- automatic video recording;
- a "reminder" service, which alerts the viewer when a selected program (or a program covering a selected topic) is about to be shown;
- restrict access to TV channels that are deemed inappropriate;
- search facilities that allow subscribers to find programs with a particular theme on a specified time or date;
- control disk storage devices in set-top boxes; and
- allow subscribers to display their favorites at the top of a menu, highlight favorite themes, or limit the number of functions that are displayed onscreen.

The user interface is fully customizable, allowing network service providers to add their own look and feel (reflecting their marketing identity). For instance, the EPG used by the WebTV set-top client is just a sophisticated Web page, so designers can change the user interface with minimum effort. The look and feel of most EPGs are based on a grid design. They are easy to read and understand with complementary color schemes that make the EPG look attractive to the viewer. Some advanced systems even allow subscribers to program the EPG to make it look the way they want it.

Typically, an EPG gives information for seven days of programs on every channel available in the MPEG digital stream. In addition to using the SI data contained within the MPEG digital stream, advanced EPGs also utilize program data from third-party TV listings companies.

Let's take a closer look at how an advanced EPG application works on a broadband digital network. The diagram in Figure 9.1 depicts the technical architecture and data flow interfaces of a complete EPG solution.

The first step in developing an advanced EPG-based service is to select a data services company that specializes in collecting information about programs and television channels.

The network operator in consultation with the data services company will then need to define the level of detail that is required for the EPG. Once the level of detail has been agreed upon, the third party will prepare the data and format it in a way that integrates with the operator's head-end. Most companies offer a wide range of pre-set file and database formats. Once the TV data has been converted to a partic-

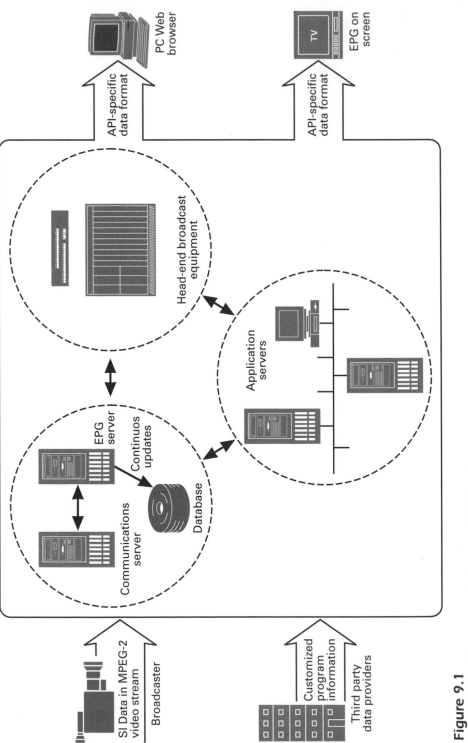

Figure 9.1
Technical architecture of advanced EPG system

ular file format, it needs to be delivered via a communications server to the head-end database servers. Currently, e-mail is the most popular option, but other mechanisms like FTP and diskettes are also being used. It is also possible to automatically deliver new or changed TV information to the head-end servers on a regular schedule. The program information is then used to update the database on the EPG server. In addition to storing program information from the data services company, this server also receives and translates SI data from the MPEG digital stream. This server interfaces with the head-end broadcast equipment to deliver program information to the EPG client application in a suitable format. The format of the data that is broadcasted to the set-top box is linked to the application software running on the operator's broadband network. For example, if the operator has chosen MediaHighway, then the EPG data that is transmitted over the broadband network needs to be in MediaHighway format.

Once the program information is received by the EPG client application, it is parsed and is displayed on the subscriber's television set or PC Web browser. It is worth highlighting that some versions of advanced EPGs do not run locally within the set-top box and are downloaded from the incoming digital broadcast stream. Broadcast-based EPGs generally require a large amount of bandwidth because the data contained within the EPG requires cyclic transmissions. This is fine for cable-based networks, but in bandwidth-constrained networks such as terrestrial, satellite, and MMDS platforms, the service provider needs to keep the advanced EPG application and accompanying multimedia data to a minimum.

One cannot describe the functionality of an advanced EPGs without making a brief reference to the subject of intellectual property rights. Gemstar, in the United States, licenses patents relating to the functionality and the look and feel of an advanced EPG. The intellectual property rights for these technologies are then licensed to companies that are involved in the development of EPGs. At the beginning of this year, Gemstar was locked in a patent infringement suit it had filed against set-top box manufacturer Scientific Atlanta. This was not the first, Gemstar had previously filed suits against General Instruments, Pioneer Electronics, and United Video Satellite Group. Gemstar holds the international patent rights on the typical guide grid design. This grid layout is familiar to most consumers, therefore most EPG developers prefer to pay the license fees rather than engage in a lengthy and expensive legal suit with Gemstar. Even Microsoft struck a licensing deal with Gemstar to allow them to have flexibility in developing EPGs for the TVPAK platform. Our next section takes a closer look at the various types of EPG layouts.

WHY EPGs LOOK THE WAY THEY DO . . . .

Before diving into future EPG developments, let's have a look at current EPG conventions. Currently, most EPGs are based on a framework of two conceptual axes: one of the axes displays the available channels, the other axis is used as a (linear) time axis. Although alternative formats, such as list-wise EPGs and Mosaic-based EPGs, are occasionally used, the most widespread form is the matrix. Generally, the EPG exists as two modes: the *zap mode* and the *full mode*.

The zap mode has the form of a partial overlay on the video; it is a more passive mode that generally looks quite modest, because in this mode the audio-visual information has the highest priority. In the full mode, however, things are the other way around: one uses this mode for more active inquiries into the program offerings. This mode is more a "pull mode."

In fact, the information to be provided in the zap mode is confined to answering the questions: "What's on now?" and "What's on next?" Preferably, the answer to these questions should also be available with either a "favorite" or a "theme" filter on, and there should be a possibility for "extended info on request" on programs of interest. The full EPG mode should support active inquiries into the program offerings. This mode should allow people to plan what to watch, tag programs for viewing/buying/ recording, and find more detailed information on a particular bouquet, service, or event. Given the current broadcast infrastructure as well as technology limitations, from a business point of view this format is quite optimal: it's a fact of life that broadcast is linear, "published" channel-wise, and tied to strict program schedules. From a usability point of view, users accept this format, since, especially in America, it closely resembles the format they were used to in the printed paper guides.

The further we progress in the digital age, however, the more the pattern described above will be overtaken.

FUTURE EPG DEVELOPMENTS . . . .

Enhanced EPG development is still in its early stages. Future EPGs will be far more sophisticated than the ones that are currently available to consumers. In this section of the book, we look at the latest EPG technologies that are being developed by Philips Electronics. Being a consumer electronics company with a stake in set-top boxes, Philips sees EPG development as a serious investment.

Philips started with digital EPG development in 1995, when EPG design was still clearly limited by technological constraints, in terms of look-and-feel as well as functional design. As for the graphics, EPGs could only be text-based, and had serious color limitations. As for the functionality, there were limitations for several reasons originating at several locations in the end-to-end chain. Now that technology limitations are mostly lifted, current EPGs face the risk of drowning in overload.

The overflow of features offered is in contradiction with the requirement to make the user feel in control. Tests show that the average user can/does use only a relatively small percentage of the functions provided by extensive EPGs. But it's not so easy for EPG providers to just cut things off, since different users appear to have different preferences, while expecting EPGs to offer extensive functionality because of the value-for-money idea.

Personalization and intelligence are two currently discernible trends that could offer a way out of the complexity. Making a shift to a richer information format could be another one. Philips Research are experimenting with these themes. At the time of going to press, the company was working on more "TV-friendly," agent-based EPGs as well as on TV-advisor systems; EPGs that know you as a user, learn from you and "talk your language." The main goal of these new technologies is to give the user an alluring and carefree TV-experience in all respects. Within this context, we will now describe two projects that are based on a number of different EPG technologies.

The Mediators (1997)

The goal of the Mediators project was to explore if and how anthropomorphic guides can aid users in selection and navigation to content in an interactive TV environment. An anthropomorphic guide is an interface that minimizes attention levels for consumers. It

Figure 9.2
An anthropomorphic interface

is used in as natural a way as possible, and provides an unambiguous three-dimensional display. A graphical image of an anthropomorphic interface is shown in Figure 9.2.

After studying a series of interfaces developed for digital TV services, the conclusion was drawn that:

1. General solutions that focused on computer-like interfaces were labeled as unacceptable to domestic television users.
2. Large quantities of EPG choices make searching, finding, and navigating to content very complex and time consuming.
3. Repeated use of the interface demands original solutions to maintain user interest and to offer ways of accommodating usage patterns and user preferences.

The conclusion of the project was that yes, users like a "TV-friendly" interface with anthropomorphic characters (since it raises engagement and simplifies navigation), but no, they should not look too much like real humans.

TV-internet EPG Project

Philips Research started this project in 1998 in an attempt to find a "TV-friendly" solution for the scenario when TV and Internet will meet. This project is still running. In this project the EPG contains, for example, an information section that is designed to be a "space" that lays out a lot of program-related information and hosts a personal TV-advisor character. Again, the character is based on agent technology: it can (a) give you an overview of programs that are of interest to you according to your personal profile, or (b) give you detailed information on a particular program, when selected.

For those users that want more detailed information, the TV-adviser (passively) provides them with this extra detail. All the objects in the screen are selectable. They are linked to more extended info. The data that is inserted into the program related information clusters (e.g., "director," "cast list," or "history") are drawn from an Internet site.

CASE STUDY ·

In 1997, Cable and Wireless Communications (CWC) embarked on an ambitious program to be the first cable provider in the U.K. to offer customers a truly interactive digital cable television service. This service would utilize the unique return path that cable provides to give consumers full interactivity through their television. This would eventually allow consumers to have access to e-mail and the Internet as well as interactive broadcasts that include multiple angle camera shots at sporting events, near video-on-demand, and play-along game shows.

It was obvious that an EPG would be the main integrator of these services. With this in mind, CWC chose to follow an open standards approach and base their interactive services on an HTML and JavaScript platform. They selected Liberate Technologies (formerly NCI), to provide their DTV Navigator platform on a set-top box that was being manufactured by Pace Electronics.

The EPG was designed to cater primarily to two groups of customers, higher educated families and younger actives. Both of these groups are seen by CWC as "best match" groups for the market factors that they were trying to cover. These included a higher than average disposable income, a high propensity toward technical products, and a high use of "similar" products like video rental.

While these groups were the target market, CWC did not want to exclude other users so CWC commissioned futura.com to research viewer reaction to the EPG and the Preview channel.

The major findings were that customers would expend extra effort to watch their favorite program. They preferred surfing to planning. They (surprisingly to CWC) liked the idea of a program grid, not considered to be a well-established way of showing information to viewers in the U.K., and they liked the idea of being able to search for programs by subject.

So CWC set about designing an EPG that had the following design principles:

- avoid alienating any users,
- easy to use,
- easy to read,
- supports TV viewing, and
- minimum steps to reach popular features.

While the primary target audience was considered to be techno-savvy, CWC wanted all users to want to use the EPG. They were, as with all EPGs, up against the very established traditional printed TV guides that consumers are used to.

This makes ease of use, ability to read, and the ability to support TV viewing while looking at listings very important.

It wasn't just the consumer/interface requirements that were driving the EPG design. CWC also had to consider the requirements that the business had. These included the usual business-type requirements like the maximization of revenue, embodiment of company and brand values, and to provide a platform for future enhanced TV programs.

On the technical side, CWC chose to follow the open standards Web-based approach using Liberate software on the client. CWC also chose to use a DVB standard back-end to deliver MPEG video and service information through the in-band stream. This leaves the out-of-band path free to deliver Web and other interactive content via an MCNS cable modem.

With all of this in mind, CWC designed an EPG that had 80 percent of the most useful functionality contained in two overlay screens that can be called up by a single button pressed while watching television.

The Now & Next bar appears each time a user changes channel, or when they specifically call it using a handset button. The most basic functions of showing what is on now and next is provided without the user having any interaction, but users can scroll down to find out what is on later, and scroll sideways to view what is showing now and later on other channels.

The other overlay is the favorite channels overlay. CWC have implemented this as a list of channels that the user can apply channel orders to. This allows users to have their favorite channels listed in the order they want at the top of their list, while CWC maintains the ability to insert new high priority channels at the top of the original channel list. This would mean they are inserted into the consumer's channel list below their favorite channels, thus eliminating the problem of unhappy consumers who do not like their favorite numbering altered.

While these two screens will offer 80 percent of the EPG functionality to all users, the more techno-minded consumer can delve deeper into the EPG, to customize it and use the extra functionality.

The extra functionality that users will find are sections such as the TV Choice, an editorial style magazine section where CWC can highlight programs in more detail, and use the opportunity to drive more customers to recommended programming. Other areas include program grids and subject searches.

The EPG can also be used to book TV on-demand events. Once booked, these will be inserted into the diary. The diary can also store other program events, and a consumer will be visually reminded of their program shortly before it starts. As with other things in the EPG, a more technical user can customize the length of time before an event reminder appears. In the future, it is envisioned that this diary functionality will be developed into a more complete personal organizer function.

Other areas that the EPG allows users to access are enhanced television services, for example interactive television game shows. There is also access to the TV Internet product and e-mail. The designs for these allow for the user to maintain this small screen TV that is available in other parts of the EPG to watch TV while writing e-mail or browsing a website.

Overall the CWC-advanced EPG is the central portal to the CWC Interactive Digital Television experience, and initial customer response has shown that CWC has done a good job at providing this for their consumers.

SUMMARY . . . .

The digital EPG is the gateway to a portal of interactive digital services such as banking, shopping, games, Internet applications, and on-demand television. An EPG needs to be imaginative and compelling to win new customers and retain a company's existing subscriber base.

Basic and advanced EPGs are important keys to the future of digital television, without them people would not be able to navigate through the complexities of the new multichannel and services world. Simplicity is paramount when we speak about the development of EPGs. A basic EPG informs a viewer what is on now and what is on next. For service providers, an EPG provides an attractive prospect of improved profits through new advertising models. Subsequently, a second category of EPG has emerged—the enhanced EPG. These types of EPG contain several menus that give television viewers access to different portals of interactive services. They provide viewers with detailed information on programs, channels, and even actors. Other features include the ability of subscribers to personalize the EPG to meet their own needs.

Creating an advanced EPG is time consuming and very expensive. In addition to the development issues, advanced EPGs are also plagued with problems with intellectual property rights. In the future, network service providers will be able to buy off-the-shelf EPGs to meet their specific needs. Due to media-environmental changes, future EPGs will certainly look different from the way they do now. The fact that digitalization will probably overthrow the linearity of current broadcasts will surely have its impact. The Philips experiments that have been described in this chapter are attempts to "shape the future" in this respect. The chapter concluded with a brief analysis of the advanced EPG that was developed by CWC.

10 Set-top Server Architecture

In this chapter…

Digital TV subscribers often don't realize that behind the simple end-user interface they see on their television screens is a series of powerful servers that work together to deliver TV, Internet, and Intranet services to their set-top box. The servers that reside at the head-end help to reduce the demands made on small footprint set-top clients by providing them with storage, user management, and data processing services. In addition to offloading some of the processing tasks from the set-top box, servers also integrate into the following head-end systems:

1. subscriber management and billing,
2. conditional access,
3. customer services,
4. digital TV processing equipment,
5. firewalls, and
6. network management.

For network operators who are considering the deployment of an advanced digital TV environment, it is important that they understand the role each server plays and how they interact with each other. Once the role of each server is understood, the next step is to design an architecture that suits the needs of your particular business. This chapter provides you with a description of the main responsibilities of each server in an integrated digital TV environment.

OVERVIEW OF SERVER ARCHITECTURE . . . .

Figure 10.1 illustrates how the servers needed to support a variety of Internet- and TV-based services are integrated into a digital head-end system. Note that because we are concentrating on the data side of the TV business, we have deliberately omitted the digital processing devices, CA equipment, and billing subsystems from the diagram to simplify the explanation.

The following systems should be in place before installing the various servers:

- A bank of modems is required to provide network connectivity between the subscriber household and the servers located at the network operations center.
- Every network provider who offers Internet-based services will require a firewall for security reasons.
- A fast network to route TCP/IP data from connected set-tops to the various servers.

The types of servers used by set-top client applications are explained in the following subsections.

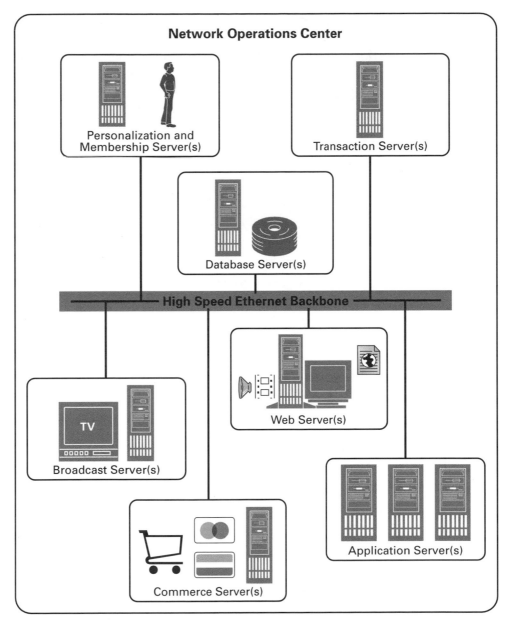

Figure 10.1
Sample head-end server configuration

Application Server(s)

An application server is typically part of a client/server network. The application processing occurs on both the client device and on the application server. In the context of a digital system, the application server's main function is to store and process set-top Intranet applications. Because several set-top users may run applications on the server at any one time, it needs powerful processing resources.

Examples of application servers include:

- E-mail servers, for organizing, processing, and managing e-mail.
- News servers, for processing newsgroups.
- Proxy servers, for reducing the workload of other servers and improving response times for digital TV customers.
- Chat servers, for a range of online chat services.
- Directory servers, for maintaining subscriber details.
- TV Ticker servers, for network operators who wish to offer an up-to-the-minute news ticker service from companies like CNN and NBC.
- DNS servers, for mapping server names to IP addresses.

Database Server(s)

The second type of server system is a database server. These servers control user access to data contained within databases stored on the local hard disks. Hence database servers typically need large amounts of disk storage with a high level of reliability. They typically have two processors and include support for dual processing. Their dual processing capabilities increase the number of subscribers that can simultaneously access the servers' databases. A database server receives requests for data from a variety of set-top applications, retrieves the data, and returns it to the requesting application.

Web Server(s)

World Wide Web servers, or Web servers for short, store HTML pages. The Web server communicates with the set-top client by responding to HTTP requests. When a subscriber wants to view a particular Web page, the server will retrieve the page from the hard disk and send it over the broadband to the set-top browser, where it is displayed on the television screen. A Web server provides an open, standards-based object architecture that is ideal for developing and deploying interactive TV and Internet services in a digital environment. Web servers can be categorized as middleware software because they link a subscriber's set-top browser to the HTML pages they are visiting. The hardware platform chosen needs to be capable of doing a large amount of computational work, particularly when using CGI, Java, or other server-based languages.

In sizing a Web server, the amount of memory required is a major consideration. A sensible entry-level server for network operators rolling out advanced services will come with 256 MB of RAM. To cope with the large number of Web page requests that it typically handles, it's important that a Web server has fast input and output subsystems. Another major consideration is storage. This needs to be fast and plentiful. If the budget permits, use an UltraWide SCSI because, when configured in a RAID array (several hard disks holding the same information), it will give operators added reliability and redundancy capabilities. Because most Web servers are available 24 hours a day, 7 days a week, 365 days a year, their various hardware subsystems need to be dependable. A Web server is identified to set-top users by its IP address, and often by a domain name as well.

Transaction Server(s)

Transaction processing is best described as a type of processing where the computer automatically deals with subscriber requests. Each request emanating from a digital TV subscriber is regarded as a transaction. Automatic teller machines are a good example of transaction processing. Transactions can be processed in two different ways: online transaction processing (OLTP) or batch processing.

OLTP occurs when the computer deals immediately with subscriber requests. Batch processing occurs when a batch of requests are stored and then processed all together. A transaction server is a software application that is designed to process transactions. It receives a transaction from a subscriber and initiates a number of functions to process the transaction. Our example in the previous chapter about purchasing the U2 CD is a good description of transaction processing.

A transaction server is the hardware platform required to support the processing of transactions within a digital TV environment. Examples of transaction servers include: Netscape Enterprise Server or Microsoft Transaction Server.

Commerce Server(s)

Commerce servers are used to conduct electronic commerce over various types of networks, including a broadband digital Intranet. They are relatively new in the server marketplace and form an integral part of the back-end architecture for the e-commerce set-top application. They host storefronts for business-to-consumer merchant sites that have partnered with the network operator. A *storefront* is the term given in e-commerce to describe the home page of an online merchant. It typically contains hyperlinks to a product catalog, where subscribers can choose to purchase goods using their remote controls. Commerce servers allow digital TV subscribers to register, browse products, place products in virtual shopping carts, and securely purchase a variety of goods. Commerce servers make life easy for merchants who want to set up shop on the digital TV network. For example, most servers can:

1. Create a new store from scratch using sample templates and wizards.
2. Connect the storefront to an inventory database containing details about products and services for sale.
3. Process transactions such as purchase orders, payments, and invoices.
4. Many commerce packages offer a variety of authoring tools that can be used to design and optimize pages for the set-top box.
5. When the storefront is up and running, the merchant will need to maintain it. Site analysis and monitoring tools allow the merchant and network operator to monitor the store's performance. For example, they can generate reports on how many sales have been made according to product, price range, date, and so on.
6. Commerce servers provide network operators with a comprehensive set of advertising features that can be easily used to generate additional revenue.

Commerce servers are available from a variety of vendors, such as Microsoft, Oracle, Netscape, and IBM. They vary from high-powered, full-featured servers, to less ambitious products that allow smaller network operators to set up an e-commerce application with minimum expense. Because commerce servers handle secure financial transactions, they must be capable of supporting the SSL encryption protocol. As previously discussed, this provides a secure link between the set-top client application and the servers in the head-end. In addition to SSL, most modem commerce servers also support a credit card payment standard called Secure Electronic Transactions (SET). SET has been endorsed by virtually all of the major players in the e-commerce arena, including the main credit card companies, Microsoft, IBM, GTE, Verisign, Oracle, AOL, and Sun Microsystems. SET affects an online purchase only after the customer has decided to pay for their goods with a payment card. The main parties involved in a typical SET transaction are:

1. the credit card holder,
2. the merchant of the products or services,
3. the financial institution used by the merchant to process payment card authorizations,
4. the CA system,
5. the merchant's bank, and
6. the card-issuing bank.

SET has been slow to take off because it requires special software for buyers, sellers, and banks, plus a digital certificate to vouch for the identity of each party. Most e-commerce payments today are made under the SSL protocol, however, over the next two years SET is expected to establish itself as the industry standard for e-commerce transactions over digital TV networks. When choosing a commerce server, it would be wise to choose one that supports both SSL and SET. This will allow you to run your interactive TV business using SSL now and then move to SET later. Commerce servers have similar hardware requirements to transaction and application servers—like them, their hardware must be extremely reliable.

Personalization and Membership Servers

Personalization enables the delivery of custom content based on the subscriber's personal profile and supports targeted promotions and one-to-one marketing. These servers contain tools that allow service providers to create direct e-mail marketing campaigns based on subscriber profiles and preferences. They can also be used to efficiently manage secure access to specific broadband content. So once a subscriber connects to the digital network, the appropriate browser favorites, user preferences, and e-mail address book are made available to the set-top user.

Broadcast Server

The main function of a broadcast server is to retrieve and aggregate content from multiple data sources and inject or carousel this information into the MPEG-2 digital stream. The basic operational model of a broadcast server in a digital environment is described in the following steps:

1. The server checks a scheduling file to determine the times for data retrieval.
2. The server then uses the HTTP protocol to fetch or "pull" the EPG data, ticker data, Web content, and authorization rights from various sources.
3. The data is then converted to a format that is supported by the set-top client.
4. Once the data is formatted it is then forwarded to either the multiplexer or IP multicasting interface to the broadband network. IP multicasting is a term used to describe the broadcasting of data to numerous people. This means only one set of data packets is transmitted for all destinations.
5. The data content is then "pushed" over the broadband digital TV network to the subscriber's set-top box.

Similar to our approach in earlier chapters of this book, we investigated the marketplace to identify some commercial products that could be used to build a server-based architecture. All of the middleware set-top software suppliers we described in chapter 4 provide operators with an accompanying suite of servers. Unfortunately due to book length restrictions, we decided to limit our review to a suite of servers that has an existing subscriber base and a suite of servers that was beginning to gain ground on the established players at the time of going to press. Subsequently, the next couple of subsections will provide you with an overview of the OpenTV suite of servers and Microsoft's TVPAK server platform.

OPENTV ....

OpenStreamer is OpenTV's solution for television operators seeking to broadcast interactive content via standard digital broadcast facilities. This software allows broadcasters to multiplex data with audio and video signals for reception by OpenTV-enabled digital set-top boxes, and is the first interactive head-end solution capable of updating the data stream in real-time, allowing up-to-the-second transmission of sports scores, stock quotes, or other time-sensitive data. OpenStreamer is OpenTV's successor to its FlowCaster product. In addition to real-time data updates, OpenStreamer adds the capability to broadcast multiple streams of data reliably and efficiently. It reduces deployment and maintenance costs by relying on a fixed-hardware architecture capable of interfacing with any standard multiplexer broadcast system. And since OpenStreamer is based on the popular Windows NT operating system, it reduces training and maintenance costs through standardization while relying on a proven and reliable server architecture.

The two main components of OpenStreamer are the Application Streamer and Broadcast Streamer.

Application Streamer

The Application Streamer runs the OpenTV interactive application, responds to external data sources and updates the data in real-time, and then plays out the stream to the Broadcast Streamer. Essentially, an Application Streamer is divided into four parts:

1. The application-specific portion of the Application Streamer is responsible for providing data as needed. Each Application Streamer is written for a specific application, which requires a specific data source to provide data in a fashion that is required by the application. But while written for a specific application, much of the code written for an Application Streamer can be reused in other Application Streamers (e.g., applications that share the same database can use the same code for those data queries).

2. The data processing portion is responsible for managing the data provided by the application-specific portion and transforming input data into OpenTV directories, modules, or SI information, or into Transport Stream data format.

3. The communication portion of the application server provides synchronous and asynchronous message-passing to and from the Broadcast Streamer.

4. The final part of the server provides updates to an SNMP management system.

Broadcast Streamer

As mentioned, the Broadcast Streamer then multiplexes multiple MPEG-2 transport streams and data from the Application Streamer and outputs the streams to the multiplexer. The configuration and operation of the Broadcast Streamer can be performed from an OpenStreamer Console, the FlowMaster Graphical User Interface (GUI), or a start-up script.

Employing the latest technology, OpenStreamer forms the head-end of OpenTV's end-to-end interactive television offering, allowing broadcasters to provide the most advanced interactive applications to their viewers while leveraging their investment in their current digital broadcasting infrastructure.

Both the Broadcast Streamer and the Application Streamer will run on most Windows NT workstations. Specific requirements are:

- an Intel-based PC (Pentium Pro or Pentium II recommended),
- 200 MHz or faster,
- 128 MB RAM recommended,
- Output PCI board on PC server,
- CDROM drive, and
- Windows NT SP4.

MICROSOFT TV SERVER . . . .

Microsoft TV Server is the server component of the Microsoft TV Platform Adaptation Kit (TVPAK). Its suite of software components instantly gives network service providers the tools to provision, manage, and operate a large-scale, commercial-grade interactive TV service. It has been optimized to work with digital set-top boxes that use the Microsoft TV client software.

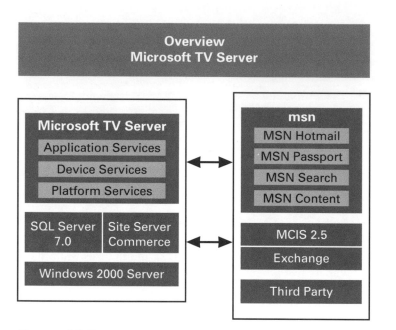

Figure 10.2
Overview of Microsoft TV server

From Figure 10.2, we can see that the server software is based on the following Microsoft technologies:

Windows 2000 Server Family

The Windows 2000 Server operating systems are the next generation of the Windows NT Server series of operating systems. The Windows 2000 Server builds on the strengths of Windows NT Server 4.0 by delivering increased reliability, availability, and scalability with end-to-end management features that reduce operating costs. It provides a comprehensive set of Web and Internet services that allow TV operators to take advantage of the latest Web technologies. The Windows 2000 Server family consists of three editions: Standard, Advanced, and Datacenter. The Standard edition is expected to be the most popular version for small- to medium-sized businesses. The Advanced and Datacenter editions are designed to meet the needs of mission-critical deployments in large corporate organizations, Internet service providers, and interactive TV operators.

Site Server (Commerce Edition)

Site Server 3.0 Commerce Edition is a comprehensive Internet commerce server that enables network service providers to engage digital TV customers, transact business, and build commerce Web sites more effectively. Additionally, it provides operators with a comprehensive range of site analysis tools to help them understand the buying habits of their customer base and thereby deliver more relevant information to improve the subscriber's viewing experience. These tools also improve an operator's ability to promote and merchandise products dynamically, run a more efficient online business, and derive revenue from targeted advertising campaigns. Microsoft customers worldwide have deployed Site Server to run large, medium, and small e-commerce sites, including some of the most visited sites on the Internet, such as Dell Computer (http://www.dell.com), Barnes and Noble (http://www.barnesandnoble.com), and The Gap (http://www.gap.com).

SQL Server 7.0

SQL Server 7.0 provides the database platform for the interactive TV applications. With SQL server, TV operators can scale this platform to support terabytes of interactive TV data and support hundreds of thousands of subscribers. SQL Server 7.0 seamlessly integrates with Windows 2000 and its Internet Information Server (IIS) technology, as well as Microsoft Site Server, to provide the ideal database platform for conducting electronic commerce on a broadband TV network. Other features of SQL Server 7.0 include:

- Support for data warehousing—this enables effective business decision making based on timely and accurate information.
- Reduced cost of ownership through simplified management and administration.
- Capable of replicating data across a broadband TV network.

TVPAK Server

The TVPAK Server platform is largely based on WebTV backend technologies. It includes the ability to remotely manage digital set-top boxes, optimize Web content for a television environment, cache frequently accessed content, and authenticate subscribers. Additionally, this server also acts as an application server storing the companies' EPGs and associated data. From a subscribers perspective, this server will also facilitate the downloading of new software updates to the digital set-top box. On the head-end side of the equation, this server integrates very tightly with existing subscriber management systems and supports a wide range of customer care tools.

Microsoft Commercial Internet System

The Microsoft Commercial Internet System (MCIS) offers network operators a suite of powerful and highly integrated applications for deploying Internet-based services. It consists of the following server components:

Membership System • The MCIS Membership System is the foundation block of the MCIS Server suite. It integrates with other MCIS services to make it easy for operators to manage and deploy Internet services for a large-scale set-top membership community. Membership provides a way for providers to authenticate users and authorize access to digital TV and Internet-based services. Membership is also integrated with personalization capabilities so that cable operators can tailor their services to the interests and needs of their membership.

MCIS Mail • MCIS Mail is a commercial-grade mail system that can scale from thousands to millions of subscribers. MCIS Mail supports open Internet standards, such as SMTP, POP3, MIME, and IMAP4. Because of the growing problem on the Internet concerning unsolicited commercial e-mail (SPAM), Microsoft SMTP service, by default, does not allow mail to be relayed through it to an external e-mail address. This feature allows administrators to block unsolicited mail, which is not bound for a user on their broadband network.

MCIS News • MCIS News is an Internet standards-based service for hosting electronic forums and discussion groups. MCIS News delivers a commercial-grade implementation of the Network News Transport Protocol (NNTP), designed to meet the high-traffic loads associated with mission-critical applications. It is based on the highly scalable master-slave architecture, which enables it to support tens of thousands of concurrent users. MCIS News provides public, read-only, moderated, and authenticated news groups.

Exchange Chat Service • The MCIS Chat Service is an Internet or Intranet server that facilitates text-based real-time collaboration on a broadband network. It supports all chat-enabled digital set-top boxes. Chat enables real-time one-to-one, one-to-many, and many-to-many conversations among set-top user communities.

Site Server • As mentioned, Site Server is a rich suite of server products that are used to build compelling commerce-enabled Web sites. As we can see from Figure 10.2, Microsoft has unbundled the Site Server product from the MCIS server family and implements it as a standalone server within the Microsoft TV Server platform.

Personal Web Pages • MCIS 2.5 Personal Web Pages (PWP) service allows network operators to provide large numbers of subscribers with simple personal Web sites. In this service, each user is allotted his or her own directory in the operator's head-end. A subscriber can create Web pages on their own computer or advanced digital set-top box, and can upload those files to the head-end using the traditional File Transfer Protocol (FTP). MCIS also contains a component called the Internet connection services which allows operators to integrate their telecommunications side of the business with their digital TV offerings.

MSN Portal Services

As part of Microsoft's strategy to accelerate the global deployment of next-generation interactive TV services, the company has decided to integrate their Web properties into the TVPAK software solution. These services are used by network operators to enhance their subscriber's viewing experience by delivering co-branded services that are powered by the MSN network of content centers. Microsoft Web properties include MSN Hotmail, MSN Search, Microsoft Passport, Expedia Travel, and MSNBC.

NETWORK MANAGEMENT . . . .

Today's digital broadband systems offer enormous potential for operators to generate a range of new revenue streams. However, these networks occasionally develop problems that can have catastrophic effects. To minimize the risks associated with network downtime, operators need to proactively manage their servers, communication links, and set-top clients. Under this proactive approach, certain considerations need to be made. One of the most important points to remember when implementing an end-to-end set-top solution is to check all new hardware before adding it to the network. Never assume that just because something is new, it must be faultless. Another important consideration for proactively managing a digital TV network is to test redundant elements. A redundant network device duplicates the functionality of some critical part of the network. It acts as a spare in case the main component fails. If a problem can arise in the main network components, it can arise in spare devices too. Detailed maps of the physical and logical architecture of the set-top network need to also be created. While drawing these maps, network operators should also compile an inventory of all network resources. For example, an operator should obtain the following items of information about each set-top box on their digital network:

- processor type,
- amount of memory,
- disk drive,
- types of data interfaces,
- physical address,
- version of real time OS,
- version of set-top middleware, and
- version of set-top applications.

Servers play an extremely important strategic role within the broadband TV network. When a server goes down, the set-top client is unable to function properly, resulting in loss of revenue for the TV operator. Constant monitoring of the servers is required to reduce downtime. Server management entails:

- measuring the performance of the various servers,
- determining the status of a server,
- troubleshooting common problems, and
- backing up important user information.

A high level of reliability is expected from consumer electronic products such as set-top boxes. Cable operators need to proactively manage their set-top boxes. Client management entails:

- reviewing set-top inventory in order to determine whether the boxes require software or hardware upgrades;
- installing and upgrading software in all the set-tops on the broadband network, which is automatically done from the head-end servers;
- software metering, which enables support staff to keep track of set-top software licenses; and
- reviewing set-top error messages to detect and trace unusual problems.

Typically, cable operators use a network management system to keep a close eye on local Intranet servers and remote set-top clients. A fully operative network management has the ability to reduce operational costs and server downtime for network operators involved with deploying interactive TV applications. The management system uses Simple Network Management Protocol (SNMP) to control and monitor the digital Intranet. SNMP operates over the TCP/IP communications protocol. Most of the servers and set-tops available today are compliant with the SNMP standard. SNMP is an application layer protocol, which is used by the management software to retrieve data from the various network devices. The types of data gathered from a broadband network falls into three distinct categories: alerts or alarms, current status, and statistics.

Alerts will inform the IT personnel at the head-end about unusual activity on the network. Alerts and alarms are always sent when a set-top is having problems in the subscriber's premises. For example, if a set-top box fails to load the electronic program guide (EPG), then an alarm is sent to the management process. Data on the current status is collected on a regular basis to determine whether the set-top is operational or not. Network statistics, such as traffic levels on the broadcast and return path networks, are collected by the management system on a daily basis. Networks can perform well or badly and it is important to be able to recognize when performance is below par. The data gathered by the management system is then used by IT personnel to optimize the performance of the digital network. An optimized network improves the delivery speed for set-top Intranet- and Internet-based applications.

A typical network management system is comprised of an application and a database stored on a computer called the Central Management Station (CMS).The CMS uses the SNMP protocol to communicate with the following network devices:

- network servers,
- encoders and compression equipment,
- CA hardware systems,
- hardware systems for customer services,
- digital set-top boxes, and
- wide and local area networking devices.

The diagram in Figure 10.3 depicts the CMS interfacing with the various components of an end-to-end digital system.

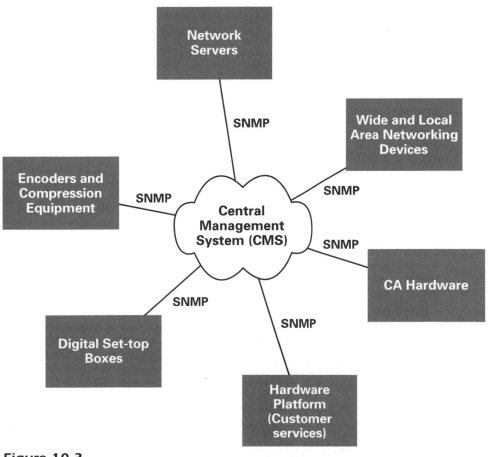

Figure 10.3
Network management interfaces

Each one of these network components is preloaded with a software module called a *management agent.* This agent interfaces with the CMS and contains detailed information about the component. For example, TV operators can use the CMS in conjunction with the agent to gather data from application servers about: hardware and software configurations, usage and performance statistics, and identification and authorizations.

In addition to gathering data, management agents are also responsible for passing alerts to the CMS. If, for example, the cable operator's link to the Internet goes down, the agent will send an alarm to the CMS so that action can be taken to restore the Internet link. Management agents use embedded databases called Management Information Bases (MIBs) to store information about network devices. The information in an MIB is standardized so that all network management processes can use it.

As you can see, the management of an end-to-end digital network requires a high level of operational and systems expertise. The increasing complexity of networks has meant that many of the cable companies have begun outsourcing the management of these complex network architectures.

SUMMARY . . . .

A high speed broadband TV network consists of several computer servers, set-top boxes, video processing devices, and peripherals that are cabled together in a particular geographical area. This chapter focused on the types of servers that are required to support a range of interactive TV applications. We began the chapter by reemphasising the crucial role that servers play within the context of a digital TV environment. Nowadays, the variety of tasks that servers must perform is varied and complex. Subsequently, computer servers that are required to accommodate the expanding needs of digital TV subscribers have become more and more specialized.

This chapter listed, defined, and described the role of specialized computer servers within a digital TV environment. People want to do more over the Internet than ever before. They want to chat with a friend, shop for products, collaborate with a coworker, and conduct transactions with business partners. Just as they want to do more, they expect more from their service provider. TV operators are facing an increasingly competitive marketplace, driven by innovations and new services. No longer can operators survive by offering their customers basic TV and PPV services; they must offer a wide variety of value-added services.

Subsequently, we decided to identify and explain two commercial server products that were able to support these new challenges: OpenTV and Microsoft TV Server.

People nowadays expect a high level of reliability from their network service provider. So we decided to allocate the last part of this chapter to managing and monitoring the many complex components that make up an end-to-end digital TV system.

11 Set-top Smart Card Technologies

In this chapter…

They are set to revolutionize the way we shop, bank, travel, browse the Internet, and make phone calls. With a Smart card, consumers will have the capability to carry multiple currencies when traveling; make secure purchases over the Internet anytime, anywhere; pay for public transportation and public phone calls; and finally, access a range of home entertainment services via their set-tops.

They look very similar to a standard credit card and are called Smart cards. The Smart card stores and processes information through the electronic circuits embedded in silicon in the plastic substrate of the card. Over the next five years, they are expected to dispense with the need for petty cash and will make phone cards and credit cards gadgets of the past. Already used in most European countries, they are fast replacing debit cards as the primary method of purchasing goods and services. The Smart card market is estimated to reach approximately $2.8 billion by the year 2002. Today, the TV industry is moving rapidly to a world where Smart cards with multiple applications will provide subscribers with secure access to their range of digital TV and Internet based services. By providing extra convenience, these multifunction Smart cards open new opportunities for network service providers to retain and strengthen existing customer relationships, attract new customers, and stay ahead of the competition.

Another major benefit of Smart cards for service providers is their ability to hold multiple applications. Consequently, subscribers are reducing the number of cards in their wallets by combining the functionality of existing cards into one single Smart card. Some of the most common Smart card applications used on a digital TV network include electronic cash, secure identification in CA systems, subscriber loyalty schemes, and credit transactions.

This chapter will provide an introduction to the basics of Smart cards and examine the security mechanisms of these devices within the context of a digital TV environment. In addition to addressing the fundamental concepts of Smart cards, we also present a brief overview of the most popular Smart card operating systems that are competing for a share of this rapidly growing market.

Smart cards are plastic cards that contain a microprocessor and up to 1 MB of memory. Because of their microprocessor, Smart cards have a limited range of features that allow them to store and process local information about the holder of the card. They can be used for such purposes as e-commerce, securing e-mail, personal identification, and storing customer's preferences. They can store up to 100 times more information than magnetic stripe cards. As you can see, owning a Smart card is like having a desktop PC in your wallet.

In terms of Smart card technologies, the set-top industry is more advanced in comparison to the PC industry. At the moment, moves are under way to develop PCs with built-in Smart card readers. In contrast, there are several million Smart card-enabled set-top boxes that have been successfully deployed in residential homes across Europe.

ARCHITECTURE OF SET-TOP SMART CARDS . . . .

A Smart card is just a very simple computer. It has an 8-bit CPU, a small quantity of RAM, ROM for the operating system, and approximately 64 KB of EEPROM. It doesn't have interfaces for keyboards and monitors, but it does have a serial I/O interface. Figure 11.1 illustrates the architecture of a Smart card and the function of each component is explained in the sections that follow.

CPU

The CPU is the brains of the Smart card and is used to process mathematical operations. Current Smart card processor designs are based on an 8-bit architecture. The speed of the processor ranges from 3 MHz to 5 MHz and is dependent on the requirements of the specific set-top applications. Many of the Smart card manufacturers are,

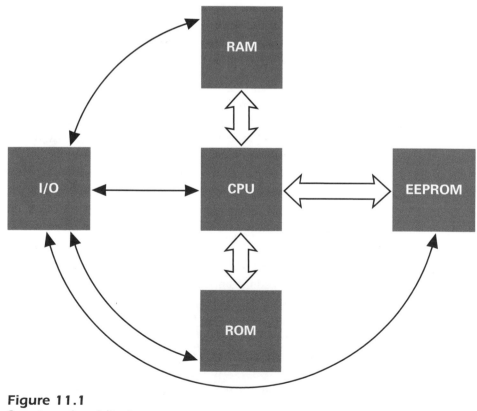

Figure 11.1
Smart card architecture

however, beginning to produce processors running at speeds greater than 5 MHz in response to market demands.

RAM

The chip contains between 128 bytes and 256 bytes of RAM. This figure is expected to grow over time as set-top e-commerce applications become more complex. Accessing data in RAM is much faster then retrieving data from other Smart card memory types.

ROM

The contents of ROM are normally defined during the production of the Smart card, usually called the *masking* process. It stores a number of resident applications, including the real time operating system. The network service provider is unable to alter the contents of this Smart card component. The size of ROM varies from card to card, however, ROM sizes are growing at a very fast pace to meet the demands of increasingly complex applications that are emerging from the digital TV industry.

EEPROM

An EEPROM is another type of memory used by the Smart card to store information such as a subscriber's profiles, passwords, electronic wallets, and various files. The EEPROM within a Smart card has pretty much the same functions as a hard drive in a PC, only much more limited. As in the case of hard drives, the contents of this silicon chip are re-writable. Today, the data storage capabilities of an EEPROM ranges from 1 KB to approximately 64 KB. As with RAM and ROM, EEPROM sizes are expected to increase over time.

I/O Serial Interface

All of the components described in previous subsections are connected to an I/O hardware component called the universal asynchronous receiver transmitter (UART). The UART in turn is connected to the pins that physically interface with the set-top Smart card readers. The physical layout of these pins has been recently standardized by the International Standards Organization (ISO).

These cut-down computers require approximately 5 volts of power to operate within a digital set-top box. However, thanks to the advancements made in the world of power management, the next generation of set-top Smart cards will require only 3 volts to operate successfully.

SMART CARD SECURITY . . . .

One thing that is very specific to Smart cards is that they are always used for secure storage. So a significant amount of effort and money has been invested in improving the security of Smart card systems. They offer far greater security protection to the consumer than today's magnetic stripe cards. The security of a Smart card is broadly categorized into four main categories: authentication, authorization, nonrepudiation, and cryptography.

First and foremost, a subscriber needs to *authenticate* himself or herself to the Smart card and the Smart card needs to authenticate itself to the set-top box. For example, suppose a subscriber wants to connect to the digital TV network and access a particular interactive service. First the customer inserts the card into the reader and the set-top checks to see if the card is acceptable. Once that is done, it needs to identify the subscriber to the set-top box. The network service provider has a choice of authentication methods to use. At present, entering a PIN code is the most popular means of authenticating an individual subscriber. Once the subscriber has been authenticated, the process of authorization commences. Authorization means deciding who can access particular services. Authorization determines who has access to what parts of the Smart card file system. From an operator's perspective, this security feature allows a group of subscribers to be authorized for a particular event. Nonrepudiation becomes increasingly important in the digital world as thousands of subscribers use remote controls and set-top boxes to carry out e-commerce transactions on their TV sets. Because there is no physical presence of a seller or a buyer during these transactions, a third party is required to verify that the transaction actually took place. This mechanism of authenticating actual transactions is called *nonrepudiation*.

The last part of the Smart card security model is cryptography. *Cryptography* falls into two main categories: symmetric and asymmetric algorithms.

Symmetric cryptography functions by using the same key for the encryption and decryption of a digital transaction. This is analogous to having a locksmith make two keys for the same lock. The most commonly used system based on symmetric cryptography is the Data Encryption Standard (DES). In DES, the key for encrypting and decrypting the data is normally 56 bits, but it is possible to generate keys with greater lengths. Symmetric cryptography is also known as private key cryptography. Asymmetric cryptography, or public key cryptography, on the other hand, uses a different process of encrypting and decrypting keys. Instead of using a single key, asymmetric cryptography uses a pair of keys for encryption and decryption of digital TV transactions. One key (the public key) is used to encrypt a transaction, and the other key (the private key) is used to decrypt the transaction. A private key is the inverse of the corresponding public key. The keys for this cryptography system are derived from a complex mathematical algorithm. RSA is currently the most commonly used public key algorithm. Created in 1978, the RSA algorithm was named after its creators, Ronald Rivest, Adi

Shamir, and Leonard Adleman. RSA is also one of the most extensively tested algorithms in the digital TV world.

So how do all these security standards apply to a Smart card that has been inserted into a subscriber's set-top box? First and foremost, the Smart card that is issued to the subscriber will contain the key(s) that are used to decrypt the EMMs and ECMs, which are broadcasted from the operator's head-end. Once decrypted, the set-top box uses the access rights contained in the EMM and ECM messages to decrypt a variety of digital services.

In addition to decrypting authorization and access rights, the security features of a Smart card are also used by network operators to store and protect electronic wallets. These wallets allow subscribers to transfer electronic cash from their bank accounts onto their card. The Smart card can then be used to purchase PPV and IPPV events.

SMART CARD SOFTWARE . . . .

Though typically only a few thousand bytes of program code, the operating system for the Smart card microprocessor must handle such tasks as:

- data transmission over the bidirectional, serial terminal interface;
- loading, operating, and management of applications;
- execution control and instruction processing;
- protected access to data;
- memory management;
- file management; and
- management and execution of cryptographic algorithms.

In contrast to personal computer operating systems such as Linux, DOS, and Windows, Smart card operating systems do not feature user interfaces or the ability to access external peripherals or storage media. The size is typically between 3 and 24 KB.

To date, no single operating platform dominates the Smart-card industry, meaning that companies must adapt their Smart-card applications for each environment. Visa is pushing it's own open platform, while MasterCard supports the Mondex electronic cash system and the MultOS system, designed so that cards with different operating systems can work together. In October 1998, Microsoft announced an extension of its Windows operating system aimed at Smart cards. And last but not least, Sun Microsystems has demonstrated its enthusiasm for the Smart card OS arena with it's development of the Java Card specification. We'll briefly consider each of these operating systems in turn.

Java Card from Sun Microsystems

Java Card technology is Sun Microsystems' blueprint for building applications to run on Smart cards. It is based on the many benefits of the Java programming language—productivity, security, robustness, tools, and portability. Sun has licensed the scalable Java Card platform to over 30 Smart card manufacturers and developers. Smart cards that have been enabled with the Java Card technology platform come with an integrated API that allows developers to create a myriad of new and exciting applications. Additional technical information about Java Card specifications is available from Suns' Web site at http://java.sun.com/products/javacard/index.html.

MultOS from MasterCard

MultOS is a high-security, multi-application operating system for Smart cards, enabling a number of different applications to be held securely on the card at the same time. Although it was originally developed by Mondex, it is now becoming an open de facto industry standard. A consortium, called MAOSCO, has been created from a group of the world's leading players in the Smart card industry, to progress multOS as an open industry standard. At the time of going to press, the current members of MAOSCO included American Express, Dai Nippon Printing, Discover Financial Services, Europay International, Fujitsu, Glesecke & Devrient (G&D), Hitachi, Keycorp, MasterCard International, Mondex International, Motorola, and Siemens. For more information on developing applications for set-top Smart cards, use your remote control and browse to the following Web site: http://www.multos.com/.

Microsoft's Smart Card for Windows

The Microsoft Smart cards for Windows is an 8-bit, multi-application operating system for Smart cards with 8K of ROM. It is designed to be a low-cost, easy-to-program platform. Smart cards for Windows use the same development tools—Microsoft Visual C++ and Visual Basic—that millions of independent software vendors and in-house corporate developers use. Smart cards for Windows are expected to cost in the region of between $2 and $4 each. This is expected to be a very attractive price point for a variety of potential card issuers, from consumers to TV operators, looking for a low-cost card solution for their set-top boxes. Read all about this exciting new Smart card platform at: http://windows.microsoft.com/windowsce/smartcard/.

Visa Open Platform

Visa's Open Platform is a specification that the company licenses free to Smart card developers. Visa has chosen Java to become the basis for its Open Platform. The company has also publicly stated that they will support other Smart card operating systems such as Microsoft's Smart card for Windows platform. The open platform solution is comprised of three integrated elements: the Visa Open Platform card specifications, the Visa Open Platform terminal specifications, and the Visa Open Platform workbench tools. To learn more about the open platform solution for set-top Smart cards, make a visit to the following Web site address: http://www.visa.com/nt/suppliers/open/main.html.

SUMMARY . . . .

A standard Smart card looks and feels like a credit card but acts like a computer. It can be used to replace the assortment of cards that are part and parcel of modern life. Smart cards have an in-built processor and an interface that allows the card to communicate with a digital set-top box. A Smart card also contains some integrated memory, which allows TV operators to download applications and data onto the card. Smart cards require a high degree of security, ensuring that unauthorized users cannot access digital services. Authentication, authorization, nonrepudiation, and cryptography are the main security technologies implemented by Smart cards.

In the new world of digital television, a Smart card can be programmed to function as an electronic purse. The card is loaded with a monetary value and inserted into one of the Smart card readers at the front of the digital set-top box. The electronic cash is then used to purchase goods and services at one of the online retailers. The chapter concluded with a brief description of the most popular Smart card operating systems currently available to subscribers of digital TV services.

12 Set-top Enhanced TV

In this chapter…

A couple of years ago, most industry analysts viewed the Internet as a competitor to traditional TV. Now, they complement each other. Network operators are finding that the novelty of full Internet access for new digital TV subscribers wears off after a few months. Consequently, operators are beginning to harness the power of a new technology called enhanced or interactive television, which brings these two compelling media forces together. Popular TV shows and new releases in the cinema develop companion Web sites to provide consumers with detailed information about the event. Broadcasters are increasingly showing interest in using the Internet as a medium to deliver programs to diverse audiences across the world. Enhanced television is a new paradigm that merges appeal and mass audience of traditional television viewing with the interactivity of the Web. It is an integral part of the new television experience.

In this chapter, find out about the fundamental concepts and benefits of enhanced TV technologies. Gain an insight into the mechanisms that are used to author and deliver content that has been optimized for the TV world. Learn about the methodologies surrounding the authoring of content for set-top boxes that are compliant with international standards. And finally, gain an understanding of the levels of interactivity that can be applied to enhanced TV content.

FUNDAMENTALS . . . .

Content for an enhanced TV environment is relatively easy to create because it is based on existing Web standards—HTML and JavaScript. This enhanced content allows broadcasters and network operators to offer their subscriber base a new layer of engaging information that complements normal TV viewing. An enhanced TV program can vary between a very simple production that includes links to related Web sites on the Internet to highly involved interactivity that merges a TV image with menus, rich multimedia components, and supporting text all timed to appear in synchronization with a particular show. Enhanced TV content can normally be accessed through a small interactivity icon that appears on the television screen. Once the subscriber has finished with the interactive content, one click on the remote control returns him or her back to regular TV viewing. For a sense of what enhanced television has to offer, picture a subscriber viewing a soccer game and clicking a remote control button to look up individual player and team statistics while the game is still in progress. Once the subscriber has finished reviewing these details, he or she may want to enter a chat room and chat with other viewers about the game while watching it.

BENEFITS OF ENHANCED TV . . . .

Enhanced TV creates a number of benefits to the following groups:

Subscribers • Enhanced TV will create a richer more engaging experience for TV viewers. Viewers will be able to access a range of value-added and graphically rich information about specific programs. This type of environment gives more reason than ever for digital subscribers to tune in.

Content Developers • For the content providers, having millions of digital set-top boxes running Internet technologies means that companies can use off-the-shelf Web authoring tools such as Frontpage, PageMill, and Macromedia Dreamweaver to produce enhanced TV content. Developers will also require an image editor like Adobe Photoshop or Paint Shop Pro for making TV graphics. The reuse of these tools enables access to a large pool of content developers. Consequently, there is no need to learn new tools or train new people to design enhanced TV content. Early adopters of enhanced TV will establish a unique niche as the competition heats up. Content developers who adopt enhanced TV technologies at an early stage will become market leaders of the digital revolution as advanced digital set-tops become more widely available.

Broadcasters and Network Operators • At the moment, network operators and broadcasters are seizing the market potential of enhanced TV. They are using this new paradigm to:

- create compelling content that complements the underlying video and background audio;
- reinforce branding and develop a competitive advantage;
- differentiate their programming offerings;
- retain and engage viewers;
- earn extra money by selling space in the interactive portion of the screen to advertisers and deriving revenue through a percentage of e-commerce sales conducted online;
- increase advert and marginal revenue per subscriber;
- offer local information services such as city guides, yellow pages, classified ads, and financial services to their subscriber bases;
- link viewers to the broadcasters own Web site; and
- build loyalty and affinity with their subscriber bases.

Advertisers • Advertisers will value the ability to more directly target their potential customers. Content that has been designed for an enhanced TV platform will provide advertisers with a one-to-few rather than a one-to-many connection. Through this direct connection, advertisers will be able to identify and track customers that are showing an interest in the product or service that is being advertised. Based on previous interests, advertisers will be able to target recommendations to certain customers. Additionally, if the customer is happy with the item on offer, they can use the set-top return path to order the product or service with another press of a remote control button. The ability to offer direct connections to prospective customers, and complete a sale using a simple remote control, will revolutionize the television advertising business.

GENERAL PRINCIPLES OF DESIGNING FOR A TV ENVIRONMENT . . . .

The principle of enhanced TV is to integrate Web data with digital video broadcast systems. The end-to-end architecture of an enhanced TV platform is based on a handful of Internet standards—TCP/IP, HTML, HTTP, and JavaScript.

With the advent of enhanced TV, content providers will be faced with the difficult challenge of creating and delivering compelling interactive services to billions of TV viewers across the globe. It is important to remember that set-top-based services are very different than PC- and Internet-based services. Television offers many exciting possibilities, but it is a new medium for most content providers. Therefore it's worth taking some time to investigate the design issues that need to be borne in mind when developing for a digital TV environment. We explore these development issues in the following subsections:

Screen Resolution

The most important thing to remember for people considering the move into the set-top content development industry is that the resolution and screen display characteristics of a TV screen are significantly less than that of most computer monitors. Pages that are designed specifically for the PC screen will be unattractive or even unreadable on a TV.

Even though computer monitors and television screens both rely on the same cathode ray tube (CRT) technology, they differ in terms of resolution. *Resolution* is frequently used to describe the overall size of a screen measured in pixels. For example, the resolution of a typical TV screen is 560×420 pixels. Resolution can also refer to the clarity of a screen image. For example, complex pages designed for display on a computer monitor does not always look as impressive when displayed on television using a digital set-top box. This is due to the low resolution of TV monitors as compared to the higher-quality resolution of computer monitors. Fine details, such as small text or graphical images, are difficult to read on TV screens. Also, certain backgrounds that look really good on computer screens tend to display distorted and unreadable on TV screens. Accordingly, the resolution of the television is a problem for set-top content authors.

Navigation

How a digital TV subscriber uses a set-top box to access information on their TV sets is totally different than how a PC user would access information on their monitor. For instance, most TV viewers are not accustomed to scrolling to see content or using click and drag technologies. Most set-top Internet- and Intranet-based set-top applications will not support horizontal scrolling and text wraps accordingly. Hence, the creation of long pages need to be avoided. Therefore, wherever possible, break the content into pages that fit on the TV screen without the need for scrolling.

The navigation tools for a set-top box are normally limited to a standard remote control with no steerable cursor control. Most television users will not use a keyboard and find them cumbersome to use while sitting on a couch or a chair. Consequently, developers need to reduce the number of user interface controls on the screen at any one time and avoid long forms that ask customers to enter large amounts of text. Complex navigational menus will also need to be avoided.

Keeping this audience in mind, content authors need to develop user-friendly set-top pages that can be easily navigated by a TV viewer.

Font Dimensions, Colors, and Lines

In general, people who watch television sit further away from their screens than those who sit in front of a computer monitor. On average, set-top users will sit on a couch 8 to 10 feet away from their TV set, whereas computer users sit between 1 to 2 feet away from the monitor.

To make it easy for set-top users to read and understand interactive content, authors need to avoid small font sizes. Designers need to avoid inserting small text into standard graphics because the text will be impossible to read on the subscriber's TV set. With regards to deciding a color scheme, some color combinations that look good on a PC monitor don't display very well on a TV screen. For example, most pages on the Internet have white backgrounds. This background color is not a good choice for set-top content. Full white or full red backgrounds cause screen distortion and can degrade the overall viewing experience. A recommended color scheme for set-top pages is light-colored text against a dark-colored background. The creation of thin lines with a thickness of less than two pixels should also be avoided because they display very poorly on today's television screens.

Computer and Multimedia Standards

Due to the constrained memory environment of the set-top box, it is nearly impossible for manufacturers to support all the various types of multimedia formats available on the Web. Hence, many of the set-tops currently available will not properly display complex set-top pages that contain multimedia formats such as Macromedia Flash, ActiveX, and RealAudio on a TV screen.

Audiences

Enhanced television is a new medium, designed for use by viewers who are comfortable watching traditional television programs, but who may or may not be as comfortable navigating a computer system. Consequently, the design of any enhanced TV content needs to be easy to use, improves the consumers TV viewing experience, and works properly. In comparison to computer users, TV viewers have a relatively low attention span and are not used to a high level of interaction with their televisions—other than adjusting the volume level or changing to a different channel. In order to appeal to a mass TV market, set-top content authors need to understand the underlying geographic and demographic characteristics of their target audience. Additionally, authors will need to gain insight into the types and levels of interactivity that is required to capture the audiences' attention. Another fundamental difference between PC users and TV viewers is the *lean forward* versus the *lean back* experience. A PC user looking for information on a particular subject will connect to the Internet, retrieve the details, and log out. In contrast, a TV viewer will sit back and expect to be passively entertained. The differences between the two experiences should be kept at the forefront of content developers' minds when developing for the television medium.

Download Times

Unlike PC users, people who watch television are not accustomed to waiting long periods of time for Web pages or multimedia files to download. Accordingly, content providers need to keep Web pages as simple as possible and within bandwidth size constraints to increase response times for the subscriber. For instance, if the maximum amount of content that can be broadcast over an MMDS network is 500 KB, then the enhanced TV content would be less than this value. Otherwise the set-top user will skip the page if the requested page is taking too long to display on their television screen. The hardware configuration of the client set-top box is also a consideration. The download times for cable modem-enabled set-tops will be very quick. However, MMDS, terrestrial, and satellite customers typically connect to the head-end servers through a modem and telephone line, and is therefore subject to particularly long load times.

CONTENT STANDARDIZATION FOR SET-TOPS . . . .

One of the main goals of producing enhanced TV content is to enrich the customers' viewing experience. Another key requirement is that any content that is produced needs to be capable of running on a variety of different set-top platforms. This requires a standards-based approach. In an effort to promote a common set-top authoring environment, three draft specifications are being finalized for the content development community: Advanced Television Enhancement Forum (ATVEF), DTV Application Software Environment (DASE), and Multimedia Home Platform (MHP). We explore these specifications in the following subsections.

Authoring Enhanced TV Content for ATVEF-compliant set-tops

In August 1998, ATVEF released version 1.1 of a specification that defines the fundamentals of creating content based on Web standards for a variety of client devices, including analog and digital set-top boxes. Since this time, ATVEF has been striving to build agreement between it's own members and across industries to develop this specification. The most recent updates to the document were made in February 1999 and the updates were posted on their Web site. The specification is divided into three separate parts:

1. types of content,
2. specifications for delivering enhanced TV content, and
3. binding to an IP network.

Before we describe the various methods that are being used to author content for digital set-top boxes, let's take a closer look at the content formats that are being referenced by the ATVEF specification. Central to the organization's strategy of developing a specification for enhanced TV was to use existing standards wherever possible and to minimize the creation of new standards. Consequently, the foundation blocks for ATVEF content is based on the following standard Internet specifications.

HTML 4.0

This is the language used by content providers to describe the presentation of text, graphics, video, and other multimedia components on a TV screen. As discussed earlier, it is the de facto language for publishing documents on the Web. It has a nonproprietary format and can be created using simple text editors or sophisticated authoring tools. HTML uses tags such as `<h1>` and `</h1>` to structure text into headings, paragraphs, lists, hypertext links, and so on. Working groups within the W3 consortium have produced a number of recommendations for the HTML language. These are essentially detailed specifications that act as guidance documents for companies who are developing software for different HTML environments. HTML 4.0 is W3C's recommendation for the latest version of HTML, following from earlier work on HTML 3.2 and HTML 2.0. HTML has been specified into three broad flavors:

1. HTML 4.0 Transactional—This variant is suitable for people who are authoring content for the general Internet community. The idea behind this flavor of HTML is to take advantage of the various new features of the language but keep the Web page-compatible with versions of browsers that do not support HTML 4.0.

2. HTML 4.0 Strict—A suitable version of HTML for Web designers who want to remove the need for tags within the structure of the document.

3. HTML 4.0 Frameset—This is the variant that is supported by ATVEF and is used by enhanced TV content authors for partitioning the TV screen into two or more frames.

When designing a Web page for an ATVEF-based set-top box, you need to specify which of these variants you are using by inserting a line at the beginning of the document. For example, one of the pages at the set-tops.com portal site starts with a line, which informs the target browser that it is using HTML 4.0 Frameset.

```
<!DOCTYPE html PUBLIC "-//set-tops//DTD HTML 4.0 FrameSet//EN">
<html>
<head>
<title>Set-tops.com enhanced TV Web Page </title>
```

HTML 4.0 contains many new and exciting technologies that are detailed in the completed specification, which is available for download at: http://www.w3.org/TR/REC-html40/

TV HTML Extensions

ATVEF have added a number of TV-orientated extensions to the HTML language to allow television and Web content to coexist on the same page. The additions to the core HTML language can be classified into the following groups of features.

Picture in picture • Displaying a live video broadcast within a Web page. The OBJECT and IMG tags may be used in conjunction with the .tv broadcast protocol to insert a live video signal directly into a Web page. The .tv protocol can also be used to specify channel names or numbers. For example:

```
<img src = "tv:Irish Multichannel" width = "320" height ="220">
```

Overlays • Displaying a Web page over a TV channel. The BODY tag is used to specify TV as a full screen background of a Web page, for example: `<body background="tv:">`

Windowing • By definition, windowing allows digital subscribers to use their remote controls to resize, close, or hide the video picture on a television screen. The new HTML extensions that have been developed by ATVEF allow content authors to create multiple windows and position them anywhere onscreen.

Transparency • Image file formats that support this technology are able to make certain designated pixels wholly or partially transparent, so that the background color or texture shows through. HTML tags associated with this feature allow enhanced TV designers to control how Web content integrates with a standard television screen. The normal technique used by designers is to position the television screen in the background and overlay the picture with Web content. Using new transparency tags, designers are then able to show through particular sections of the live video.

Positioning of components • Laying out a page for a low-resolution television screen is different than page layouts for a high-resolution computer monitor. The use of tables in designing enhanced TV content offers designers a great deal of control over the exact positioning of multimedia and text components on a television screen. New attributes have been defined by ATVEF to improve the layout of Web pages on TV screens.

Triggers • The development of advanced interactivity usually involves the addition of special instructions called *triggers* to the broadcast streams. They are used to choreograph the sequence of events within a TV channel. The ATVEF specification has defined a trigger as a real-time event that is comprised of a URL, a name, an expiration date, and script attributes. Triggers are text-based, and their syntax follows the basic format of the Electronic Industries Association specification EIA-746-A (`<url> [attr₁:val₁] [attr₂:val₂]...[attrₙ:valₙ] [checksum]`). The contents of the square brackets are best described as an attribute/value pair. This specification is available for purchase on the global engineering document's site at http://global.ihs.com/.

The syntax defined in version 1.1 of ATVEF specifies that all interactive TV triggers must begin with ASCII "<" and contain some or all of the following attribute/value pairs.

URL • The URL is contained within angle brackets and contains the address of the interactive TV content (e.g., http://www.set-tops.com/communities.html). This is the only required attribute/value pair of an ATVEF-defined trigger. The availability of a return path is not always available in digital set-top boxes, consequently, some enhanced TV content needs to be delivered by a local identifier URL scheme (lid:). The syntax of the "lid:" URL is as follows: Lid://www.set-tops.com/index.html

The "lid:" URL scheme enables content creators to assign unique identifiers.

Checksum • The checksum is used to detect data corruption.

Name • The name attribute/value pair provides digital TV subscribers with a drop-down panel that displays information about the interactivity content, after they select the onscreen Web link icon. The attribute can accommodate a string of between 20 and 30 characters, depending on the size of the font that is used by the designers. The attribute is contained within square brackets, as shown in the example below.

```
<http://www.set-tops.com/voiceactivation.html>[name:Tell me more!!!!]
```

Expires • This attribute specifies the expiration date for the interactive TV link. Once this date has been reached, the digital set-top box will ignore the link. The expires attribute can be abbreviated as the single letter "e." For example:

```
<http://www.set-tops.com/voiceactivation.html>[e:19991025]
```

Script • This attribute triggers an action on the target Web page of the interactive TV link. The script is executed when the page is opened. For example:

```
<http://www.set-tops.com/voiceactivation.html>[s:latestnews()]
```

CSS

Short for cascading style sheets, it is a new extension to the HTML language that gives both Web site developers and Internet users more augmented control over how pages are displayed on a television screen. Furthermore, the CSS standard can also give enhanced TV designers control over voice, pitch, and other aspects of how the text will sound when rendered into speech. The W3 consortium has actively promoted the use of style sheets on the Web since it's inception in 1994 and has produced two recommendations (CSS1 and CSS2), which have been integrated with newer versions of Web browsers. ATVEF has decided to base their content on CSS1.

CSS is a powerful way to specify the look and feel of HTML documents. It allows Web site and enhanced TV developers to separate layout and style from content. CSS is a simple declarative language that allows authors to apply stylistic information (concerning font, spacing, color, and so on) to structured documents written in HTML. You can define styles either within an HTML document or in an external file attached to the HTML document. As an external file, a single style sheet can affect multiple pages, even a whole Web site. This makes site-wide changes much easier to implement. You can specify how elements are rendered by associating them with *properties*, *classes*, and *values*. For example, suppose that you are a developer and you want to change the font size of the text on a TV web page. You begin by defining the style within the header of the document.

```
<HEAD>
<STYLE>
.set-tops {
font-family: Arial;
```

```
font-size: 10pt;
font-weight: bold;
color: brown;
}
</STYLE>
</HEAD>
```

This style sheet, which is contained within the opening and closing <STYLE> tags, defines a class (*class* essentially means a particular style of text) named *set-tops*, where the name of the class is preceded by a period. The set-tops class has four unique properties, all of which are contained between the two brackets that follow. The type-face is Arial, font-size in this class is 10, the font-weight is bold, and the color is brown. Once you've defined a class in a style sheet, you can apply that class to any of the text contained within the enhanced TV Web page.

```
<DIV CLASS = "set-tops">
New online chat service for members
</DIV>
```

Here, the set-tops class is applied to the text " New online chat service for members." Consequently, this code declares to a CSS-enabled browser that the elements of the set-tops class should be 10-point bold brown text in an Arial typeface. Defining styles in the headers of an enhanced TV page is useful if you want to affect the contents of only one TV HTML page, but what if you want to use the same styles for several pages. To facilitate this flexibility, CSS allows developers to create an external style sheet and link to it from your enhanced TV pages. The first step is to create your style sheet and save the file with a .css extension. Next, start developing your enhanced TV Web page and add the following link to the header of the page.

```
<HEAD>
<LINK REL=STYLESHEET HREF="filename.css" TYPE='text/css">
</HEAD>
```

This instructs the set-top Web browser to find and apply the external style sheet to a specific range of enhanced TV pages. In addition to specifying font sizes and type-faces, there are many more CSS properties that allow you to specify everything from the font and color of individual paragraphs, to the size of margins, the distance between lines, the type of bullet points, background textures, and a great deal more. Another important feature of CSS for enhanced TV developers is the ability to control the position and layout of elements on their pages. CSS positioning opens up a whole new level of control over Web pages. Instead of building awkward tables to hold objects, you can place each object exactly where you want it on the page. The positioning of HTML and multimedia elements can be broadly classified into absolutely-

and relatively-positioned. Absolute positioning occurs when you set the element's exact distance from the edges of the TV screen, whereas relative positioning offsets an element from other multimedia components on the enhanced TV page. Developers can also update the coordinates of the page at any time to create various types of animated effects on the television screen.

As you can see, CSS constitutes a complex topic and a detailed discussion of all its components is beyond the scope of this book. Accordingly, we suggest that you download a detailed description of the CSS1 specification from the following URL: http://www.w3.org/TR/REC-CSS1

ECMAScript

For all practical purposes ECMAScript has the same functionality as JavaScript. It is the result of a project between Netscape, Microsoft, and several other companies to compile a unified definition of the languages that were modeled on Netscape JavaScript. This powerful new scripting language allows enhanced TV authors to add interactivity and synchronize HTML content with the broadcast video signal.

In addition to defining a common standard, the companies involved in the project have also committed to reworking their own implementations of JavaScript to conform to the new standard. Due to its simplicity and openness, ECMAScript is ideally suited to developing content for the TV world. Additionally, it is used to build applications for the digital set-top box. The ATVEF implementation of ECMAScript closely matches the JavaScript and Microsoft's Jscript implementations, but there are differences.

Document Object Model

When originally conceived, the Web lacked the technology required to build full-scale, interactive applications. The static nature of HTML limited the development of engaging Web content in the early days. Later, the introduction of client-side scripting and more advanced servers facilitated the development of rudimentary interactive browser applications. But these advancements relied on the server for interactivity and there was no way to modify an existing page without loading an entirely new one. Because many of the digital systems across the globe support one-way broadcasting of data, ATVEF uses Document Object Model (DOM) Technology to help remove the dependence of the client set-top box on the servers located at the head end. DOM is a programming interface for HTML documents. It defines the logical structure of documents and the way a document is accessed and manipulated. DOM is used by enhanced TV creators to dynamically change the appearance of Web pages after they have been downloaded to a subscriber's set-top browser. DOM is a W3C recommendation that describes how objects in a Web page—text, images, headers, and hyper-links—are represented. It defines what attributes are associated with each object and how the objects and attributes can be manipulated. And it provides full support for keyboard and mouse events on all page elements, so TV content creators will be able to delete, add, or change elements on the fly. For example, developers could create an enhanced TV application that is dynamically updated with new headlines without refreshing the Web page that is stored in the subscriber's set-top box. The completed DOM specification has been reviewed by W3C members and has been endorsed by the director as a W3C recommendation. Rather than attempting to cover the entire DOM W3C recommendation in this book, we suggest that you download the file from the following Web address: http://www.w3.org/TR/REC-DOM-Level-1/.

Cookies

One final requirement for ATVEF compliance is the support for a Web personalization technology known as "cookies." A cookie is best described as a message that is trans-mitted from a server to the set-top browser. The set-top browser stores the message in a text file called cookie.txt. Because the majority of digital set-top boxes do not have hard disks, the cookie.txt file is normally stored in ROM. ATVEF has specified that all set-top boxes are required to assign 1 KB of memory for storing cookies. The main pur-pose of these cookies is to identify subscriber habits and customize enhanced TV pages for them. Cookies are widely used on the public Internet. Amazon, for example, uses this technology to improve sales and Yahoo uses them for personalization purposes.

The best way to understand how cookies can be used on a broadband digital TV network is to look at a practical application. Suppose you are the owner of an e-com-merce store that is selling goods and services to a number of digital TV subscribers. You would like to find out more information about their buying habits and customize some of the enhanced HTML pages for them. The first step is to develop a form and post it to your e-commerce site. When customers enter your site, they will be asked to fill out the form, providing such personal information as name, age, hobbies, and home address. This information is then packaged into a cookie and stored in set-top ROM for later use. The next time the customer visits your site, the set-top browser will send the cookie back to the server in the head-end. The server can then use this infor-mation to present your customers with personalized enhanced TV pages. So, for exam-ple, instead of seeing just a welcome page on the TV screen, your customer might see a welcome page with their name on it.

Additional Content Support

In situations where the enhanced TV content developer knows the specific software capabilities of the target set-top box, data can be sent over an ATVEF-compliant network that is outside the basic content formats that have been defined in version 1.1 of the specification (HTML 4.0, CSS, ECMAScript, and DOM). In which case, rich multimedia technologies like Shockwave, Dynamic HTML, XML, and streaming technologies could be integrated with enhanced TV content in the near future.

ShockWave • Developed by Macromedia, ShockWave is a technology that enables content providers to access and design very sophisticated multimedia applications for digital set-top boxes. Enhanced TV developers can use Shockwave to produce games, animations, movies, and interactive presentations for a digital TV audience.

Dynamic HTML • Dynamic HTML (DHTML) is a term used by some vendors to describe the combination of HTML, style sheets, and scripts that allows documents to be animated. DHTML is not a scripting language, like JavaScript or VBScript, it is an application program interface for HTML. It allows an author to take advantage of the processing power of the client to create pages that can be modified on the client, without having to access the server for each change. And it provides TV authors with enhanced creative control so they can manipulate any page element on a television screen at any time.

XML • XML is a markup language for documents containing structured information. Structured information contains both content (words, pictures, graphs, etc.) and some indication of what role that content plays (for example, content in a section heading has a different meaning from content in a footnote). XML was created so that richly structured documents could be used over the Web. The only viable alternatives, HTML and SGML, are not practical for this purpose. Almost all documents have some structure. A markup language is a mechanism to identify structures in a document. The XML specification defines a standard way to add markup to documents. The number of applications currently being developed that are based on, or make use of, XML documents is truly amazing (particularly when you consider that XML is not yet 2 years old)! In the context of XML, the word "document" normally refers to traditional documents, but it can also describe other XML formats such as mathematical equations and e-commerce transactions. Industry analysts are predicting that we will begin to see XML-enabled set-top boxes in our living rooms toward the middle of the year 2001.

Streaming technologies

Millions of people on the Internet use streaming technologies on a daily basis to enjoy live audio and video entertainment shows from around the world. Streaming technology, also known as streaming media, lets a consumer view and hear digitized content—video, sound, and animation—as it is being downloaded. In order to enjoy these technologies, people need to have special software called a "player" loaded on their computer. The player then does all the work of taking the audio and video from the incoming digitized stream and translating it into a format that can be heard and seen by PC users. The most popular player currently on the marketplace, with an installed base of more than 65 million users, is RealPlayer G2 from RealNetworks. At the time of going to press, RealNetworks announced a strategic agreement to distribute its RealPlayer G2 multimedia software in Liberate Technologies television set-top boxes.

Authoring Enhanced TV Content for DASE-compliant set-tops

A language called Broadcast HTML (BHTML) is used to develop content for DASE compliant set-top boxes. It is based on well known and well used Internet technologies, which allows manufacturers to deliver a range of products with varying levels of digital services. It is a modular language that is primarily based on the XML language. A draft specification of the BHTML language was made available on the Internet in October 1998. It is a detailed document, that outlines three different HTML profiles that can be applied to developing interactive TV content.

1. W3C HTML—A version of HTML that is widely used on the public Internet and suitable for full Web connectivity.
2. Broadcast HTML—Suitable for TV-centric networks.
3. Compact HTML—This version of HTML is a well-defined subset of HTML 2.0, HTML 3.2, and HTML 4.0 recommendations, which is designed for small information appliances.

Each of the three HTML profiles contain a collection of document type definition (DTD) sets that can be combined to allow content developers to author content for a variety of platforms. Off the shelf Web authoring tools can be used to produce BHTML content for an enhanced TV environment. BHTML allows network operators to add their own customizations and branding to existing Web content. BHTML has defined Java instead of JavaScript to add interactivity to content developed for the DASE-compliant receivers. The BHTML specification does not specify set-top hardware features however it does specify particular attributes. For example, set-tops that run the BHTML platform should be able to support the following technologies:

- Animation;
- Real-time 3D objects;
- ATSC Subtitling; and
- Streaming audio.

An important feature of the DASE specification for set-top box manufacturers is the fact that a Web browser is not required to view BHTML content. This reduces the memory and processing requirements for a DASE-compliant set-top which subsequently reduces the manufacturing costs. Similar to the ATVEF specification, BHTML also facilitates the linking of program related Web sites to broadcast channels. Additionally the BHTML supports the following enhanced TV features:

Timing relates to the relationship between the set-top decoding, rendering of a multimedia object, and a particular clock source.

Synchronization refers to beginning and ending the playback or rendering of multimedia objects with respect to time and other objects.

Transitions are a set of properties that let an enhanced TV content developer specify the way in which multimedia objects appear or disappear on the television screen.

An addendum to the core BHTML proposal has been developed to describe these enhancements and is available for download at: http://toocan.philabs.research.philips.com/misc/atsc/bhtml/sync_atsc_1_0.html.

Authoring Enhanced TV Content for MHP-compliant Set-tops

Before you commence development of content you need to examine the data formats that are supported by the target device. The formats supported by MHP-compliant devices can be categorized into two distinct groups.

1. Internet content standards—JPEG, GIF, and PNG.
2. Broadcast streaming formats—MPEG-2 I-Frames (still pictures), MPEG video clips, DVB subtitles, monomedia audio, and various types of fonts.

The HTML family of technologies is an optional part of MHP for Enhanced Broadcast. The application lifecycle of an MHP system takes into account the possibility of including HTML as well as the necessary signaling and delivery mechanisms. When developing content for this environment, you need to be aware that MHP has profiled HTML broadcasting as follows:

- Enhanced broadcasting—This profile uses content that is provided via a service provider, without the use of a return channel.
- Interactive broadcasting—This profile assumes the existence of a return channel. HTML content will be carried to the MHP-enabled set-top box via the television channel and/or via the return channel (assuming sufficient bandwidth on the response channel).
- Internet access—This profile will allow full set-top browser support.

To finish our discussions on the MHP platform, I'd like to give you a brief description of the transport methods that are used by MHP to deliver content to a digital set-top box.

In a two-way system, HTTP and TCP/IP protocols are used for accessing content on the Web.

Two different transport mechanisms can be used to deliver HTML content in a one-way digital system.

1. The DVB DSM-CC Object Carousel can be used for transport of HTML family content. HTML content can be distributed via this protocol by reflecting the pieces of content in the hierarchial file system of the Object Carousel. Content, which uses relative addressing, can be maintained unchanged when using this way of distribution. Multiple files can be packaged in one module for efficient compression.

2. For some instances it might be preferable to be able to use a protocol stack that is based on the IP protocol for broadcast delivery. Because of the unidirectional nature of the broadcast transport, the higher level protocols need to be different.

An existing transport method for such delivery is the Unidirectional Hypertext Transfer Protocol (UHTTP). UHTTP is a simple, robust, data transfer protocol designed to deliver data efficiently in a one-way broadcast-only environment, including retransmissions and a forward error correction mechanism. Data sent using the UHTTP protocol is divided into a set of packets, encapsulated in UDP. Typically, these packets will be delivered via multicast IP using DVB Multi-protocol Encapsulation.

DELIVERING ENHANCED TV CONTENT . . . .

Once you've designed and authored enhanced TV content (e.g. video, adverts, graphics, and Web links), it then needs to be combined and encoded into the TV signal. Specialized enhanced TV tools and powerful servers are required to complete this particular function. The enhanced TV content can then be transported to both computers and televisions using cable, MMDS, terrestrial, or satellite technologies. Powerful broadcast servers located at the head-end are used to assemble and inject enhanced TV content into the digital signal. The main purpose of these servers is to collect enhanced TV pages, encapsulate them within standard TCP/IP packets, and pass them to the encoder. Once encoded, the TCP/IP packets can then be transmitted to the set-top box using the HTTP protocol in an analog or digital broadcast stream.

The main phases associated with delivering enhanced TV services to subscribers are graphically illustrated in Figure 12.1.

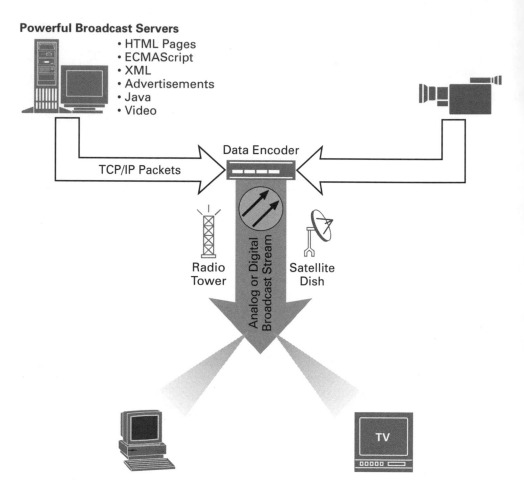

Figure 12.1
Phases related to delivering enhanced TV content to a digital set-top box

LEVELS OF INTERACTIVITY

Similar to most software and content development projects, labor costs are the largest expense item associated with producing enhanced TV content. Typically a team of people developing enhanced TV content for a digital set-top box will have a detailed knowledge of Web technologies and authoring tools. Content that is being currently designed for set-top boxes can be grouped into two broad categories: basic interactivity and advanced interactivity.

Basic Interactivity

The simplest way of adding the richness and interactive nature of the Web to a TV program is to add a link onscreen that connects the viewer to a specific piece of information on the Web. This information that the link would lead to could either be a home page of an associated Web site or a specific page on an advertiser's Web site. A Web link appears onscreen as an icon and can be activated using a standard remote control or wireless keyboard. This icon is customizable and could look like the one shown in Figure 12.2.

Web links are easily customized and are normally transmitted to the subscriber's set-top box within the television broadcast signal. Links are easy to create and are typically comprised of a URL and a number of associated attributes that point to specific items of information on the Web. The convergence between the Web and the television benefits producers of programs because they can engage the audience by providing links to sites that complement the program itself. For example, a technology show about digital set-top boxes is being broadcast. The viewer would like to view more detailed information and possibly buy one of these new devices. Consequently, the viewer selects the remote control or wireless keyboard to select the Web link icon on the screen. The home page of www.set-tops.com appears onscreen and the viewer browses the site to identify specific items of interest. The content developer controls the look and feel of how the Web page appears on the television screen. For instance, you may decide to place the technology program over the Web page and allow viewers to interact with the set-top's site while continuing to watch the main program. Developers can also embed the display of the technology program within the set-top's home page. The first step in creating links between a TV program and various Web sites is to identify the software platform that is running at the network operator's head-end and in the subscriber's set-top box. As we saw in Chapter 6 most set-top software vendors will supply authoring tools that are optimized for their own platforms.

The next step is to either identify relevant Web sites that complement a particular program or else develop new Web pages. It's a much better idea to design Web pages or identify sites that are related to what's happening in a TV show than to simply link viewers to unrelated Web pages. For instance, many viewers will not appreci-

Figure 12.2
Web link icon

ate a soccer game with links to PC manufacturers' Web pages. If, however, you can identify or develop Web content that complements the game, such as player statistics, then viewers will continue to watch the game and read the player's statistics at the same time.

Advanced Interactivity

Once content producers and subscribers have become reasonably comfortable with adding and using Web links to TV programs, the demand for advanced interactivity features will increase. Advanced interactivity is not limited to complementing programs with specific Web content. Under this method of delivering enhanced TV, service providers and content developers can broadcast information that is not thematically connected to the associated program—for example, local news, stocks, financial data, weather, opinion polls, and sports headlines. With advanced interactivity, developers can actually change the interactive content in response to particular events that happen within the film. This type of enhanced TV is very compelling to set-top users. However, developing this sort of TV content requires a range of new skills and abilities.

As mentioned previously, the methods and tools used to develop enhanced TV content will depend on the software environment that is resident in the set-top box. For example, providers who want to author content for an OpenTV-based set-top will need to use a specialized authoring tool called SNAP.

SUMMARY . . . .

Enhanced TV is a technology that allows a consumer to receive both television broadcasts and Internet access across the same screen at once. The term "Enhanced TV" was originally introduced by NCI (now called Liberate Technologies) in 1997.

Using this technology, consumers are able to shrink the TV broadcast to a desired size in a corner of the screen and use the rest of the space for the Web. The graphics and text for enhanced television applications are created using common Internet-based technologies and skills. Many network operators have seized the market potential for enhanced TV content and have begun to embed Web content within their normal digital broadcasts. In addition to network operators, the enhanced TV revolution will also bring huge benefits to the following groups of people: consumers, content developers, service providers, and advertisers.

Putting a Web page on a television screen is very different than displaying the same page on a computer monitor. We must remember that the television has been with us for many years so there will obviously be limitations in developing for this platform. Three different specifications are defined for enhanced TV programming: ATVEF, DASE, and MHP. All three specifications define a common set of protocols for the transmission of multimedia content and services over cable, satellite, and broadcast video systems, both analog and digital.

We concluded the chapter with a description of the two main categories of enhanced TV content. The most basic approach uses Web links that are related to the program that's being broadcasted. The second approach is more sophisticated and integrates very closely with the events that take place within a digital program.

13 Advanced Set-top Features

In this chapter...

Some analysts have predicted that advanced digital set-top boxes will replace PCs for home use. One of the reasons for this assumption is because a digital set-top box is less expensive to purchase or lease than a standard multimedia PC. Also, set-top boxes require less maintenance than PCs and software purchase costs do not generally apply to set-tops. Clearly, we can expect to see a great deal of activity in the area of set-top middleware, development, and authoring tools in the future. Personal Java, JavaScript, and HTML are likely to remain the approaches to providing consumers with enhanced TV capabilities. Between now and the end of the century, the digital set-top box will likely play a greater role in managing and manipulating the rich multimedia content that enters the homes of the future. Manufacturers are already working on set-top products that integrate with DVD players, game consoles, and videophones. Some industry experts speculate that the set-top could go a different route, essentially disappearing as its functions are integrated into the television set. This scenario is highly unlikely because keeping the box separate from the television will enable service providers to continue to control access to interactive services, instead of yielding that authority to television manufacturers. So looking ahead, what type of a set-top box will the living room of the future embrace? This last chapter of our guide presents you with a sample of some of the more advanced features that will be supported in the telecommunication hubs of the future—digital set-top boxes.

MPEG-4 SUPPORT . . . .

MPEG-4 is an ISO/IEC standard developed by MPEG (Moving Picture Experts Group), the committee that also developed the Emmy Award-winning standards known as MPEG-1 and MPEG-2. These standards made interactive video on CD-ROM and digital television possible. MPEG-4 is the result of another international effort involving hundreds of researchers and engineers from all over the world. MPEG-4, whose formal ISO/IEC designation is ISO/IEC 14496, was finalized in October 1998 and has become an international standard at the beginning of 1999. MPEG-4 builds on the proven success of three fields:

- digital television;
- interactive graphics applications (synthetic content) ; and
- interactive multimedia (World Wide Web, distribution of and access to content).

MPEG-4 provides the standardized technological elements that enable the integration of production, distribution, and content access paradigms of the three fields. The MPEG-4 standard enables a whole spectrum of new applications, including mobile audio-visual communication, multimedia-rich electronic mail, electronic newspapers, interactive multimedia-rich databases, virtual reality games, and 3D computer imagery. Thanks to the development of software implementations of an MPEG-4 player, the MPEG-4 TV picture compression standard could be in people's homes before long—a development that opens many exciting possibilities. The MPEG-4 player is currently available for digital set-top boxes and plans are underway to incorporate the technology into the next generation of digital set-top boxes.

HOME NETWORKS . . . .

The boom in PC sales continues unabated with approximately 30 million homes in the United States having two or more PCs. If you are a resident of a house with multiple electronic devices, imagine how cool it would be to have your PC located in your home office connected to a noisy printer in the garage and simultaneously being able to access pictures stored in your digital camera in the kitchen. The concept of interconnecting electronic devices within a residential home is called *home networking.*

Home networks allow consumers to share files between family members without putting them on a floppy disk, share the use of expensive peripheral devices such as DVD players, and play multi-user games. Over the next year, Anderson Consulting is predicting that manufacturers will integrate computing powers into everyday electrical appliances such as refrigerators, light switches, heaters, alarms, coffee makers, and microwaves. The addition of home networking technologies to electrical appliances would then allow consumers to remotely manage their house via the Internet. Home networks have a couple of basic requirements. They need to be simple to install and quality of service is required since the network carries real-time audio and video data.

Today, most members of a family would like to have access to the Internet without the constraints associated with installing and running separate telecommunication links. Home networks can deliver significant savings and greater entertainment value by allowing all family members to share a common high speed Internet connection.

The growth of multiple-PC households using highspeed broadband devices such as cable modems, digital set-top boxes, and Asymmetric Digital Subscriber Line (ADSL) modems accessing the Internet creates a fertile environment for manufacturers and service providers across the globe. Consequently, major heavyweights from the cable, networking, software, and PC manufacturing industries are jumping into the home networking arena. These companies are launching products that are simple to install and maintain.

Convergence between home networks and the Internet is providing a revolution in home entertainment. Through this phenomenon, physical walls within a home are slowly being broken down and replaced with virtual walls that bring entertainment into any and all rooms within the house. For cable operators, home networking is another opportunity to increase the use and revenue streams of broadband interactive data and video services. Everybody who installs a digital set-top box is a potential home networking customer for cable companies. Special home network kits and technologies are currently available that allow consumers to connect multiple PCs to their broadband connection via the set-top box. Some TV companies are even talking about ways of exchanging information between different conditional access systems within the home. Under this approach, the conditional access system would then become a full network resource. Digital signals floating around a home network is a hacker's dream come true. Realizing this, a number of working groups and committees have been established to develop various methods of safeguarding copyrighted material.

In the next section, we examine some of the technologies and commercial products that promise to deliver the holy grail of home networks without the need to run hundreds of yards of new cables inside the walls of your house.

Wireline Home Networks

Telephone Lines

Until recently, home networks depended on special cables (typically requiring professional installation) to link PCs, audio/visual equipment, and peripheral devices together, which could be expensive and problematic if the hardware components were in different rooms of the house. Now, thanks to recent technological developments, consumers can use their already installed telephone wiring system to link multiple computers and digital appliances around the house.

Phone lines offer consumers an established in-house wiring system for networking devices in different parts of the house. However, phone wiring does have some problems, such as:

- The quality of cables may not be of a high enough standard for sending data quickly and reliably.
- Telephone cables generally meander through the walls of a house instead of running back to a central location. The telephone wiring structure within each home is unknown and even changes on a day-to-day basis.
- Susceptible to electronic interference from other home devices such as answering machines, phones, heaters, air conditioners, microwaves, and fax machines.

An organization called the Home Phoneline Networking Alliance (HomePNA) has been established to define standards and technologies that will overcome these technical issues. The HomePNA is a group of more than 70 companies seeking to develop specifications for interoperable, home networked devices using existing phone wiring. HomePNA has defined a standard specification that simplifies the

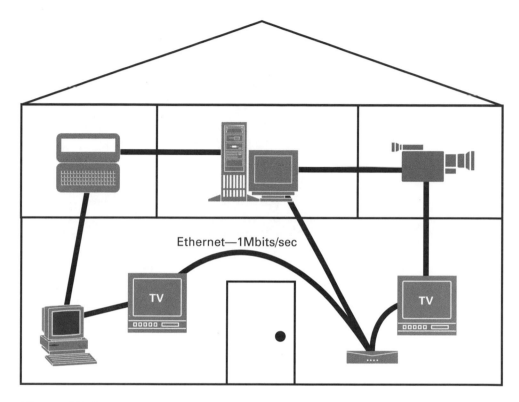

Ethernet—1Mbits/sec

Figure 13.1
Typical Implementation of a home network

implementation of a home network over the phone lines. Figure 13.1 shows a typical implementation of a home network using the phone lines wiring system.

Let's examine each component of the network and see how they work together.

Network transport technologies

The Alliance has chosen to standardize on Ethernet-based technology available from Tut Systems, allowing consumers to link devices at speeds up to 1 Mbps over existing home telephone wires. Ethernet is a popular and internationally standardized networking technology (comprising both hardware and software) that enables computers to communicate with each other.

Ethernet was developed by DEC, Intel, and Xerox. The Institute of Electrical and Electronics Engineers (IEEE) later standardized it as IEEE 802.3. As a result, people tend to use the terms Ethernet and IEEE 802.3 interchangeably. The fact that IEEE 802.3 has been chosen as a networking technology allows HomePNA to leverage the tremendous amount of Ethernet compatible software, applications, and existing hardware in the market today.

The IEEE 802.3 standard was designed to support the CSMA/CD access method. CSMA/CD stands for carrier sense multiple access with collision detection. Let's briefly explore what this means. On a home network that uses the CSMA/CD access method, the devices can send data at any time, so there's multiple access. When an electronics or PC device has data to send, it listens to the phone line to see if it is busy. The device is sensitive to any carrier on the line—that's why this access method is said to have "carrier sense." If there's traffic on the line, the device waits, in other words, it enters waiting mode. If the line is free, the station transmits its data immediately.

Let's say that another device in another part of the home decides to send data at the same time. In such a case, a collision may occur. Collision detection allows the two devices to detect this event and perform the required recovery. The devices back off for a period of time before re-transmitting. Of course, it's essential that the two devices do not back off for the same length of time. If, for example, all appliances on the home network were set to back off and retry after half a second, the same two frames would collide again. To prevent continual collisions, each appliance on the network backs off for a random amount of time.

An additional requirement of home phone line networking is the coexistence of multiple services on a single piece of telephone wire. For example, members of the household will need to make telephone calls, while other members of the family use the home network for enhanced TV purposes. One of the most common methods for simultaneously operating multiple data and voice services over a single pair of wires is Frequency Division Multiplexing (FDM). This is a multiplexing technique that assigns each communications service a frequency spectrum that is different from all others. Through the use of frequency-selective filters, appliances using one type of service can exchange information without interference from other services that communicate in another frequency band. The diagram in Figure 13.2 depicts how FDM

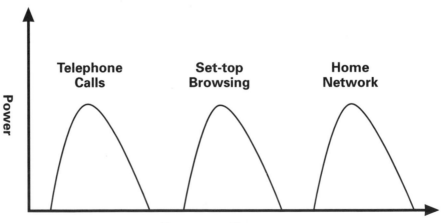

Figure 13.2
Different frequency ranges used by FDM

allows a consumer to simultaneously make a phone call and use the home network to access the Internet via a digital set-top box.

Wiring

The Ethernet technology found in corporate office environments was originally designed to support four types of wiring systems:

1. thick coaxial cable,
2. thin coaxial cable,
3. unshielded twisted pair, and
4. fiber-optic cable.

These types of expensive cabling systems are not available in most residential houses. Consequently, HomePNA decided to leverage existing infrastructure provided by phone wire inside the home. The use of the phone wiring system means that every RJ-11 modular jack in the house becomes a port on the home network as well as a phone extension. RJ-11 is a standard telephone line connector.

The first HomePNA specification operates at maximum distances of at least 500 feet between nodes on the network and is capable of achieving data rates of 1 Mbps. Each appliance that forms part of the home network is known as a node.

Network Interface Cards

All the computers on a HomePNA-based home network needs an adapter to control the I/O to the network. Essentially, an *adapter* is a piece of hardware inside the PC or digital appliance that allows it to communicate with the external home network. Adapters transfer data between one electronic device and the external network, whether it is a network operator's broadband network or another digital appliance located in a separate room. An adapter has one interface to the digital appliance and another to the home network.

Home phone line network interface cards (NICs) are separate cards that cost around $100 that plug into the computer's expansion bus. This allows you to create a home network using the existing in-home phone wiring system. Some HomePNA certified adapters also come with connectors known as RJ-45. These interfaces are slightly wider than RJ-11 connectors and can be used to connect into a sophisticated data wiring system. HomePNA are also working with various manufacturers to incorporate their interface into the next generation of computers, consumer electronics products, and communications devices, making the cost of networking nearly transparent to the end user.

Software

Every device on a home network needs an OS with networking capabilities. Once an NIC is installed in a PC, a driver is required to communicate with other appliances on the network.

Next Generation of Technologies HomePNA

To keep up with the availability of high-speed access technologies such as digital set-top boxes, ADSL, and cable modems, HomePNA intends to extend its initial 1 Mbps to 10 Mbps.

Companies like Epigram are proposing a scalable Home Ethernet network running at 10 Mbps today, with the ability to increase to speeds approaching 100 Mbps in the near future—while maintaining backward compatibility across previous generations of HomePNA-compatible equipment, including the HomePNA's 1 Mbps specification. The new technology would use selective portions of the 2–30 MHz frequency band to achieve these data rates. In addition to increasing data speeds within the home, the HomePNA is working to incorporate their technologies into a range of electronic appliances, including: PC's, ADSL modems, cable modems, digital televisions, set-top boxes and IP based Web phones. Compaq for example, agreed to install equipment from Californian manufacturer Tut Systems in its off the shelf personal computers. Similar developments are to be announced by set-top box manufacturers in the near future.

AC Power Lines

This is an emerging home networking technology that allows consumers to use their already existing electrical wiring system to connect home appliances to each other and to the Internet. Home networks that utilize high-speed power line technology can control anything that plugs into an outlet. This includes lights, televisions, thermostats, and alarms.

Many of the power line devices that are designed for in-home electrical wiring systems use the X-10 carrier protocol to allow compatible devices throughout the home to communicate with each other. Using X-10, it is possible to control lights and virtually any other electrical device from anywhere in the house with no additional wiring. The X-10 technology and resource forum design, develop, manufactures, and markets products that are based on this standard. Today, scores of manufacturers make X-10-compatible products that at $10 to $30 scarcely cost more than their incompatible counterparts; more than 100 million such products have been sold, according to the X-10 group. These home automation products are called "power line carrier" (PLC) devices and are often installed by builders who want to offer home automation as an additional selling feature. The home automation line consists of "controllers" that automatically send signals over existing electric power wiring to receiver "modules," which in turn control lights, appliances, heating and air conditioning units, and so on. With the X-10 standard, you can literally walk into a nearby electronics store and purchase all of the necessary equipment to automate your home with the X-10 standard. X-10 is not the only method of delivering data over lines that previously delivered only electricity. A company in the United States called Enikia is providing a range of products and competing technologies that allow home electronics devices such as set-top boxes to connect to a powerline home network via the nearest electrical outlet. Similar to HomePNA technologies, Enikia also bases its home networking technology on the IEEE 802.3 standard. Enikia's chipset technology is capable of transferring information around your house at speeds of 10 Mbps. In regard to security, Enikia-enabled devices encrypt data before sending the signal through the electrical wires.

IEEE-1394

The IEEE-1394 standard, also known as the FireWire Bus, is a new interface alternative for high-speed data transfer between digital set-top boxes and personal computers. The FireWire Bus standard, originally created by Apple Computers, was born out of the need for a low-cost, consumer-oriented connection between digital-video recorders and personal computers. It grew into a standard called the IEEE-1394 for low-cost, high data-rate connections. In 1994, an organization was formed to support and promote the adoption of the 1394 standard. Today, the organization is comprised of over 170 member companies from all over the world.

Many of the major consumer electronics companies are currently working to incorporate IEEE 1394 ready ports into the next generation of digital set-top boxes. In order to understand how an IEEE 1394 port operates in a digital set-top box, we need to examine the standard itself in more detail. IEEE 1394 is a very complex serial bus protocol that is capable of bidirectional data rates at 400 Mbps. There is, however, a roadmap in place to eventually bring the speed of an IEEE 1394 port up to 1.6 Gbps. The cabling required to interconnect devices on an IEEE 1394-based home network is quite similar to that of Ethernet. Unlike other home networking technologies, IEEE 1394 requires the installation of new wires. The IEEE-1394 cable medium allows up to 16 physical connections (cable hops), each up to 14 feet in length. This gives a home network using IEEE-1394 a total cable distance of 224 feet. Similar to Ethernet and other high-speed networking systems, IEEE 1394 adopts a layered approach to transmitting data across a physical medium. The physical layer provides the signals required by the IEEE 1394 bus within the set-top box. The link layer takes the raw data from the physical layer and formats it into recognizable 1394 packets. The transaction layer takes the packets from the link layer and presents them to the set-top application.

IEEE 1394 supports Plug-and-Play (PnP) which gives consumers the ability to plug a device into the back of the set-top and have the set-top box automatically recognize the new appliance and configure it for use.

For a more detailed description of the IEEE 1394 standard, we suggest that you download the complete specification from any of the Internet draft repository sites. Companies like Sony have already begun to lay the groundwork for using the IEEE 1394 home networking standard for interconnecting a range of hardware products within the household. In 1998, General Instruments (GI) announced that they would license Sony's i.LINK interface and associated software modules for use in their DCT-5000+ set-top boxes. The i.LINK interface is based on IEEE 1394 and allows devices on a home network to send and receive digital streams, such as video or audio, at up to 400 Mbps. In addition to licensing the i.LINK interface, GI will also include a new home networking software module in the DCT 5000. The new software module is a middleware product that provides the bridge between the set-top interactive applications and the i.LINK high-speed interface at the back of the set-top box.

Wireless Home Networks

Basic Principles

On the wireless side of the home networking spectrum, data is transmitted over the air. Wireless solutions are ideal platforms for extending the concept of home networking into the area of mobile devices around the home. Consequently, wireless technology is portrayed as a new system that complements phone line and power line networking solutions. At the core of wireless communication is a device called a *transmitter* and one called a *receiver*. The user interacts with the transmitter—for example, inputting a URL into a PC. This input is then converted by the transmitter to electromagnetic (EM) waves and sent to the receiver, which could be built into the set-top box. The receiver then processes these electromagnetic waves.

For two-way communication, each user requires a transmitter and a receiver. Consequently, many of the home networking devices have the transmitter and receiver built into a single unit called a *transceiver*. The operation and functionality of a wireless and wired home network remain the same. However, there are distinctions in the technologies used to achieve the same objectives.

The two main technologies used in wireless home networks are: Infrared (IR) and Radio Frequency (RF).

Most of us are familiar with everyday devices that use IR technology, such as remote controls for TVs, VCRs, and CD players. IR transmission is categorized as a line-of-sight wireless technology. This means that the workstations and digital appliances must be in a direct line to the transmitter in order to operate. An Infrared-based network suits environments where all the digital appliances that require network connectivity are in one room. IR home networks can be implemented reasonably quickly, however, people walking across the room and moisture in the air can weaken data signals. The other main category of wireless technology is Radio Frequency. RF technology is a more flexible technology allowing consumers to link appliances that are distributed throughout the house. RF can be categorized as narrow band or spread spectrum. Narrow band technology includes microwave transmissions. Microwaves are high-frequency radio waves and can be transmitted to distances of up to 50 km.

Microwave technology is not suitable for home networks, but is used to connect networks on separate buildings, for example.

Spread spectrum technology (SST) is one of the most widely used technologies in wireless home networks. SST was developed during World War II to provide greater security for military communications. As it entails spreading the signal over a number of frequencies, spread spectrum technology makes it harder to intercept it. There are a couple of techniques used to deploy SST, a system called frequency hopping spread spectrum (FHSS) is the most popular technique for operating wireless home networks. FHSS transmissions constantly hop over entire bands of frequencies in a particular sequence. To a remote receiver not synchronized with the hopping sequence, these signals appear as random noise. A receiver can only process electromagnetic waves by tuning to the relevant transmission frequency. The FHSS receiver hops from one frequency to another in tandem with the transmitter. At any given time, there may be a number of transceivers hopping along the same band of frequencies. Each transceiver uses a different hopping sequence that is carefully chosen to minimize interference on the home network.

When implementing a wireless home network, you need to install specific hardware to complete the connections. Similar to phone line, IEEE 1394, and Powerline networking, you need to connect your network nodes in the house to the transmission medium. To do this, you install a wireless NIC. The NIC hardware is comprised of a card with an onboard transceiver, a fixed or external antenna, and all cable connections. To install the card, you remove the cover of the digital appliance and slide the card into one of the free slots. To complete the hardware installation, you connect a fixed antenna to the rear of the NIC. Or else you connect an antenna cable for mounting an external antenna. Usually the external antenna is placed as high up as possible on the wall or ceiling to improve coverage. The antenna resembles a TV aerial, in the sense that where you locate it is important in relation to signal transmission and reception. In addition to installing the wireless NIC, you must also complete a number of software installation steps. This entails configuring and loading device drivers. If the nodes on the network are PCs with Windows 98, then the software configuration will be performed automatically. The layout of digital appliances on a wireless digital network is normally dictated by the physical layout of the house.

Let us now examine a standard body that has been established to promote home networking technologies—HomeRF.

HomeRF

The HomeRF Working Group (HRFWG) was formed in March 1998 to develop and open an interoperable specification for the next generation of wireless home networks. At the time of writing, the current membership of the group had exceeded 70 companies and is made up of leading companies across the personal computer, consumer electronics, peripherals, communications, software, and semiconductor industries worldwide.

At the beginning of 1999, the group announced an open industry specification called Shared Wireless Access Protocol (SWAP), which may be used for wireless digital communication between PCs and consumer electronic devices anywhere in and around the home. In addition to ratifying the standard, 13 companies have also committed to building products based on SWAP. Products that adhere to the SWAP standard will carry voice and data traffic between various portable appliances within the home without using a wiring system. Additionally these products will interoperate with the public telephone network and the Internet. SWAP technology is derived from technologies deployed in the cordless phone world combined with FHSS. SWAP operates in the 2.4 GHz section of the RF spectrum. A SWAP home network can operate as either a basic communications network or as a managed home network. In a basic SWAP network, all appliances have equal control over the operation of the network. The managed network uses a connection point to coordinate activities on the home network. The connection point acts as a gateway to a range of time-critical voice and data services. The connection point is normally a PC, but some consumers may want to use an advanced digital set-top box for this purpose. A SWAP home network is capable of accommodating a maximum of 127 digital appliances.

Set-top Home Networking Middleware

As mentioned earlier, *middleware* is a software product that interconnects two separate applications together. In the world of home networking, we encounter many types of hardware devices from different manufacturers. To provide interoperability between these diverse systems a number of home networking middleware applications have evolved.

HAVi • HAVi is an abbreviation for Home AV Interoperability. It is a project that was started by Sony and Philips in 1996. Since then, six other companies have joined— Thomson, Hitachi, Toshiba, Matsushita, Sharp, and Grundig. It is a software system that is based on the IEEE 1394 standard and is integrated with home entertainment devices such as digital set-top boxes. The middleware itself contains certain software elements that allow a set-top box to interoperate with different brands of entertainment appliances.

Jini • Jini is Sun Microsystems' home networking software solution. It is a layer of Java software that allows devices to plug directly into a home network without the hassle of installing drivers and configuring operating systems. Jini technology provides simple mechanisms that enable devices to plug together to form an impromptu community—a community put together without any planning, installation, or human intervention. Each device provides services that other devices in the community may use. These devices provide their own interfaces, which ensure reliability and compatibility. Sun Microsystems is currently working with a number of manufacturers to

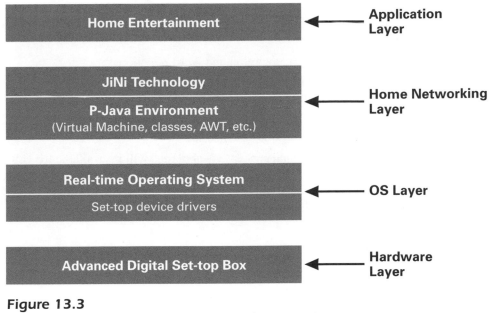

Figure 13.3
Jini integrated with Java-based set-top box

integrate the Jini home networking technology into the next generation of digital set-top boxes (see Figure 13.3).

In the world of digital set-top boxes, competition is going on at certain levels. At the time of writing, news was coming through of Microsoft's entrance into the nascent set-top home networking market with its Universal Plug and Play (UPNP) technology. Other players include: HomeAPI, HomePnP, and LonWorks.

VOICE RECOGNITION ....

Imagine the convenience of sitting on your sofa and issuing voice commands to your digital set-top box on top of your TV screen. No more clumsy cables, remote controls, or wireless keyboards.

Digital set-top boxes of the future will be able to recognize and respond to naturally spoken speech. Companies like Microsoft, Philips, and Lernout & Hauspie are actively involved with integrating speech technologies into the next generation of set-tops. Voice-driven interfaces are being developed that provide speaker independent and dependent recognition in high noise environments. Advanced features include:

- Spelling recognition and word rejection.
- Subscribers can begin using a speech-enabled set-top box immediately without training with "factory shipped" vocabularies.
- End-users can add their own vocabularies with speaker-dependent commands, such as "Launch my EPG."
- Speaker-independent vocabularies will be available for U.S. English, U.K. English, Japanese, French, Spanish, and German set-top boxes.

Speech-enabled set-top boxes are expected to be commercially available in mid-2000.

PERSONALIZATION TECHNOLOGIES . . . .

Research suggests that consumers want a more personal and convenient system of viewing television. To meet consumer demands, we will see the deployment of intelligent set-top boxes that will track consumers' viewing habits, scan through the myriad of digital services available on broadband network connections, and record information. When a subscriber comes home from work in the evening, their intelligent set-top box will display a suggested schedule of programs and services to choose from. Additionally, these new advanced devices will give subscribers the ability to pause and apply slow motion to specific films. In other words, consumers will decide when and what they want to watch on their televisions and not the network service provider. This technology is already available from a U.S. based company called—TiVo (http://www.tivo.com). It does, however, require you to purchase a dedicated dial-up set-top box and a monthly subscription to use this type of technology. Looking ahead, we expect this type of intelligent personalization software to be incorporated into the next generation of digital set-top boxes.

SUMMARY . . . .

Set-top boxes currently offer support for content that is based on a mix of Internet and proprietary-based technologies. In the future, we believe that the set-top box will evolve into a powerful platform capable of processing and displaying a myriad of different 3D visualization technologies. This vision is on the horizon and will be implemented through the incorporation of a multimedia standard called MPEG-4 into future generations of set-top boxes. MPEG-4 is an emerging digital media standard that will enable users to view and manipulate audio, video, and other forms of digital content.

Numerous analysts foresee the set-top box becoming the center of the networked homes of the future. Parents can surf the Web to plan a family vacation while the kids use an online search engine to help with their homework. As more and more consumer electronic devices such as videos, cameras, PCs, and set-top boxes make their way into consumers' houses, the home network will become more and more important. Home networks need to be simple to install and maintain. The term "cable spaghetti" is probably a good description of the wiring systems that run through most of our homes. Two approaches are being promoted to bring home networking to the masses. The first approach focuses on using either the existing wiring system or designing a new wiring system. The second approach is based on avoiding the "cable spaghetti" and using wireless technologies instead.

Technologies have already been developed to allow you to use your telephone and electrical wiring systems to carry data at speeds of 10 Mbps and above. If your in-home wiring system is not up to the job, then you should consider a new cabling system based on the IEEE 1394 networking standard. On the wireless front, you can choose between two main home networking wireless solutions—IR and RF. Home networks require software and there are numerous products on the market that provide interoperability between different brands of digital appliances—Havi, Jini, Microsoft's Universal Plug and Play, and many more. Voice-enabled set-top boxes are expected to be available in mid-2000. The proliferation of digital TV around the world is expected to fuel new personalization technologies that allow subscribers to create their own personal portals of digital- and Internet-based services.

Only one thing is certain about the future of digital set-top boxes—things will change.

For Further
Information

PowerTV product technical details
> http://www.powertv.com/product/product.html

VxWorks product technical details
> http://www.vxworks.com/

PSOSystem product technical details
> http://www.isi.com/

OS-9 product technical details
> http://www.microware.com/ProductsServices/Technologies/os-91.html

Microsoft product technical details
> http://www.microsoft.com/tv/

JavaOS, Java and Personal Java technical details
> http://www.sun.com

MHEG technical detail
> http://www.mhegcentre.com/
>
> http://www.dtg.org.uk/

OpenTV product technical details
> http://www.opentv.com

Mediahighway product information
> http://www.canalplus-technologies.com/

Liberate product information
> http://www.liberate.com

PlanetWeb product information
http://www.planetweb.com

Product details on device mosaic
http://www.spyglass.com

Information on XML
www.xml.com

Information on DASE and BHTML
http://toocan.philabs.research.philips.com/misc/atsc/bhtml/sync_atsc_1_0.html

Smart card software details
http://www.litronic.com/whitepaper/scoper.html

MPEG-4 information
http://www.cselt.it/mpeg/standards/mpeg-4/mpeg-4.htm

http://www.homepna.org/docs/wp1.htm

FURTHER READING . . . .

Anyimi, C., (November, 1998) Flash memory: What it is and how it will change set-tops in 1999. *Communications Technology*

LSI Logic white paper on the architecture of Integra

Sutherland, F., (July, 1999). Remote Overload: Too much too soon? *Cable and Satellite*

Index